MONEY AND POWER

Volume 66, Sage Library of Social Research

Sage Library of Social Research

MONEY
AND
POWER

Banks and the World Monetary System

Jonathan David Aronson

Preface by SUSAN STRANGE

Written Under the Auspices of the Center for International Affairs

Volume 66
SAGE LIBRARY OF
SOCIAL RESEARCH

SAGE PUBLICATIONS   Beverly Hills   London

For information address:

SAGE PUBLICATIONS, INC.
275 South Beverly Drive
Beverly Hills, California 90212

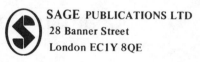

SAGE PUBLICATIONS LTD
28 Banner Street
London EC1Y 8QE

Printed in the United States of America

Library of Congress Cataloging in Publication Data

Aronson, Jonathan David.
  Money and power.

  (Sage library of social research ; v. 66)
  Bibliography: p. 199
  Includes index.
  1. International finance. 2. Banks and
banking, American. I. Harvard University. Center
for International Affairs. II. Title.
HG3881.A774   332.4'5   78-6630
ISBN 0-8039-0998-5
ISBN 0-8039-1046-0 pbk.

FIRST PRINTING

To my parents and my brothers

In our profession . . . there are certain few . . . whose respect for the law is quite immeasurable; whose knowledge of it is encyclopaedic—men of honor and integrity. . . . For us, the law is sacred. Inviolable. Not to be touched—but it can be *eluded*. . . . When we are confronted with the law's great edifice—majestic; immovable—there rising in front of us, across the path we, and some distinguished client may wish to travel—do we run our heads against it? By no means! First we bow, to show our respect; then, find our way round, over, or under it.

Bonnefoy in Moliere's
"The Imaginary Invalid"

CONTENTS

ACKNOWLEDGMENTS

I gratefully acknowledge the aid, encouragement, criticism, and intellectual stimulation I received from the most formative stages of this research until its completion. David Kay and Edward Shaw helped immensely during the earliest formulation. Robert Russell and Hyman Minsky tendered excellent advice on many key points. John Barton and Alexander George guided me back from the abyss when my focus strayed. Joseph Nye, Jorge Dominguez, and Raymond Vernon contributed valuable criticism as the work began to take form. James Burtle, Janet Kelly, and Rob Paarlberg provided insightful comments on the entire first draft. Peter Cowhey did likewise on the second draft. John Odell granted me access to his excellent interview transcripts with officials concerned with U.S. international monetary policy and provided me with astute and sensitive comments on each chapter as it rolled from the typewriter. Scott Pearson and James March tried to prompt me to walk the line between focus and vision. Robert Keohane read so many drafts of this work that he practically can recite it from memory. He was sage in his moments of encouragement while forcing me constantly to develop and rethink my analysis.

This book would still be unfinished without the cooperation of nearly 200 bankers, businessmen, and government officials who opened their offices and minds to me. However, I could never have reached them without much appreciated financial help from the Carnegie Endowment for International Peace and the International Studies Association. Finally, I am grateful to Joseph Nye, Samuel Huntington, and Raymond Vernon for inviting me to spend the 1975-1976 academic year as a graduate research associate at the Harvard Center for International Affairs. The CFIA's stimulation, particularly from those participating in the transnational relations seminar, immensely improved this work as it progressed. Needless to say, no other person or institution should be held responsible for errors of fact or analysis which remain.

Jonathan David Aronson

PREFACE

Novelists are often heard to remark that a book, once started, is apt to take on a curious life of its own, so that characters develop all by themselves and even shape their destinies independently of the writer. Academic books, in sensitive and creative hands, can be the same. An author may start out with an idea, but as the research proceeds, the subject begins to modify the original intention and the material starts to tell a different and even sometimes an unexpected tale.

Jonathan Aronson's book about the role of banks in the world system of recent times seems to me to be such a book. Begun as a study of the role of US banks as a pressure group in the making of US foreign economic policy, it quickly developed into something far more radical, interesting and important.

What he is saying in this book—and it seems to me an observation that deserves very wide attention—is that the bankers seldom act—as G. K. Chesterton and many of his American muckraking contemporaries liked to believe—as puppeteers of powerless politicians. But that the power they exercise on the financial chessboard (as distinct from the foreign policy, international relations chessboard) may actually and in the long run be far more important. It is their indirect impact that counts. By countless transnational operations, banks have radically changed the environment, domestic as well as global, within which the policy-makers lived and worked and made their decisions.

Beavers busy about their own business make dams, create ponds, change the habitat of other wild-life. Bankers, similarly, have busily sought their own profits and freedom in directions least taxed and regulated by governments. As Aronson says, "The pressure generated by bank and MNC actions was not usually intentional. Private actors merely attempted to make profits in relatively predictable environments" (p. 136). But, as a result, the activity of the various international capital markets became, within a brief decade, too great, too complex, too quick altogether for the monetary authorities of the industrialized countries to keep up with or control.

In consequence, governments did not so much choose to change the rules of the game, and resort to more flexible exchange rates. They were under such inexorable pressure from the markets that they had precious little option to do anything else. The international monetary reform so much discussed and written about in the 1960s proved, when it came in the early 1970s, not to be reform at all, but the acknowledgment of impotence by governments immobilized in a Catch-22 situation to which they themselves had contributed. Unable to return to fixed rates because they could not hold them against the markets, they were equally unable to allow "clean" floating for fear of the economic consequences. The vested interests here were political, not financial. They were found not among bankers but among governments who shared a compelling need to maintain confidence in the international monetary system even though it lacked rules, lacked a central authority and even any agreement on priorities for monetary management. Yet nobody wanted to see it collapse. A certain conspiracy of silence resulted.

Yet, as Aronson explains, the situation was not in the last resort one of the banks' making. They were only responding to regulations made in a context of domestic politics in the major states concerned—primarily the United States and, to a much lesser degree, Britain, West Germany, Canada and Japan. The New Deal regulations for US banks were strict at home but loose abroad. In London, regulation was loose for British banks operating in currencies other than sterling, and looser still for US banks.

This carefully documented demonstration of the backward linkage to domestic politics and economics in a sparsely cultivated field is one of the book's major contributions. Only a few economists have shown the way—notably Charles Kindleberger, Stephen Clarke, Alexander Swoboda and Marcello de Cecco. Only one doctoral thesis that I know of, by Nikita Harwich, has dealt with the international problems raised by consortium banks.

But the linkage is not a simple one, and it can vary with market conditions. An important point about national regulation of banking activities that comes out particularly well in Chapter 6 and again in the concluding chapter is that banks are curiously ambivalent about their watchdogs. Though they are impatient of regulations and controls, they also cannot operate without them. So although they profited in their transnational operations from the loopholes left by national regulations, they were quick to scurry back to the protection of national authorities when danger threatened. When the going gets rough—as it did after the Herstatt collapse in June 1974—and when competition between banks threatens to destroy either the competitors or the system, "private firms . . . expect governments to straighten things out." Whether they will always be able to do so without the overriding authority of a world central bank to act as a lender of last resort is one of the key questions raised in this study.

Indeed, a second and perhaps still more important contribution made by the book is the explanation of the forward linkage between banking operations and world politics—the politics of managing a global credit and monetary structure. Not only have the banks created the active international financial markets which had such a predominant influence on the network of international payments and exchange rates that this environment redefined the limits of international bargaining; they have also added to the future agenda of international monetary diplomacy. By their overeager and uncoordinated lending to developing countries in the aftermath of the oil price rises in 1973, they have vastly added to the LDC's total debt, and to their burden of debt servicing in relation to exports. Aronson even suggests this may be "the preeminent issue in relations between the industrialized and developing worlds in the next decade."

But it is by no means the only issue. There is also the question of who should coordinate the management of credit provided by Western banks and their customers for the economic development of Soviet bloc countries. There is the question raised by the exodus of US banks to the Cayman Islands and other tax havens. This frees a large and lucrative part of the profits made in the private sector of any responsibility for the provision of public goods and services—including the defense services on which their operations totally depend.

I can only add the hope that bankers find the time (in between their profit-making acrobatics), that policymakers display the farsighted vision to perceive its relevance, and that academics in economics and in political science have the humility to read this book.

London,   *Susan Strange*
April 1978

Chapter 1

INTRODUCTION

The growing complexity of the international system makes it extremely important for governments to cooperate in formulating their foreign economic policies. Without cooperation, successful adaption of the world economic system to changing future developments is unlikely. Without understanding the roles and relationships of the major actors in the economic system, sensible policies and policy changes are impossible. In the past, system crises and collapse spiced with a touch of charisma allowed for periodic restructuring of the world economic system, but evolution and adaption through collapses and near-misses is precarious—and becoming more so. As global interdependence continues to rise, the potential cost of collapse rises as well. Nations can no longer trust crises to lead to system change.

Management of the world economic system requires an understanding of the relationship between governments and markets and between governments and market participants. In the international monetary realm, it is particularly important that governments and private banks are aware of their own interrelationship and its impact on system stability. To this end, scholars, bureaucrats, and private executives must consider the interaction and relative power of actors in the monetary realm. This study attempts to begin providing such analysis by examining the roles and power of private banks in the international monetary system.

The public perceives bankers as conservative men in grey suits who exercise tremendous power over the lives of people, the fortunes of corporations, and the policies of governments. It sees them as princes of global finance who control international trade, investment, and lending and whose ways are typified by David Rockefeller, a diplomat for private enterprises, a politician serving capitalism. But while the conclusions of popular myths about bankers are clear, few Americans understand the workings of the domestic and international money and banking system. If the public believes bankers are extremely powerful, they also admit to understanding little about the mechanisms of bank influence because these paths of influence are shrouded by the complexity of financial operations.

The world of scholarship has done little to clear up the mysteries surrounding the banking industry. There is a dearth of research on the nature and scope of banks' political influence.[1] Even the excellent existing studies concerning the political economy of international money are surprisingly barren in describing private enterprises' activities.[2] Instead, we are engulfed by biographies of famous banks and bankers, assailed by textbooks on money and banking, and pummeled by explanations of the techniques and developments of the marketplace. There is also an abundant documentation of the recent, rapid expansion of international banking, but almost no information on the political consequences of banking globalization.[3] Although studies analyzing the political power of extractive and manufacturing multinational corporations (MNCs) are appearing, the paucity of research on the political influence of international banking, insurance, construction, transport, consulting, advertising, and other service industries is striking.[4]

This study tries to fill the void. It does so by examining a simple proposition: that multinational enterprises may have an important impact on international political relations. The key word of this proposition is "important." (It would be impossible to believe the banks had no impact.) There are a number of ways to define important impact. This work tries to go to the central issue at stake. It seeks to determine whether bank behavior exerts pressure on government decision-makers to adopt policies or take decisions which they do not favor. If so, how and why might the level of bank pressure change over time? This book examines the nature, dimensions, and mechanisms of American commercial banks' political power within the international monetary system since 1958. It begins to assess the appropriate relationship between public and private actors in the international economic system.

As a first step, it is necessary to define what is meant by bank power now and in the past. The prevalence and effectiveness of traditional forms of bank influence must be examined. Possible changes in the nature of bank influence mechanisms should be investigated. Only then can we turn to analysis of bank power within international monetary issue areas and suggest a reasonable form of government and business interaction in those realms.

To make the research manageable, four areas of inquiry are addressed. Specifically, what implications did the activities of U.S. commercial banks have for: (1) the passage, effectiveness, and eventual removal of U.S. exchange regulations between 1963 and 1974? (2) the development and resolution of U.S. and British foreign exchange crises since 1964? (3) the changes in international monetary system between 1958 and 1977? and (4) the access, conditions, and vulnerability of lesser developed countries seeking international financing? In each of these four areas, the relative level of pressure exerted by banks on government decision-makers is examined. In addition, the impact of banks' actions on monetary outcomes is considered.

This research agenda means that the present volume departs from standard treatments of international monetary developments since 1958.[5] Existing studies do not seriously consider the role of the private sector as a whole, much less the activities of individual industry groups and companies.[6] In contrast, I shall focus on private influence on monetary politics specifically and downplay aspects of the monetary system dealt with admirably elsewhere.

The balance of this chapter defines the key concepts recurring throughout this study. Then it presents a series of suppositions to guide the explanation of the major case studies. It concludes with a brief methodological review and an outline of the remainder of the book.

Power and Monetary Politics: Definitions and Clarifications

Our arena of action is the international monetary system comprising the "rules and conventions that govern financial relations between countries."[7] Operationally, the international monetary system may be classified according to exchange rate mechanism, by principal reserve asset or assets employed, by the degree of management involved, or even by the quality of its internationalism.[8]

Defining and operationalizing bank pressure and bank impact are more difficult. In a sense, this demands operationalizing "power" within the international monetary context. For most political scientists, power involves the ability of an actor to induce a second actor to do something the second actor would not otherwise have done.[9] When political scientists write about the exercise of power or influence by one actor over another, they imply that one actor *intended* to exercise sway over the other. Starting from this conception, it is not surprising that political scientists focusing on public-private interaction usually examine bank and corporate power over government officials who concern them.

The process of interaction is clearest when public and private officials disagree on the wisdom and necessity of policies. One can then operationalize power in terms of the ability of private executives to lobby, co-opt, bribe, or otherwise persuade government officials to take certain actions they might not otherwise have taken. In this manner a number of studies have examined a wide array of issues and investigated power of private actors over policies of their home governments as well as the policies of governments in nations where private actors have invested.[10]

This type of analysis is important and is employed here. It also points to a second form of influence that cannot be captured by research examining the international use of influence by one actor or group of actors over another actor or group of actors. This second variety of influence entails the ability of an actor to mold the decision environment of another actor, thereby limiting the scope of options available to the second actor. Even when the first actor does not intend to prevent the second actor from taking a certain action, the action may be precluded because the cost of taking the action for the second actor has been raised too high. In an extreme case, options may become so inconceivable that neither actor realizes power has been exercised. In addition, the power of one actor over another may be great or meaningless depending on the extent to which viable options are limited. Thus bank-induced globalization of unregulated international capital markets limited government's ability to prevent politically undesirable exchange rate adjustments, for which banks were not blamed.

Although this second definition of power can be subsumed under the first, the two will be separated here. *Direct* power or influence will refer to instances where an actor or group of actors exercises control over another actor or group of actors. Operationally, banks exercise direct power over government officials through (1) lobbying within the excutive and legislative branches of governments, (2) rotating bank officials into government positions, and (3) publicly calling for changes in policy. The prevalence and effectiveness of these direct influence channels will be analyzed. Although banks may use bribery and other means to pressure governments, these are difficult to measure. Indeed, measuring direct power accurately is impossible because so many activities can slip by undetected.

Banks also limit the options available to government officials. They can use their international structural flexibility and legal loopholes to *circumvent* the impact of government regulations. Circumventing influence is most effective when legislation is specifically designed to control the activities of market participants. Sometimes government officials even design regulations to encourage some private sector evasion. Within the international monetary system, banks can employ national regulatory disparities, unregulated capital markets, rapid global communications facilities, and flexible structure to dampen regulatory effectiveness. Such circumvention eventually may impel government officials to revamp regulations. As a side effect, regulatory circumvention may disrupt monetary policy. Nonetheless, banks normally circumvent government regulations simply to insure the profitability, competitive position, and planning stability available to the bank and its customers.

Banks and MNCs also exert *indirect* influence over government officials when they shape outcomes by overloading or saturating the channels governments and international monetary agencies employ to stabilize international capital flows and control the international monetary system. Indirect influence is most effective when government attention is focused on the regulation of the international economic system and not specifically at market participants. Overloading and saturation occur when regulatory authorities are inundated by flows or "hot" money or contradictory information too great to be digested by existing cooperative government arrangements. Recent international monetary developments have increased banks' opportunities (and temptations) to maximize their internationally generated profits even when this brings substantial pressure on government officials to change their monetary policy.

Indirect and circumventing influences are operationalized in three ways. Conflicting national regulations inadequately control international capital markets and allow banks to exert indirect and circumventing influence through (1) their actions in the foreign exchange and (2) Eurocurrency markets, as well as through (3) use of their international structural flexibility. Banks also exert indirect and circumventing influence through Eurobond, commercial paper, and other international market operations. A complete mapping of banks' indirect and circumventing power is precluded here. However, because other mechanisms of banks' indirect and circumventing influence seem to reinforce the constraints on outcomes initiated through the foreign exchange and Euromarkets, they will not be dealt with specifically here.

The implications of intentionality for this research should be articulated. Direct influence is by necessity intentional. Circumventing behavior involves the purposeful evasion of regulations but may or may not be designed to influence government policies and choices. Similarly, indirect influence may be wielded intentionally or be a side effect of banks' efforts to protect their positions and profits. In the latter two cases, it is rarely possible to demonstrate that bankers intended to pressure governments into certain revisions of their policies by limiting their alternatives. Therefore, while political motivations of bankers are discussed where evidence exists, bankers' intent is not the overriding focus. Indeed, bankers frequently seem unaware of the ultimate impact of their activities on decision-makers. It is the impact, not the reasoning behind the actions which is critical.

Table 1.1: Types of Influence Employed by Banks in the International Monetary System

	Direct Influence	Circumventing Influence	Indirect Influence
Response to:	Existing or proposed legislation or policies	Policy and legislation aimed at market participants	Policy and legislation designed to control the economic system
Channels:	Lobbying Personnel transfer Public appeals Bribery	Capital flows Currency exchanges International structure	Capital flows Currency exchanges International structure
Strategy:	Persuasion	Evasion	Coercion
Impact on:	Policy-making	Policy-effectiveness	Economic outcomes
Intent:	Conscious	Conscious at a primary level. May have unintentional side effects	Conscious or unintentional at both primary and secondary levels

To aid readers, these relationships are summarized in Table 1.1. It will be reintroduced and supplemented at the end of each chapter treating substantive areas.

Expectations and Suppositions

It is customary in political science to lay out a series of hypotheses to be tested throughout the work. This study departs from this procedure in part by initially illustrating the *types* of hypotheses found in each chapter. The formulation of more general hypotheses is reserved for the conclusion of this study.

How can one think about the use of direct influence? Friends and critics alike claim that the rapid overseas expansion of international businesses and their vast productive capacity provide multinational executives with increased direct power over governments.[11] While few claim that multinational banks "want" to replace governments as the central international decision-makers, some argue that multinational enterprises (MNEs) force governments toward policies compatible with private sector goals.[12] If so, American multinational banks might be expected to consciously and directly induce government officials to alter their policies. Perhaps the internationalization of bank operations and perspectives and the growth of banks' foreign exchange and Eurocurrency activities enable bankers to more effectively lobby government officials on international monetary matters. This supposition does not concern banks' indirect and circumventing influence. While these processes are considered, changes in the extent of banks' international operations and market control need to be linked to lobbying effectiveness.

How can one conceive of indirect or circumventing influence? It is possible that the conversion of banks into genuinely multinational enterprises and the growth and development of foreign exchange and Eurocurrency markets allowed banks to circumvent national regulations aimed at them and to overload the capacity of national governments to control international money markets. In this way banks pressed officials to adopt bank-favored monetary policies by limiting the scope of available policy options. In addition, changes in the global bank structure and market operations, when supplemented by low government resolve and private uneasiness about government policies, may have stimulated bank impact on international monetary outcomes. Private impact on the emergence of floating exchange rates in March of 1973 is a case in point.

Presumably banks are aware of the impact of their activities on monetary policy-making and outcomes, but they often seem oblivious to the ramifications of their actions. Apparently, few bankers consider the impact of their indirect and circumventing behavior on government decision-makers and on the monetary system. It is plausible that government officials are also frequently unaware of the indirect impacts of bank activities on governments' freedom of choice. Although some public and private officials undoubtedly perceive the interactive consequences of banks' global expansion and market activities, most view the monetary system in different terms. Such tunnel vision probably hinders government policy efficiency, allowing government officials to adopt programs destined to be undermined by private activities. But regardless of their limited perspective, they are being caught up by the indirect or circumventing influence.

The examples considered thus far are fairly straightforward. More difficult cases shall also be encountered. While examining banks' international monetary influence, the magnitude of bank power over outcomes and policy choice should, over time within certain issue areas, vary because bank power is redundant when government officials already concur with business' opinions. Differences in regulatory effectiveness across issue areas may also depend on the aim of government constraints. When government policies aim to control private actors rather than the international monetary system, banks evade regulations without directly or indirectly inducing government officials to reorganize regulations aimed at them. On the other hand, changing bank influence within issue areas need not be related to banks' failure to exert indirect influence. Even when free of government regulatory hindrances, internal, private sector competition may influence monetary developments.

More formally, changing business relationships or the introduction of new actors into the market may affect the level of private pressure exercised over government monetary officials. To verify this expectation, an analysis of the internal workings of the private sector, a task not usually undertaken by political scientists, is needed. This supposition implies that government officials should look beyond the surface of issues to predict impending private pressure.

Scope and Methodology

A brief explication of this study's methodology may aid those unfamiliar with political science techniques. Economic data are unavailable or unusable in addressing questions posed here. While aggregate data on international monetary flows exist, disaggregated information on commercial bank activities do not.[13] To treat direct, circumventing, and indirect bank influence, specific, disaggregated information was required because different banks have different goals (and even when goals are similar, diverging strategic perceptions create variations in bank behavior). To gather data on bank influence and its consequences, it was necessary to interview involved individuals about their thoughts and actions at key junctures. Interviews were conducted with bank executives, government officials, and others involved or concerned with international financial dealings.[14] Differences in interviewees' positions precluded the use of standardized interview forms. Thus, while the evidence presented here is empirical, the interview results were not quantifiable.

This approach has an inherent methodological difficulty which must be faced forthrightly. Information was collected on the impact of numerous actors on the monetary system and on monetary officials. Still, it is impossible to account for all major private pressures in play. Thus while interviews provided large amounts of information on which to base this analytical account, they also underscored differences in attitudes among major actors in the monetary system. As a result, since the information available is far from a complete compilation, conclusions drawn here must be cautious in nature and scope. The permutations of the topic, the difficulty in reaching all the prime market participants, and the complexity of public-private interactions make it unwise to claim too much. This study provides a base from which others may wish to proceed: it does not delimit the exact impact of commercial banks on international monetary developments.

Basic Outline

This research is organized around issue areas. Chapter 2 reviews the political role of banks before 1958, focusing mainly on banks' direct influence, and argues that the efficacy of bank power before 1958 varied immensely. Influence differences are linked to bankers' goals and to the extent that they participated in governments' monetary decision-making. Chapter 3 examines American banks' direct influence since 1958. The expansion of U.S. banks' international operations are examined and the growth and evolution of the foreign exchange and Euromarkets are reviewed. Evidence suggests that publicized changes in the monetary system did not necessarily enhance banks' capabilities for exercising direct power.

Chapters 4 through 7 address the broader problems of banks' circumventing and indirect influence within the monetary system. Chapter 4 analyzes the impact of circumventing bank behavior on U.S. exchange regulations, and concludes that while bank evasions may have undermined the efficiency of exchange restraints, their attempts to influence policy-making were ineffective and even counterproductive. Chapter 5 investigates bank indirect influence during American and British exchange crises after 1964. Here, the role of European banks is also briefly considered because it diverged from U.S. banking behavior at critical points. Chapter 5 argues that the impact of banks on exchange crises varied substantially over time, but that their influence was often misperceived by government officials. Chapter 6 studies the subtle, indirect role of private actors in the search for effective monetary reform. It is argued that private actors' changing preferences effectively delimited the range within which official negotiators could seek to build a new monetary order after August 1971. Chapter 7 investigates the supposed political power derived by commercial banks in their lending activities to richer, developing nations. The focus in this chapter is on the implications of bank lending to developing nations for relations between nations and for the stability of the monetary system. It is argued that, contrary to expectations, borrowing nations and not commercial banks may have the better bargaining position.

The final chapter starts from a broader perspective and posits that internal, private sector competitive processes may help predict the level of indirect and circumventing influence exerted on government officials at various moments. While no prediction of how policy-makers will respond to growing private pressure is offered, the concluding chapter hypothesizes that greater attention to indirect and circumventing influence and to industry competition may help officials design more reasonable, efficient policies for the future.

NOTES

1. The best research on banks' political influence investigates the pre-World War I era. See, Herbert Feis, *Europe the World's Banker 1870-1914* (New York: W. W. Norton, 1965); David S. Landes, *Bankers and Pashas: International Finance and Economic Imperialism in Egypt* (New York: Harper & Row, 1969); Bray Hammond, *Banks and Politics in America* (Princeton, N.J.: Princeton University Press, 1960); and Bray Hammond, *Sovereignty and an Empty Purse: Banks and Politics in the Civil War* (Princeton, N.J.: Princeton University Press, 1970).

2. See, Richard Gardner, *Sterling-Dollar Diplomacy* (New York: McGraw-Hill, 1969); Richard Cooper, *The Economics of Interdependence: Economic Policy in the Atlantic Community* (New York: McGraw-Hill, 1968), Fred Hirsch, *Money International* (Harmondsworth, England: Penguin, 1967); Susan Strange, *Sterling and British Policy* (New York: Oxford University Press, 1971); and C. Fred Bergsten, *The Dilemmas of the Dollar* (New York: Council on Foreign Relations, 1976).

3. Stuart Robinson, Jr., *Multinational Banking* (Leiden, Netherlands: Sijthoff International Publishing Company, 1972); Francis Lees, *International Banking and Finance* (New York: John Wiley, 1974); and Janet Kelly, *Bankers and Borders* (Cambridge, Mass.: Ballinger, 1976).

4. Before his death, Stephen Hymer was investigating the political implications of the structure of international business in such works as, "The internationalization of capital," *Journal of Economic Issues* 6 (March 1972): 91-111; and "The multinational corporation and uneven development," *Economics and World Order,* pp. 113-139, edited by J. N. Bhagwati (Toronto: Macmillan, 1972). Ronald Müller is working along similar lines and beginning to focus more and more on international bank structure. Also, Theodore Moran, *Multinational Corporations and the Politics of Dependence: Copper in Chile* (Princeton, N.J.: Princeton University Press, 1974). Morton Keller's *The Life Insurance Enterprise, 1885-1910* (Cambridge, Mass.: Harvard University Press, 1963) is the only major study of the political influence of insurance companies. Noël Mostert's *Supership* (New York: Warner Books, 1975) is a revealing but unsystematic look at the world of supertankers. To my knowledge, there are no major studies of the political influence of construction, consulting, or advertising industries.

5. There are excellent studies of the economics of the monetary system. See, for example, Leland Yeager, *International Monetary Relations* (New York: Harper & Row, 1976).

6. Three superior books detailing governmental actions and cooperation in international monetary politics have recently appeared. These are: Robert Solomon, *The International Monetary System 1945-1976* (New York: Harper & Row, 1977); Fred L. Block, *The Origins of International Economic Disorder: A Study of United States Monetary Policy from World War II to the Present* (Berkeley: University of California Press, 1977); and Susan Strange, *International Monetary Relations: 1958-1971* (New York: Oxford University Press, 1976). For a more anecdotal treatment by one who believes the dollar could and should have been more vigorously defended in 1971 and 1973, see, Charles Coombs, *The Arena of International Finance* (New York: John Wiley, 1976).

7. Richard Cooper, "Prolegomena to the choice of an international monetary system," *International Organization* 29 (Winter 1975): 63.

8. This follows C. J. Morse, "The evolving monetary system," *Finance and Development* 11 (September 1974): 14-15.

9. Robert Dahl, *Modern Political Analysis* (Englewood Cliffs, N.J.: Prentice-Hall, 1963): 25-26, 47-48.

10. See, E. E. Schattschneider, *Politics, Pressure and the Tariff* (New York: Prentice-Hall, 1935); and Raymond Bauer, Ithiel de Sola Pool, and Lewis Anthony Dexter, *American Business & Public Policy: The Politics of Foreign Trade* (Chicago: Aldine-Atherton, 1972). More conspiratorially, Lenin, Hilferding, C. Wright Mills, and to an extent Herbert Feis assume that a single elite controls both the public and private sectors. Therefore, governments and companies of a nation work together toward nearly identical goals.

11. Relatively friendly accounts include Charles Kindleberger's introduction to his *The International Corporation: A Symposium* (Cambridge, Mass.: MIT Press, 1970): 1-13; Raymond Vernon's *Sovereignty at Bay: The Multinational Spread of U.S. Enterprises* (New York: Basic Books, 1971); and his *Storm Over Multinationals* (Cambridge, Mass.: Harvard University Press, 1977); and George Ball, "Multinational corporations and nation-states," *Atlantic Community Quarterly* 5 (Summer 1967): 247-253. Publicized negative assessments have come from Harry Magdoff, *The Age of Imperialism* (New York: Monthly Review Press, 1969); Richard Barnet and Ronald Müller, *Global Reach* (New York: Simon & Schuster, 1974); and Stephen Hymer, "The multinational corporation and the law of uneven development." An old, but excellent summary of the issues is: Detlev Vagts, "The multinational enterprise: a new challenge for transnational law," *Harvard Law Review* 83 (February 1970): 739-792; and more recently, Robert Keohane and Van Doorn Ooms, "The multinational firm and international regulation," *International Organization* 29 (Winter 1975): 169-209.

12. See, Omer Carey (ed.) *The Military-Industrial Complex and U.S. Foreign Policy* (Pullman: Washington State University Press, 1969); Kari Levitt, *Silent Surrender: The Multinational Corporations in Canada* (New York: St. Martin's, 1970); and Jean-Jacques Servan-Schreiber, *The American Challenge,* translated by Ronald Steel (New York: Avon Books, 1969).

13. The best available data on international banking is provided in the speeches and papers of Andrew Brimmer presented between 1966 and 1974 during his tenure as a Federal Reserve Governor. See particularly, "American international banking: trends and prospects," paper presented before the Bankers' Association for Foreign Trade, Boca Raton, Florida, April 2, 1973; and "Multi-national banks and the management of monetary policy in the United States," paper presented before a joint session of the American Economic Association and the American Finance Association, Toronto, December 28, 1972. Substantial amounts of data are also available in the papers and supplements to the FINE report of the House Committee on Banking, Currency and Housing. *Financial Institutions and the Nation's Economy. Papers and Supplement.* 94th Cong., 2nd sess., 1976.

14. A total of 161 formal interviews and many more conversations were held in gathering materials. Of this total, 115 bankers representing 16 U.S. commercial banks, 5 investment banks, and 9 foreign or consortium banks were interviewed. Although bankers at all levels were interviewed, from trainee to Board Chairman, a particular effort was made to interview individuals in certain key positions. Twenty-three of the interviewees were present or former heads of foreign exchange and Eurocurrency operations in London (13) or in the United States (10). Thirteen interviewees were active foreign exchange dealers. Thirteen were in charge of Eurocurrency syndication in the United States or London. Ten senior international bank economists were also interviewed. To balance the bankers' views, U.S. and British treasury officials and central bankers, IMF officials, congressional committee staff members, several MNC executives, and assorted financial journalists were queried about their interactions with bankers and

their perception of critical events in the international monetary system. In all, 46 non-bankers concerned with the monetary system were interviewed. In most instances, confidentiality precludes identification of interviewees. However, in most cases institutional affiliation are provided in the notes. Unless otherwise noted, all interviews were conducted between January 1, 1974 and November 15, 1974.

Chapter 2

BANK INFLUENCE BEFORE 1958

Bank Power Before 1914

Throughout history the rise and fall of money centers has been recorded by financial chroniclers. From Roman times, traders and merchants carried gold and silver from continent to continent to profit from differences in the relative valuation of the two metals, an international arbitrage of specie and bullion which triggered severe monetary crises century after century.[1] In the early Middle Ages, Jewish money lenders often financed the crusades and lifestyles of monarchs. Eventually, they were pushed from significance when shackled by defaults they could not contest and exorbitant taxes they could not evade.[2] Slowly, banking practices and institutions developed.

Bank centers have risen and subsided in several European cities during the past millennium. Operating patterns, power bases, structures, and the extent of influence have varied, but only rarely have specific banks maintained decisive influence for more than a few decades. For example, in the first half of the fourteenth century, three Florentine companies, the Bardi, the Peruzzi, and the Acciaiuoli were described as the "pillars of Christian trade."[3] Their agents girdled Europe. By 1336, the Peruzzi, the second largest of the three, maintained ninety clerks in fifteen foreign branches extending from London to Cyprus. In 1341, the smaller Acciaiuoli had forty-three clerks residing abroad. All three companies collapsed shortly before the onset of the Black Death in 1348, apparently because of an over-extension of credit and excessive loans to sovereigns.[4] Giovanni Villani, a onetime Peruzzi employee, asserted that when the Peruzzi company failed in 1343, Edward III of England owed the "value of a realm."[5] The Italian companies' direct power was insufficient to insure that foreign sovereigns met their debts.

The community isolation of the plague years prevented rebounding bank power. Not until the early fifteenth century did the Medici Bank rise to prominence, carrying the Medici family to power in Florence. Though never as large as the Bardi and Peruzzi empires, the Medici Bank maintained branches in Rome, Venice, Naples, Pisa, Milan, Geneva-Lyons, Basel, Avignon, Bruges, and London. Garrett Mattingly suggests that the Medici bankers often served as both political and economic agents and implies that Medici power rested on the closeness of the bank and the government. This was particularly true after 1434 when it became "progressively harder to distinguish between resident representatives of the Medici bank and the political agents of the Florentine state."[6] Yet after Cosimo de Medici's death in 1464, the bank's influence declined rapidly. His son made enemies by recalling loans, and his grandson, Lorenzo, neglected his economic power base in favor of diplomacy and art. The bank crumbled so rapidly, according to Raymond de Roover, that had the Medici rule not been overthrown by the French invasion in 1494, "it might have ended even more disgracefully in a financial crash of the first order."[7]

Many banking empires surged to the heights and plummeted to obscurity between the fall of the Medicis and the rise to dominance of the British merchant banks in the latter half of the nineteenth century. In 1873, Walter Bagehot aptly described the merchant banks lining Lombard Street in the shadows of the Bank of England as "by far the greatest combination of economical power and economical delicacy that the world has ever seen."[8] London thrived as the economic hub of the British Empire and as its political cynosure. Beyond the economic power resulting from the financing of the bulk of worldwide trade and investment, the City's merchant bankers wielded tremendous political power. One monetary historian contends that:

> The carrying out of any British government policy which required money, required also the City's blessing. If the government wished to wage war, it would need the means of making payment in the war theater. Meanwhile, though government support in the shape of gunboats was available in extreme instances, the timely pulling of a remote thread in Britain's international financial network by someone in the City was generally sufficient to keep debtor governments in line.[9]

Merchant banks' power rested on their ability to funnel investment abroad and their willingness to keep British allies and colonies financially in line. The French and German banks maintained similar ties with areas critical to their countries' interests, though on a smaller scale. In 1914 French foreign long-term investment was approximately $8.68 billion, of which $3.38 billion was invested outside Europe. About $2.62 billion of Germany's $5.59 billion in long-term investment was outside Europe. In contrast, British long-term, publicly issued capital investment totaled $18.32 billion in 1914.* Only six percent of this investment was in Europe (half of that in Russia). The rest was divided almost equally between British colonies and other non-European nations.[10] The greater diversity supplied British merchant bankers with more flexibility in manipulating outcomes.

Herbert Feis in his classic study of European banking from 1870 to 1914 argued that banks and their home governments cooperated with each other in pursuing their individual international goals. In Great Britain, France, and Germany both the corporate and governmental sectors worked to further national, mercantilist objectives.[11] Banks within each of these nations cooperated with each other on international projects while competing strenuously with their foreign counterparts. When war broke out, there were few entangling alliances among the private enterprises in Great Britain, France, and Germany. However, the linkages between European banks and other nations tended to predict the alliance patterns which emerged after Saravejo. For instance, Russia used her huge debt to French banks to impel France to assist Russia politically, economically, and militarily. The threat of Russian default, which would have driven French banks into insolvency, cemented the Franco-Russian alliance.[12]

On the other hand, Lenin's interpretation of bank-government relations before 1914 focused on finance capital. He insisted that capitalist bankers dominated the foreign policies of their governments. He pointed to increased concentration of capital with a few giant banks in each European nation and noted the predilection of these oligopolies to export capital. He predicted that increasing competition among national financial oligopolies in backward, capital-poor nations would inevitably lead to confrontation between European governments, resulting eventually in the destruction of capitalism.[13] Despite their differences in interpretation, Lenin and Feis concurred that during the decades preceding World War I, European banks, and particularly the British merchant banks, were powerful beyond the narrow realm of international finance.

The nature of the gold standard, which regulated monetary relations between 1870 and 1914, provided European banks with substantial influence within the international monetary system as well. Major nations maintained

---

*These figures were provided in pounds, French francs, and German marks by Feis but have been converted into dollar equivalents for easy comparison of magnitudes. Exchange rates used were 1 pound = $4.8689, 1 French franc = $0.1020, and 1 German mark = $0.2379. These figures are for 1913 as provided by the Federal Reserve Board's 1943 *Banking and Monetary Statistics*.

two-way convertibility between gold and national monetary units at substantially fixed ratios and rarely interfered with international gold flows. A large part of the stability of the foreign exchange standard rested on the sterling balances of foreign bankers in London, which could be shifted to smooth the monetary system when strain arose.[14] In fact, bank-controlled "private short-term capital movements . . . played an important role in the functioning of the pre-1914 gold standard."[15]

American bankers were less significant than European bankers on the international scene before 1914. In 1837 George Peabody opened a London office to attract British capital to America. Other mercantilist endeavors began funneling capital from Europe to America to finance industrial and rail expansion a decade later. By the 1860s Peabody and his associate Junius Morgan, J. Pierpont's father, were leading bankers. However, while the London merchant bankers financed worldwide trade and investment, New York remained preoccupied with financing domestic American economic expansion and paid little attention to the development of an international market. Until shortly before World War I, America remained a net borrower in London and other European markets.[16]

Within the United States individual bankers grew steadily more powerful after the Civil War.[17] The elder J. P. Morgan, in particular, was consistently involved in critical decisions affecting the government's ability to control its economy. For example, without Morgan's support it is questionable whether the United States could have remained on the gold standard during the 1895 gold crisis. Morgan perceived himself as a political actor with certain rights and responsibilities and proceeded accordingly. President Theodore Roosevelt noted with some surprise after a 1902 meeting that "Mr. Morgan could not help regarding me as a big rival operator, who either intended to ruin all his interests or else could be induced to come to an agreement to ruin none."[18] Morgan's influence was so great that the banking panic of 1907 was quieted when Morgan took the initiative and established liquidity reserves for others to draw on.[19]

Domestic bank power came under increased government scrutiny after the breakup of Standard Oil in 1911. On December 19, 1912, in testimony before the Pujo Committee, J. P. Morgan denied that any one man or group could monopolize money and defended existing interlocking directorships between major U.S. banks. The Pujo Committee Report directly rebuked Morgan and laid the groundwork for greater governmental control over banks under the planned Federal Reserve System. Bankers retorted in an American Bankers Association resolution which argued that the proposed system would ruin national banks, would be resisted by both national and state banks, and should not be passed into law.[20]

Nevertheless, the Federal Reserve Act was signed by Woodrow Wilson on

December 23, 1913. While placing banks under a clearer regulatory authority, it did not stifle their growth domestically, and it encouraged international expansion by allowing, for the first time, national banks to establish foreign branches. In addition, each of twelve newly created Federal Reserve Banks was responsible both to the Federal Reserve Board in Washington and to a local board consisting of three bankers, three businessmen, and three outside directors.[21] This partial control encouraged private bankers to cooperate with the Federal Reserve System and allowed them to acquiesce gracefully in its authority.

Rebuilding and Collapse: 1913-1931

While extensive materials on interwar monetary relations exist, little attention has been paid to the changing influence of public and international agencies or of the private sector. An examination focusing on shifts in interwar private bank influence during the 1920s, a period of U.S. governmental isolation but also of the fullest flowering of American international banking power, therefore provides a valuable base for considering post-Bretton Woods monetary developments.

In the economic shambles which emerged after 1919, the two dominant governmental representatives were Benjamin Strong, President of the New York Federal Reserve Bank, and Montagu Norman, Governor of the Bank of England. Norman's influence was closely linked to his government's will. Strong's preeminent position rested on the dearth of U.S. governmental resolution to participate in the rebuilding of Europe. "Strong assumed no function that this government wished to perform. The American government would have taken no initiative in promoting reconstruction and stabilization abroad, and would not have participated officially in such efforts if Strong had stayed out of the field."[22]

Low United States government interest also allowed J. P. Morgan, Jr. and Thomas Lamont, both of the partnership of J. P. Morgan & Co., to play an important role in European reconstruction. As early as 1919 Lamont served as President Wilson's financial advisor at the Versailles peace talks. The House of Morgan's importance was obvious again in 1924 when Poincaré's government borrowed $100 million from Morgan to resist speculation against the French franc. While negotiating this profitable loan, Lamont felt justified in pressuring the French Premier to insure the loan by dissuading the author of a pessimistic assessment of French economic prospects to withdraw his article from publication.[23] In large part, "the vacuum left by the United States authorities was filled by J. P. Morgan & Co."[24]

Other United bankers also played major roles in shaping American foreign economic policy throughout the 1920s. Charles Dawes, a Chicago banker before becoming Vice President of the United States, chaired the Paris, Dawes Conference in 1924, which attempted to reconcile German reparation payments to economic stability and growth in Europe. Again, at the Baden-Baden Conference held in October 1929, in connection with the Young Plan (Owen Young was a banker), the American chairmen of the conference was Jackson Reynolds, a leading New York banker. The second U.S. representative, Melvin Taylor, was head of the First National Bank of Chicago.[25] Within these financial conferences bankers consistently held important political posts. In addition, bankers were represented within the United States throughout much of the 1920s by Secretary of the Treasury Andrew Mellon, one of the nation's leading bankers.

Inevitably a certain arrogance of power arose among many bankers. Stories concerning J. P. Morgan are legion. A. P. Giannini, the founder of Bank of America, refused to wait for changes in laws banning operations he wanted to undertake. "He simply went ahead and began his arrangements . . . expecting lawmakers to catch up with him."[26] Major banking figures demanded laissez-faire capitalism and were taken seriously. In 1929 Benjamin Williams, writing on U.S. foreign economic policy, adumbrated C. Wright Mills, stating, "the political influence of the banking class is vastly out of proportion to their numerical strength."[27]

American bankers, led by the House of Morgan, were central to most financing efforts throughout the 1920s. Restabilization and reconstruction required money, and Morgan could usually be counted on to float the loan, on admittedly profitable terms. Morgan and other American bankers were, however, less influential during the political proccess of restabilizing the pound at $4.86 in 1925. Stephen Clarke makes no mention of Morgan or other bankers during the negotiations that led to restabilization.[28] In his study of this event, D. E. Moggridge is almost equally silent. He notes that Keynes and Reginald McKenna, the head of Midland Bank, opposed the restabilization, but also that the head of the National Westminster Bank favored the move.[29] He stresses that Strong and Norman consulted J. P. Morgan on his views in December 1924, but implies that the key decisions had already been made.[30] Moggridge also implies that a line of credit was extended by Morgan to the Bank of England, but this presumably was never drawn.[31] Apparently, Morgan and other bankers were listened to during restabilization preparations but did not exercise extensive influence because restoring sterling did not require major private sector loans.

Generally, bank influence was exercised in areas involving interactions among nations but not when basic revisions in the structure of the international economic system were contemplated. To an extent, this separation was fostered by the central bankers. Strong believed, and Norman apparently concurred, that the monetary system's basic weakness "was not in the motives of men, but in the structure of the monetary and banking system" which precluded effective voluntary bank cooperation to prevent crises or deal with them when they occurred.[32] This consensus led Strong and Norman to play active roles in restoring the stability of European currencies. With the help of Germany's Hjalmar Schacht and despite frequent disagreements with France's Emile Moreau, Strong and Norman helped stabilize the Belgian franc in 1926 and the Polish, Italian, and Rumanian currencies the following year.[33] In these instances private bankers were used by central bankers to supply stabilization loans but exercised less influence than during reparation negotiations.

Toward the end of the 1920s governments began restructuring their international economic roles just as the private banks became more daring in their operations. Private bankers became so enthralled by profit opportunities during the 1920s boom that they abandoned their supportive role in the monetary system. The only major bank initiative after the late 1920s took place at the establishment of the Bank for International Settlements. The BIS was designed to monitor and redistribute the German reparations under the Young Plan but the U.S. government would not officially participate since it was sponsored by the League of Nations. As a result, the original founders were privately held European central banks and J. P. Morgan & Company, the First National Bank of New York, and the First National Bank of Chicago. At least on paper the BIS is unique; both private and central bankers are members of the same international institution.[34] In practice, the Federal Reserve System sends "observers" to participate in monthly BIS meetings, from which private bankers and finance ministry officials are excluded.

The BIS began operations as economic depression deepened worldwide. The October 1929 crash of the New York stock market reverberated throughout the developed world. Some have suggested that had J. P. Morgan, Sr. rather than his son been responsible for the market's defense, the catastrophic drop might have been averted or controlled.[35] This misses the wider perspective. Bank prestige and power had already begun to wane. Bankers had lost some of their initiating power which allowed them to play a key role in stabilizing the monetary system when necessary. Nonetheless, many blamed the system's failure on bankers. Some bankers went to jail; others were disgraced.

Bankers' power and prestige also waned in Europe as the Great Depression unfolded. On May 11, 1931 Austria's largest bank, the Rothschild-controlled Kreditanstalt, failed. Briand's reelection defeat in France two days later fueled uncertainty. The political unrest prevading Europe led to such harsh terms on the proposed government salvage operation for the Austrian economy that on June 18, 1931 the Austrian government chose to resign rather than submit.

Market structure linking Germany and Austria coupled with bankers' fears refocused the growing crisis on Germany. Speculation on the reichsmark became extremely heavy. Domestic capital fled and foreign funds were withdrawn from Germany in such huge quantities that the announcement of the Hoover Moratorium on German reparation payments on July 4, 1931 failed to stem the flow or restore market confidence. The failure of Germany's largest textile concern created a run on its chief bank, the Darmstadtler Bank, which in the absence of adequate government support closed its doors on July 13. Despite extensive, extraordinary assistance from the Bank of England, the Federal Reserve System, the members of the Seven Power Conference convened to deal with the situation, and the Bank for International Settlements, withdrawals continued except for frozen, short-term funds.

The day the Darmstadtler failed, the Macmillian report revealed that £70 million in short-term bank funds were frozen in Germany. Intense pressure on the pound followed immediately and was aggravated by the French withdrawal of substantial gold from Great Britain to strengthen its own position. Breaking down responsibility for market pressure is extremely difficult, but according to Charles Kindleberger, the key pressure "seems to have come from the commercial banks in the smaller countries of Europe—Belgium, the Netherlands, Sweden, and Switzerland—which had lost liquidity through the blocking of German credits and sold sterling to increase their gold reserves."[36] This interpretation is supported by Federal Reserve figures which show that during 1931 net gold exports from Great Britain to the Netherlands were $127.3 million more than in the previous year. France, Switzerland, and Belgium also had sharply higher gold imports from Great Britain in 1931 than in 1930. Only Germany and the British Commonwealth exported more gold to Great Britain in 1931 than in 1930.[37] Bankers in gold importing nations were trying to protect their own interests and not intentionally aiming to upset the monetary system. Still, their actions were destabilizing in part because their frightened behavior forestalled equilibrating action from other parts of the banking and business community.

Pressure on the pound redoubled after July 31 when the May Committee predicted a minimum British budget deficit of £120 million and called for greater austerity. After the fall of the Labour government on August 24 and its recreation under MacDonald, a new austerity budget in early September prompted unrest among British sailors. Sensationalist reporting exaggerated the extent and severity of the "mutiny," which prompted huge flights of capital away from sterling and forced Britain to abandon the gold standard on September 21, 1931.

Without Bank of England exchange market support, sterling plummeted from $4.86 in September to a low of $3.25 in December. Twenty-five nations followed Britain off gold. Most of its empire matched its depreciation. The

United States, Germany, South Africa, and the gold bloc countries resisted the depreciation while most British trading partners allowed their currencies to dip, though by less than the pound.

Although these events were rooted in the economic context of the nations involved, banks and corporations which manipulated the flow of funds between nations and currencies were critical in preventing governments from curtailing the crisis when panic set in. Once the stream of "hot" money was turned on, extensive governmental bilateral and multilateral cooperation, marred only briefly by French intransigence in July, was unable to stem the flow. Although most bankers did not completely understand the impact of their activities on government control of the monetary stability of the system, tensions between banks and governments became as intense as the tension among governments. Control of the monetary system was divided between public and private actors.

Ragnar Nurkse's respected and disputed League of Nations study of this period argued that freely floating exchange rates such as those existing after September 21, 1931 were unlikely to provide efficient operations in the international monetary system. He argued that disequilibrating capital flows controlled by private banks and corporations undermined sterling. Nurkse suggested that during crises exchange rates were bound to become highly unstable, largely because of psychological factors and that the realization of the exchange market's inability to maintain a stable, short-run equilibrium had led to the abandonment of freely fluctuating exchange rates.[38]

Definitive evidence to define the political intent of European bankers during 1931 is unavailable. However, they were apparently motivated more by the fear of losses than the possibility of windfall gains. Even though banks were probably not directly responsible for the underlying problems which created the crisis, their prestige and influence suffered in both Europe and America. Bank links in the 1920s were primarily with central banks, even though Mellon was the Treasury Secretary. The fall in private bank prestige was repeated throughout the business community and mirrored by a drop within governments of the power of central bankers. Finance ministries in Europe and Treasury Departments in Great Britain and America rose to take the brunt of the policy-making burden. This further eroded the already declining power of commercial bankers and investment bankers since the new central decision-makers were suspicious of them.

Banks in Depression: 1932-1944

The seepage of power from the Federal Reserve System and the private sector in the United States was accelerated by Roosevelt's election. Roosevelt believed many commercial bankers had acted irresponsibly. This opinion was reinforced when Charles Mitchell, president of the National City Bank, was convicted of tax evasion and Albert Wiggin, president of the Chase National Bank, was discovered shorting Chase stock while recommending other bank officers to invest in it.[39] In this atmosphere FDR told Hamilton Fish Armstrong that while he never believed Wall Street "gave orders to the Treasury Department under the Republicans," and only that the line was always open for advice back and forth, he intended to cut that line.[40]

The new President was determined to rebuild the American economy even if it meant neglecting international economic affairs. He announced in his first inaugural that "our international trade relations, though vastly important, are, in point of time and necessity, secondary to the establishment of a sound national economy."[41] Roosevelt, never a lover of bankers, found that his first major task was to shore up the domestic banking system. His aim was to support solvent, adequately managed, small and medium-sized banks and not the huge metropolitan institutions which were in no serious trouble.[42] On March 6, 1933 he proclaimed a bank holiday. His first "fireside chat" on March 12, 1933 was aimed at reassuring the American people concerning the Bank Holiday and promised an early return to stable banking practices.

On June 21, 1933 FDR signed the Glass-Steagall Banking Act which struck at independent bank power in the United States. It gave the Federal Reserve wider regulatory power to dampen the ability of American banks to use funds brashly. In addition, banking structure was shaken by the Act's provision forcing the separation of investment and commercial banking activities. Equally important on the domestic side, was the establishment of the Federal Deposit Insurance Corporation (FDIC), which over time quieted the public's fear of bank failures and prevented runs on banks by small depositors.[43] The Glass-Steagall Act was followed by the 1935 Banking Act, which strengthened the domestic control and overall independence of the Federal Reserve System but did not address the central bank's international responsibilities.

The American economy required drastic reorganization after one third of all U.S. banks failed between 1931 and 1933. The Federal Reserve System had forfeited its international preeminence of the 1920s to the Treasury. Treasury preoccupation with international money affairs increased rapidly after Roosevelt's election. Simultaneously, the Federal Reserve became more firmly involved in domestic, regulatory matters and was granted greater authority over national banking operations. The Treasury and State Department filled the international economic policy vacuum which had existed since Strong's death in 1928. Roosevelt apparently had no firm idea of what he wanted to accomplish on the international economic front, but was forced to spend substantial amounts of time reading memoranda concerning the

World Economic Conference of 1933, to which the Hoover administration had committed U.S. participation. At that conference, it became clear that FDR's policy toward bankers differed from his Republican predecessors. Unlike the international conferences of the 1920's, bankers were almost entirely absent from the London economic conference. Only Paul Warburg of the financial elite attended, and his role apparently was quite small. The prime U.S. delegates were politicians backed by State Department officials. Treasury and Federal Reserve officials participated mainly on technical matters.[44]

This interpretation supports Kindleberger's argument that many monetary difficulties in the 1930s can be traced to lack of international economic leadership caused by British inability and American unwillingness to assume responsibility for controlling the international depression.[45] Whether or not a true "beggar thy neighbor" policy of competitive devaluations was underway,[46] there was no government, no public agency, no private enterprise and no international organization which asserted its leadership in the 1930s. American and European banks and central banks retreated and the finance ministries were inexperienced in running the monetary system. The result was a leaderless, unstable monetary environment which lasted until the 1940s.

Rebuilding the Monetary System: 1944-1958

When the Allied Nations met at Bretton Woods to design a new monetary order to govern postwar economic relations, there was no old structure to sweep away. The economic relations of nations had muddled along during the preceding dozen years. Only a festering emptiness, not outright opposition, faced those who gathered to reorder the economic scene.

Between the fall of the pound in 1931 and the emergence of the Bretton Woods system in 1944, private bankers played only a minor role internationally. In 1926 eleven U.S. banks maintained 107 branches and subsidiaries abroad.[47] By 1950, only 95 American bank branches were operating abroad.[48] More important than the decline in numbers was the conservative approach bankers adopted at home and abroad. In the 1930s and 1940s bankers lost their independent spirit. Before venturing into new international loans, they obediently consulted the U.S. government. When the government needed international financial assistance, the bankers were willing to react to their requests quickly and favorably. In fact, "reactive" is perhaps the best description of the bankers' stance. The conservative posture they adopted was honed to keep banks out of decision-makers' consciousness and slowly to rebuild their badly tarnished image among both the public and government regulators.

World War II solidified the hold of the government planners. Banks which had remained obedient to government needs throughout the war were in no position to play a major role in the rekindling of the monetary regime at Bretton Woods had they so desired. The pattern of the 1930s was not greatly altered. The key figures were not private or central bankers, but Assistant Secretary Harry Dexter White of the U.S. Treasury and John Maynard Keynes, then attached to the British Treasury.[49]

The struggle surrounding the shape of the new monetary regime pitted an internationalist British plan designed by Keynes to create new international reserve assets and force nations to relinquish substantial power to the new International Monetary Fund and the U.S. Treasury-sponsored White plan which pushed the dollar to the forefront and granted the fund less independent authority. Since Europe required U.S. assistance in rebuilding, the eventual compromise was closer to the U.S. perspective.[50]

The internal struggle between finance ministries and central banks, which had significance for private banks as well, was crystalized in a finance ministry-sponsored resolution that the central banker-dominated BIS should be abolished. This finance ministry domination was so pervasive at Bretton Woods that BIS supporters worked to make the inevitable resolution of dissolution noncompulsory rather than directly opposing it. The final resolution called for early liquidation of the BIS, but by 1946 it was evident that central bankers would not disband despite some pressure from the U.S. Treasury.[51]

Bankers, who had no voice in the IMF's formulation, were fearful of the new order. One banker attending the American Bankers Association meetings in 1944 found a tendency to approve the bank, and disapprove the fund because "it does not solve the British problem, it does not stabilize rates, exchange restrictions are continued, too wide authority is given to countries to devalue, the quota system is condemned, the United States loses control of a large amount of money, power to devalue the dollar may be surrendered, the amount of the fund is too large, etc., etc."[52] However, opinion was not united. The Bank of American executive who received this missive, believed that "the Monetary Fund [was] a sound device" and stressed that it would serve America's specific national interest.[53] Apparently, most businessmen believed that the Bretton Woods agreement distributed U.S. resources to the rest of the world. However, businessmen engaged in import and export trade generally favored the fund.

Still, bankers and businessmen had only minimal direct impact on U.S. approval of the fund and the World Bank. Many complained, some supported, but they could not and did not act. Yet the private sector rapidly accepted the newly imposed monetary regime and discovered they could live well and profitably under it. Bankers in particular adjusted their views of the new monetary order quite smoothly. Often, bankers seem to be the last to want changes in their environment, but the first to adapt to new conditions.

Despite renewed economic solidarity provided by the Bretton Woods regime and the Marshall Plan aid to Europe, parity relationships remained out of line in the late 1940s. In a move which recalled 1925, in accordance with the Anglo-American financial agreement, Great Britain attempted to restore full currency convertibility on July 15, 1947, valuing sterling at $4.03. Circumstances were not propitious. Approximately £1 billion was converted to other currencies, driving reserves downward and forcing the British to abandon convertibility on August 20, 1947 with U.S. approval.

Monetary relations were again jolted by a wave of devaluations and parity realignments in September 1949. The BIS commented in its 1949-50 annual report that during only two years since the nineteenth century establishment of the gold standard were there adjustments of foreign exchange rates "so sweeping that the expression 'wave of devaluations' has been justified. These years were 1931 and 1949."[54] Three major similarities between the devaluation waves are evident. "Both episodes fell within periods of postwar reconstructions. Both involved heavy bearish speculation. On both occasions, the depreciation of sterling touched off chain reactions of exchange-rate adjustment."[55] Differences also existed. The price declines of 1949 were gentler and of shorter duration. North Atlantic economic prospects were brighter in 1949. The 1949 experience also differed because the United States aggressively supported the newly defined monetary regime to minimize short-term chaos. Finally, strict exchange controls and the absence of internal European convertibility prevented speculators from taking control of events as they had in 1931. Thus, Britain's 1949 devaluation from $4.03 to $2.80 was instituted after a currency drain only one half as severe as the flow generated during the attempted return to convertibility in 1947.

Banks were also readjusting their international operations in the late 1940s. They remained carefully conservative in these dealings, preferring to conduct most of their international transactions from their domestic headquarters. Competition between U.S. banks became obvious as early as the beginning of 1945 when Bank of America was excluded by Eastern bankers, and particularly Chase, from participating in a loan to the Netherlands.[56] Nonetheless, syndicates of American banks were formed to aid European recovery with great frequency throughout the late 1940s. Perhaps the most publicized credits were the $75 million lent by the Chase National Bank and the Guaranty Trust Company to France one month after the 1949 devaluations and the $225 million raised for France the next year by Chase and J. P. Morgan & Co.

In the 1950s American banks continued to increase their business activities abroad from their headquarters. The lack of convertibility, however, dissuaded them from opening numerous new branches and subsidiaries in Europe. Lending policies remained conservative and banks were particularly careful to avoid the tint of political motivations. In 1955 for instance, the chairman of Bank of America described the bank's international posture in a letter to the president of the Federal Reserve Bank of New York:

> In our dealings with foreign borrowers, we are especially concerned with establishing a constructive and enduring relationship that will grow stronger year after year. Any transactions no matter how profitable, that would lead a foreign government or central bank to be critical of us could do us so much harm in the long run that it would not be worthwhile even from a purely selfish point of view. Moreover, any such criticism, if at all reasonable, would soon come to the attention of other foreign central banks and governments, and would injure our relationships with them, too.[57]

As bankers learned their way around the monetary system, they became bolder. Their conservatism faded as profit possibilities emerged, but governments retained the upper hand. For instance, growing foreign exchange markets allowed bankers to protect themselves and their corporate clients in crisis situations. Between January 1951 and January 1958, Britain alone repulsed four separate runs on sterling. Two of these crises were purely speculative in nature. In late 1956 the pound was attacked in the aftermath of the Suez crisis despite Britain's healthy balance of payments surplus. Extensive Bank of England intervention was also necessary during August and September 1957, to soothe sterling in the face of a French devaluation and German revaluation expectations.[58] In these and other cases of speculation in the 1950s, private banks backed down. Firm government resolve coupled with central bank reserves and limited currency convertibility guaranteed government dominance over private banks. Devaluations were rare even when economic indicators suggested their need. U.S. control was sufficient to insure that when devaluations were undertaken, as in 1949, it was even possible to time them to coincide with the IMF annual meeting.[59] Formal negotiations preceded the devaluations. Such openness was impossible in the 1930s or the 1960s.

Quickly retracing the major shifts in influence, it can be seen that at the close of the nineteenth century, the British merchant banks and the Bank of England controlled the system. The demise of the gold standard and the coming of World War I spelled an end to merchant banks' dominance, which had been slipping since 1890. The new realities of the economic situation after 1919 thrust American businessmen and bankers into the forefront of international activity. The government, however, was divided. America did not enter the League of Nations, and the bulk of the official burden for international restabilization of the revised monetary system fell to Benjamin Strong and Montagu Norman, aided by a handful of American bankers who were able *and willing* to play an activist international political role for a price. The shift from British to U.S. banking power was inevitable anyway as British economic power slipped and was replaced by U.S. dollar diplomacy.

Bankers reached the peak of their prestige, power, and influence about 1929. When disaster struck, they were early casualties. They retreated into the background and were replaced by the Treasury and State Department at international conferences. Federal Reserve and European central banks were similarly banished to domestic affairs and regulatory business while the running of the monetary regime was taken over by politicians and finance ministries. Unfortunately, they lacked the will, the tools, and the focus to cooperate in the construction of a new monetary system until 1944. Even at Bretton Wood the finance ministries dominated. Still, it took thirteen years for the system to approach the ideal position intended.

In these years American bankers remained conservative but began lending more frequently abroad. They were more strictly controlled domestically than before 1933 but by the 1950s discovered that major new profit opportunities lay outside the United States. In moving abroad, some bankers realized they were entering a new era of international banking, but they ignored the political implications of their activities. They were trained to seek profit, not bank history. Yet increasingly, bankers discovered that their opportunities for profits led them into conflict with governments. When the governments were certain and committed to one path, the bankers preferred to relent, but when the government hesitated, the bankers found themselves involved with politically sensitive issues which many would have preferred to avoid.

NOTES

1. Andrew M. Watson, "Back to gold—and silver," *Economic History Review* 20:1 (1967): 1-34.

2. Doris M. Stenton, *English Society in the Early Middle Ages* (Harmondsworth, England: Penguin, 1965): 194-202.

3. Giovanni Villani (1276-1348) quoted in Raymond de Roover, *The Rise and Decline of the Medici Bank 1397-1494* (Cambridge, Mass.: Harvard University Press, 1963): 2.

4. Ibid.: 2-3.

5. Ibid.: 3.

6. Garrett Mattingly, Renaissance Diplomacy (Boston: Houghton Mifflin, 1971): 69.

7. de Roover, op. cit.: 370.

8. Walter Bagehot, *Lombard Street: A Description of the Money Market* (New York: Scribner and Armstrong, 1873): 4.

9. Brian Johnson, *The Politics of Money* (New York: McGraw-Hill, 1970): 49.

10. Figures provided in Herbert Feis, *Europe: The World's Banker 1870-1914* (New York: W. W. Norton, 1965): 23, 51, 74.

11. Ibid.

12. Ibid.: 212-224. For a detailed account of French bank activity in Egypt before World War I, see, David S. Landes, *Bankers and Pashas: International Finance and Economic Imperialism in Egypt* (New York: Harper & Row, 1969).

13. V. I. Lenin, *Imperialism: The Highest Stage of Capitalism* (Peking: Foreign Languages Press, 1965).

14. William A. Brown, *The International Gold Standard Reinterpreted: 1914-1934*, 2 vols. (New York: National Bureau of Economic Research, 1940): 1: xv.

15. Arthur Bloomfield, "Short-term capital movements under the pre-1914 gold standard," *Princeton Studies in the International Finance* 11 (July 1963): 34.

16. Paul Einzig, *The Fight for Financial Supremacy* (London: Macmillan, 1932): 38.

17. For a detailed study of the political role of banks during the Civil War see, Bray Hammond, *Sovereignty and an Empty Purse: Banks and Politics in the Civil War* (Princeton, N.J.: Princeton University Press, 1970).

18. Edwin P. Hoyt, Jr., *The House of Morgan* (New York: Dodd, Mead, 1966): 257.

19. Ibid.: 279-307.

20. "Resolutions by the American Bankers' Association, August 22, 1913," in Herman Krooss (ed.) *Documentary History of Banking and Currency in the United States*, 4 vols. (New York: McGraw-Hill, 1969): 3:2241.

21. Federal Reserve Bank directors are listed in the Federal Reserve's annual report.

22. Lester Chandler, *Benjamin Strong: Central Banker* (Washington, D.C.: Brookings Institution, 1958): 30.

23. Hamilton Fish Armstrong, *Peace and Counterpeace: From Wilson to Hitler* (New York: Harper & Row, 1971): 323-325.

24. Stephen Clarke, *Central Bank Cooperation: 1924-1931* (New York: Federal Reserve Bank of New York, 1967): 48.

25. Hjalmaar Schacht, *My First 76 Years* (New York: Wingate, 1955): 251-252.

26. Marquis James and Bessie James, *The Biography of a Bank: The Story of Bank of America N.T. & S.A.* (New York: Harper & Brothers, 1954): 268.

27. Benjamin Williams, *Economic Foreign Policy of the United States* (New York: McGraw-Hill, 1929): 24.

28. Stephen Clarke, *Central Bank Co-operation*.

29. D. E. Moggridge, *The Return to Gold: 1925*, University of Cambridge, Department of Applied Economics, Occasional Paper 19 (Cambridge, Mass.: Cambridge University Press, 1969): 28-31.

30. Ibid.: 40.

31. Ibid.: 58.

32. Chandler, op. cit.: 30.

33. See, Clarke, *Central Bank Co-operation* and Richard Meyer, *Bankers' Diplomacy: Monetary Stabilization in the Twenties* (New York: Columbia University Press, 1970).

34. See, Henry Schloss, *The Bank for International Settlements: An Experiment in Central Bank Cooperation* (Amsterdam: North Holland Publishing Company, 1958): 147.

35. Hoyt, op. cit.: 376-377.

36. Charles P. Kindleberger, *The World Depression 1929-1939* (Berkeley: University of California Press, 1973): 158.

37. *Federal Reserve Bulletin*, February 1932: 113.

38. League of Nations, *The International Currency Experience* (Geneva: League of Nations, 1944): 118.

39. Margaret Myers, *A Financial History of the United States* (New York: Columbia University Press, 1970): 313.

40. Armstrong, op. cit.: 522.

41. U.S. Congress, *Inaugural Addresses of the Presidents of the United States.* 82nd Cong., 2nd sess., 1952: 227.

42. Indeed, the Bank of America suffered more in 1931 than 1933 when it was undergoing definite recovery. James and James, op. cit.: 346-374.

43. Former Treasury Secretary Joseph Barr, who became head of the Franklin National Bank after problems surfaced in May 1974, believes that Franklin was the ultimate triumph of the FDIC. Franklin's small depositors were so confident the FDIC would reimburse them in case of failure, that they did not make a run on the bank. MNCs and municipalities were the ones withdrawing funds. Joseph Barr, conversation at Harvard Center for International Affairs, October 15, 1975.

44. This interpretation was developed in conversation with Ken Oye, whose dissertation "Bargaining, belief-systems, and bullion: the evolution of international monetary politics," Ph.D. dissertation, Harvard, 1978, deals with the 1933 World Economic conference. Also see, Jeanette Nichols, "Roosevelt's monetary diplomacy in 1933," *American Historical Review* 56 (January 1951): 295-317.

45. Kindleberger, *World Depression*: 291-292.

46. Ragnar Nurkse and most other economists studying the depression argue that begger-thy-neighbor polices were consciously adopted by governments. Sidney Rolfe and James Burtle, *The Great Wheel: The World Monetary System: A Reinterpretation* (New York: Quadrangle, 1973): 19-55, dispute this view.

47. Clyde Phelps, *The Foreign Expansion of American Banks: American Banking Abroad* (New York. Ronald Press, 1927). 211.

48. George S. Moore, "International growth: challenge to U.S. banks," *National Banking Review* (September 1963): 8.

49. David Eagle Brown, the head of the First National Bank of Chicago was active at Bretton Woods. Nonetheless, there is no mention of Brown, other bankers, or banks in general in Richard Gardner's definitive *Sterling-Dollar Diplomacy* (New York: McGraw-Hill, 1969).

50. A good summary of this period is Fred Block, *The Origins of International Economic Disorder* (Berkeley: University of California Press, 1977): op. cit.: 12-137.

51. Schloss, op. cit.: 118-120.

52. Letter from Clarence Hunter (N.Y. Trust) to Otto Jeidels (Bank of America), September 18, 1944. Bank of America Archives, San Francisco.

53. Undelivered testimony prepared by Otto Jeidels (Bank of America) for a "House Committee" investigating Bretton Wodds, March 11, 1945. Bank of America Archives, San Francisco.

54. Bank for International Settlements, *20th Annual Report*, 1949-50: 148.

55. Leland Yeager, *International Monetary Relations* (New York: Harper & Row, 1966): 383.

56. Letter from Otto Jeidels to Mario Giannini, March 13, 1945. Bank of America Archives, San Francisco.

57. Letter from Jesse Tapp (Bank of America) to Allan Sproull (President, N.Y. Federal Reserve Bank) August 15, 1955. Bank of America Archives: San Francisco.

58. Fred Hirsch, *The Pound Sterling: A Polemic* (London: Victor Gollancz, 1965): 47-49.

59. See, the IMF's official history of events for the international or organization perspective of 1949 developments: J. Keith Horsefield, *The International Monetary Fund 1945-1965,* 3 vols. (Washington: IMF, 1969): 1: 231-256.

Chapter 3

DIRECT BANK INFLUENCE AND

INTERNATIONAL MONETARY

POLITICS, 1958-1976

To exert direct influence over governmental officials and their politics, bankers lobby in the executive and legislative branches, appeal publicly for policy changes, and rely on the judgment of bank-trained officials in government. In special cases, particularly in developing countries, banks directly influence government policy by granting or withholding credit. Occasionally, officials will modify policies if banks can demonstrate that existing regulations are inequitable or uneconomical. When successful, direct bank pressure persuades officials to adopt or not to adopt proposed policies or to retain or alter existing policies.

A serious difficulty prevents precision in analyzing direct influence. If little influence is found, it does not necessarily mean it is absent. Intellectual persuasion and the favorable perspective most U.S. officials maintain towards the ideals of capitalism provide a bedrock of sympathy linking corporate and government officials and minimizing the need to exert direct influence. Therefore, while the basis of cooperation may be becoming more fragile, it cannot be inferred that banks are impotent even if their efforts are often unsuccessful.

Potential Sources of Increased Direct Bank Influence

Did evolving opportunities, behavior, and visibility of banks after the return to general European convertibility at the end of 1958 help restore direct bank power over government and particularly U.S. government policies? The prospect of Europe unified by the Common Market and the return to European currency convertibility encouraged U.S. bank expansion into Europe. Foreign acceptance of U.S. banks improved in 1960 after New York City allowed foreign banks to open there. Nonetheless, at the close of 1961 only eight American banks maintained foreign branches. Only four of these had more than four branches.[1]

CHANGED BANK ATTITUDE TOWARDS INVOLVEMENT

The most straightforward reason to expect increased direct bank influence, is that bankers started to reconsider their role in international relations. Banks are no longer passive institutions, reactive to their home governments' whims, but have become activists desiring freedom from governmental contols and the right to at least participate in discussions on international monetary matters. Contrast, for example, policy statements made by heads of the international department of Bank of America a dozen years apart. In 1959 Russell Smith confidently asserted that

> the role of business for the future should be to make profits and to follow its own self-interest in maximizing production in the economy as a whole. . . . Business at the same time should continue to have a social conscience, but it should limit its welfare activities to those which are in reasonably direct relationship to its own operations.[2]

While in 1971 C. M. van Vlierden stated:

> In the coming 25 years we can expect a shift from influence by the nation-state to a new and greater influence by private, profit motivated, entrepreneurial organizations and supranational economic institutions which together can surmount (political) structure of limited geography or limited (and often unrealistic) political programmes of single nation-states.[3]

Recently, Bank of America President A. W. Clausen went even further and asserted that we can look forward to "an international corporation that has shed all national identity."[4] This change in attitude makes it probable that banks would try to influence U.S. policy, not just react to it.

Bankers have no desire to usurp governmental prerogatives, but only to avoid the latter's regulations, which are perceived as damaging banking operations. Thus, banks could reasonably be expected to try to influence officials to ignore them rather than to try to include them in policy-making groups. A banker's ideal world consists of little or no regulation of their operations and minimal barriers to their operations between countries. However, in those instances where conflict between banks and governments arise, banks hope to persuade governments of their right to operate without restraint.

BANK EXPANSION

Increased direct bank influence might also flow from the tremendous expansion of bank activities abroad. U.S. bank expansion abroad accelerated after the Voluntary Foreign Credit Restraint Program (VFCR) was promulgated in an attempt to limit the deterioration of the American payments balance in 1965. The VFCR limited the amount banks could lend from the United States to overseas customers and forced corporate treasurers to turn from New York to Europe to raise capital for use outside the United States. Large banks, no longer able to service their MNC customers from America, followed the MNCs to Europe.

Although conditions allowed for bank expansion in the early 1960s, changes in bank behavior and strategy also acted to turn U.S. banks outward. The First National City Bank* (Citibank) led the way in the late 1950s and early 1960s. Its international expansion was masterminded by George Moore and his lieutenant, Walter Wriston, who recruited the best talent available with high salaries, substantial authority, and rapid promotion. In 1963 Moore confidently predicted that "as American business increasingly looked outward for expansion, so U.S. banks would find international operations a profitable experience."[5]

Bank visibility increased as bank activities expanded dramatically throughout the 1960s. When 1960 closed, eight banks operated 124 foreign branches. The number of banks and foreign branches tripled by the end of 1966, and at the end of 1975, 126 U.S. banks operated 762 foreign branches.[6] Simultaneously, the number of Edge Act Corporations—units that allow banks to conduct international business from states other than their home state—increased from 10 at the end of 1960 to 112 at the end of 1975.[7] Inevitably, the frequency of American bank contact with government officials concerned

---

*In 1955 the First National Bank of New York and the National City Bank merged to form what became the First National City Bank. In early 1976 the name was simplified to Citibank. This name will be used throughout.

with international monetary matters increased and the intensity of these contacts rose sharply.

International bankers cheerfully acknowledge that profit opportunities are likely to continue to be more attractive abroad than in the United States, where over 14,000 banks compete for business. Although other nations have more bank branches per capita, no other country supports nearly as many distinct banking institutions. The glut of banks in the United States is accompanied by masses of regulations administered at several levels which frequently inhibit domestic profitability. Table 3.1 traces the rapid growth

Table 3.1: Total Deposits and Foreign Deposits as a Percentage of Total Deposits[a] Reported by the 17 Largest American Commercial Banks: 1964, 1973, 1976

		end 1976		6/30/1973		end 1964	
		Total Deposits	% Foreign	Total Deposits	% Foreign	Total Deposits	% Foreign
1.	BankAmerica	60.7	41	36.5	35	14.3	9.6
2.	Citicorp	49.1	64	29.4	49	10.9	16.1
3.	Chase Manhattan	37.6	47	26.2	37	11.4	12.1
4.	Manufacturers Hanover	26.2	35	15.2	31	6.1	5.4
5.	J. P. Morgan	21.5	55	13.1	44	4.8	8.4
6.	Chemical	20.9	40	13.0	27	5.4	2.8
7.	Bankers Trust	17.7	45	12.8	31	3.8	4.2
8.	Western Bancorp.	16.4	11	13.5	9	2.7	——
9.	Continental Illinois	15.8	45	11.2	32	4.1	1.2
10.	First Chicago	14.1	41	10.7	28	3.6	——
11.	Security Pacific	13.5	22	11.3	21	4.4	——
12.	Wells Fargo	10.4	7	8.3	23	3.3	——
13.	Marine Midland	9.1	30	10.0	31	1.1	1.6
14.	Crocker National	9.1	11	6.5	16	3.2	——
15.	Charter (Irving Trust)	8.7	29	7.8	26	2.8	——
16.	Mellon National	6.7	25	6.3	39	2.7	——
17.	First Boston	6.0	50	5.2	38	1.9	5.9
	Average top 3	49.1	50.7	30.7	40.3	12.2	12.6
	Average top 10	28.0	42.4	18.2	32.3	6.7	6.0
	Average all 17	20.2	35.2	13.9	20.4	5.1	4.0

SOURCES: **Business Week,** April 18, 1977; September 15, 1973; and Andrew Brimmer, "American International Banking . . . ," paper presented April 2, 1973.
a. All Total Deposit Figures in $ Billions.

of foreign deposits as a percentage of total deposits for the seventeen largest U.S. banks. In 1964 foreign deposits made up at least 10 percent of total deposits of only two U.S. banks. By mid-1973 thirteen of the largest seventeen U.S. banks received more than 25 percent of their total deposits from abroad. Simultaneously, the structure of foreign claims and deposits also shifted. At the end of 1964, 28.8 percent of $13.2 billion in U.S. commercial banks' foreign claims were at overseas offices, and by late 1971 the corresponding figures were 69.7 percent of $38.3 billion. The comparable figures for U.S. commercial banks' foreign deposits were 33.6 percent of $14.3 billion overseas in 1971.[8]

More important than growth of deposits and claims abroad is the tremendous surge in foreign profits for U.S. banks. In mid-1976, Saloman Brothers estimated that

> Since the start of this decade, international earnings of the thirteen United States banks with the largest overseas operations have risen from $177 million in 1970 to $836 million in 1975, representing compound growth of 36.4% per annum. During this same period, domestic earnings from these companies have been pale ($918 million in 1975, compared with $884 million in 1970), compounding at a rate of only 0.7%. The international contribution to total earnings for this group of banks has more than doubled over the past five years, rising from 16.7% in 1970 to 47.7% in 1975. Stated differently, growth in international earnings has accounted for 95% of total earnings increase registered by the companies since 1970.[9]

Although foreign deposits profitability lagged in 1976, the figures are still impressive. The new overseas focus of major U.S. banks after the mid-1960s brought bank executives into more intimate contact with government officials worldwide and created an arena in which direct bank influence potentially could flourish.

Some critics impute to multinational banks and corporations the intent to dictate developments in the international economic realm, others do not. However, while many Europeans and Canadians resent MNCs, which control large portions of their productive capacities, there has been no attempt to show how the invading American banks *directly* control U.S. or foreign government policies.[10] Nevertheless, some developed countries, aware of the difficulties of dislodging established branches and fearful of their possible influence, refuse to allow extensive U.S. bank penetration of their economies. American banks have only been permitted low-level activity in Scandinavia, Eastern Europe, Portugal, Austria, and Spain. Canada and Australia forbid branches. Canadian officials became so incensed when Citibank purchased the *Dutch-owned* Mercantile Bank in 1963, that they forced Citibank to divest itself of 75 percent of its equity over a period of years.[11]

While the increasing spread of bank activities and the consequent rise in bank-government interactions received high levels of publicity, global structure alone did not supplement banks' direct power over governments. As security and economic considerations became intertwined and made it more difficult for nations to plot unified strategies in their relations towards other nations, bank visibility may have led to increased regulatory attention rather than increased bank power.

However, those who argue that bank power has increased do not confine themselves to bank structure and statements. They also examine increased bank activities in the Eurocurrency and foreign exchange markets and the importance of those activities for policy-makers.

BANKS' EUROCURRENCY MARKET ACTIVITIES

The development of the unregulated, American bank-dominated, Eurocurrency market is a third factor which has persuaded many critics that bank direct influence must have climbed in recent years. Perhaps banks use these markets to circumvent government regulations, exert pressure on exchange rates, and even direct governments towards monetary reform agreements. Implicit in these arguments is the assumption that banks consciously manipulate government policy through these money market operations.

Banks and the Development of the Eurocurrency Market. The Eurocurrency market is a highly liquid market for bank deposits denominated in foreign currencies. It is the least regulated major money market in existence.[12] It remains misunderstood. Academics and market practitioners cannot agree on its origins,[13] its size,[14] or on the extent to which borrowed funds are redeposited in the market.[15] Although it is generally conceded that its development has been important for international monetary relations, a debate still rages over whether it has a stabilizing or destabilizing impact on exchange rates.[16] In the early and middle 1950s when the Bank for International Settlements contributed about 20 to 25 percent of the market's small turnover, it "could often control the market simply by phoning two or three banks and letting them know that it had funds to place. That was sometimes enough to kill a speculative burst without even putting out a dollar."[17] Throughout the 1950s the market grew slowly and quietly. Paul Einzig, a journalistic fixture in the City of London for more than four decades remarked:

> The Euro-dollar market was for years hidden from economists and other readers of the financial press by a remarkable conspiracy of silence. Bankers deliberately avoided discussing it with financial editors,

presumably for fear that publicity might attract additional rivals to the market, or that it might breed criticism in the Press and opposition in official quarters. I stumbled on its existence by sheer accident in October, 1959 . . . and when I embarked on an inquiry about it in London banking circles several bankers emphatically asked me not to write about the new practice.[18]

After the promulgation of American exchange restrictions in the early and mid 1960s, the Eurocurrency market expanded rapidly. While Eurodollar interest rates were generally marginally higher than in New York, this was acceptable to MNC treasurers as long as funds were available and planning continued smoothly.[19] At the end of 1964 the gross size of the Eurocurrency market was $20 billion. Eurodollars accounted for 83 percent of this total. Twelve years later, Eurodollars accounted for 73 percent of the $305 billion dollar Eurocurrency assets.[20] American exchange regulations certainly encouraged the growth of the Euromarkets. Indeed, it can be plausibly argued that, without American exchange restraints, U.S. banks would have grown far more slowly, and regulating the monetary system would have been far easier in the past decade.

This spectacular growth of bank-controlled liquidity provided the private sector with greater flexibility within the monetary system than ever before. But who actually controls the Euromarkets? One reasonable indicator is the distribution of loans made by groups of banks. Bank of England figures indicate that U.S. banks have recently made approximately two-fifths of all Eurocurrency loans, but Japanese banks, in particular, have been rising in importance. Although U.S. banks' share has dropped, they remain the key market-makers, particularly considering their offshore, tax-haven activities.[21]

Bank Direct Influence Through Euromarkets. The question remains: can control of the Eurocurrency markets be converted into direct influence over government policy makers? Perhaps banks and MNC's could dictate policy to government officials by threatening to manipulate exchange rates if new policies favorable to private actors were not adopted. Most banks would not lobby this way; only the largest banks with the most extensive contacts might consider latent threats.

Indeed, it makes sense to argue that large banks might cooperate in lobbying for specific international monetary policies. While large banks from major nations pursued policies closely tied to their own government before 1914, subsequently, the coordination of each nation's banks began to deteriorate. During the 1960s, banks of similar size from different nations had more compatible goals than large and small banks from the same country for at least four reasons. First, international, top management cooperation was fostered through participation in international lending syndicates and international consortium banks, which normally linked banks of the same size. Similarly, social contact between bankers increased because more and more top-level bankers attended the annual IMF-IBRD board meeting and the International Monetary Conference. Second, large banks tended to "know" each other well because old-boy networks developed among banks maintaining worldwide contacts. Third, a common petulance existed within London's more established banks towards London's newer invaders, which pushed spreads down and risk up in an effort to establish their operations. Finally, difficulties of smaller banks after late 1973 sharpened the line between banks certain to be supported by central banks in crisis situations and those which might be allowed to fail if difficulties were related to internal management rather than liquidity flows.[22]

However, large banks have tended towards conservatism in the Eurocurrency market. They have often followed innovative and aggressive smaller institutions rather than led them. The only direct influence attempt related to the Eurocurrency markets has been the consistent plea by large and small bankers alike that no Eurocontrols be imposed.[23] Bank lobbying and public pleas concerning the international monetary system have been directed almost entirely at persuading governments not to do things rather than at persuading them to change the system that had evolved. Perhaps the lack of controls in the Euromarkets can be judged a victory for bank lobbying. However, despite much talk, governments have never seriously considered such controls because no one country could institute them and no agreement among countries is likely. In fact, it does not seem that bankers have ever threatened to use the Euromarkets to manipulate government policies. On the contrary, large banks have seemed content to let the markets operate and have not spent excessive energy considering the impact of their Euromarket activities on governments as long as profits and stability were high. Small banks, believing that regulators would not pay much attention to their activities no matter what they did, have had no reason to lobby governments on most international monetary matters. Nonetheless, small bank activities may have been the most crucial in maintaining system stability. The question remains: did the development of the Euromarkets allow greater direct influence over government policies? The answer seems to be no.

BANKS' FOREIGN EXCHANGE MARKET ACTIVITIES

A fourth possible factor contributing to increased direct bank influence was the growth of the foreign exchange markets in the 1950s and 1960s. Some argue that the growth and increased integration of foreign exchange markets gave banks added leverage with which to bend government policies to their will.[24] However, as in the case of the Euromarkets, there has been extreme confusion between growing bank ability to manipulate monetary outcomes and ability to exert direct power over governments.

The role of the foreign exchange markets did become central to the monetary system after 1964, but the techniques of foreign exchange have remained remarkably constant over time.[25] No banker interviewed remembered a single innovation in technique adopted in the past fifteen years. Changes were structural (the diminishing role of the dollar as a vehicle currency) or operational (the introduction of new computer and communication techniques).[26]

The foreign exchange market is comprised of several linked markets located in London, New York, Amsterdam, Brussels, Paris, Milan, Frankfurt, Zurich, Tokyo, Singapore, and elsewhere. Each market has slightly different rules and operating procedures. For instance, in New York banks deal directly with other banks or through brokers while in London banks must deal through brokers if they are dealing with another bank with foreign exchange operations in London. Exchange rate differences between markets are quickly smoothed by arbitrageurs.[27] As a result, for most purposes the foreign exchange market can be viewed as an integrated world market in operation 24 hours a day.

London is the focal point and by far the largest single foreign exchange market. Although overall volume figures and breakdowns according to maturities of contracts do not exist, recent figures indicate that the aggregate foreign exchange contracts of foreign branches of twelve multinational banks more than doubled between 1971 and 1973 from an average of about $15 billion of both buy and sell contracts to about $40 billion of buy and sell contracts.[28] A major dealing room may transact more than $1 billion in exchange contracts each day. A large London dealing room comprises fifteen to twenty traders. Each is almost constantly on the phone making deals with a minimum size of about $1 million. One Swiss bank boasted that it could handle exchange deals up to $100 million without moving the market.[29] These observations reflect the huge size of the market.

It is generally conceded that while exchange volume increased steadily from the late 1950s until mid-1974, it dropped substantially in the wake of the collapse of the Bankhaus Herstatt.[30] Rapid expansion resumed in 1975. This growth was uneven. Frankfurt, a small market in the 1960s, grew in importance with the German mark. Spot and near forward transactions increased steadily until mid-1974 but many distant forward markets disappeared or were greatly curtailed after the two dollar devaluations and the float of sterling in June 1972.[31] * Simultaneously, the composition of

---

*Spot exchanges between currencies are transacted when the contract is made. Among banks, payment must be made within two days. Forward transactions are contracts to exchange currencies at some set future date. The distance in the future may vary, but 30, 60, 90, 180, and 360 day forward contracts are standard.

currencies traded shifted. While the dollar maintained its preeminent position, the pound has lost considerable ground to the Deutschemark, Japanese yen, and Canadian dollar in recent years.[32]

None of this translates easily, much less automatically into a rise in direct bank influence. It seems plausible that critics of MNCs and banks became so enmeshed with the role of multinational enterprises in the international system that they failed to distinguish private actor power over governments from private actor influence over outcomes.

Nonetheless, before dismissing direct bank influence, its specific mechanisms should be examined. How could influence be mobilized? Was it used and used successfully in persuading government officials to adopt policies favorable to private actors? And, despite the apparent lack of direct power derived from global bank networks, expanding foreign exchange, and Eurocurrency activities, is there evidence of rising direct bank influence in recent years on international monetary issues?

Channels of Direct Bank Influence

LOBBYING AND INTELLECTUAL PERSUASION

Lobbying in Congress. Like other interest groups, banks maintain a vast array of contacts with governments. In the United States formal legislative lobbying is undertaken by the American Bankers Association and by individual banks according to their perceived needs. According to Representative Jerry Patterson of the House Banking Committee, "the bankers are certainly the best organized (lobby) on Capitol Hill."[33] There is much truth to this when bankers throughout the country unite to fight domestic legislation which would restrict their freedom. However, on international questions bank lobbying has not been particularly effective because larger banks are internationalist while the more numerous small banks are protectionist. Harold Taylor has argued that on issues which would upset the competitive balance between local, regional, and international banks, "the big-little bank division is the first stumbling block [preventing effective lobbying]. It is hard except on housekeeping matters to get all the banks together, and the legislator is likely to feel that it is better to do nothing and disappoint both factions than side with either."[34] In fact, to counteract what they perceive as a small bank bias in the ABA, Citibank and other large banks have begun energetically to lobby state and national legislators in the past fifteen years.

The largest banks have been more consistently successful in lobbying on international structural questions. For instance, they routinely pushed for more open U.S. legislation on domestic branching and operations of foreign banks in the United States. These bankers reasoned that unless America allowed foreign bank penetration, other nations would not reciprocate. Thus, when Brazilian, Venezuelan, Philippino, and Japanese authorities threatened to impose restrictions on U.S. banks unless they received reciprocal rights in New York, the "First National Citibank proposed that the New York State banking law be amended, and a bill was evolved sponsored by the Association of New York Clearing House Banks; it was passed by the State legislature and became effective on January 1, 1961."[35] Similarly, the Bank of America spearheaded the fight which eventually changed California laws to allow foreign banks to set up branches in the state. Smaller banks, devoid of dreams of foreign expansion, fought the legislation at every opportunity.

Lobbying in the Executive Branch and Federal Reserve. Large bank lobbying on international monetary issues also takes place in both the Treasury and Federal Reserve System. Such lobbying may be formal or informal and may occur at various levels. Thus, in the mid-1960s Treasury Secretary Fowler established a high-level group of private sector executives under Douglas Dillon to advise and assist the Treasury in determining U.S. policy towards the introduction of a new international reserve unit. It appears that this group reinforced Treasury ideas and smoothed the reversal of early American opposition to the introduction of the Special Drawing Rights but that it did not initiate ideas or itself change the direction of Treasury thinking.[36]

Similarly, since its establishment on August 22, 1973, an Advisory Committee or the Reform of the International Monetary System has met regularly to suggest coherent strategies for monetary reform.[37] In addition, lower-level groups frequently draw on specialists from banking, business, and academia to supply ideas and feedback on policy ideas within the government.[38] However, these meetings at various levels have generally been more effective in circulating ideas between sectors than in introducing new ideas. It appears, in fact, that commercial bankers do not systematically lobby within the Treasury. Former Treasury Secretary Joseph Barr, for instance, found that in his years in the Treasury Department he was far more often approached by investment bankers, MNC executives, and union leaders than by commercial bankers.[39]

Commercial bankers are more effective in lobbying within the Federal Reserve System. Although Representative Wright Patman exaggerated when he labeled the Reserve Board "a wholly owned subsidiary of the American Bankers Association,"[40] by statute, some bankers are elected to each Federal Reserve Bank board. Each of the 12 Federal Reserve Bank boards elects its own president with the approval of the Federal Reserve Board. In addition, the Federal Reserve Board is required to meet at least four times each year with the Federal Advisory Council, composed of twelve leading bankers. Through these formal links banks lobby and influence Federal Reserve policy as well as partially controlling its direction.

In addition, bankers and Federal Reserve executives are in nearly constant contact concerning the developments in various money markets. This contact increases during periods of market unrest since bankers stay close to market developments and can provide information and suggestions to Federal Reserve officials. Certain bankers establish excellent reputations and can be extremely influential when officials are uncertain which way to proceed.[41]

Lobbying Abroad. Until recently most bankers, schooled in lessons of the 1930s, bent over backwards to avoid appearing to pressure foreign governments in developed countries. This has begun to change. Citibank, for instance, actively, though unsuccessfully, lobbied to retain its ownership of the Mercantile Bank in Canada and has "always felt free to discuss with local governments matters directly affecting [their] interest," while recognizing that governments "have final regulatory authority."[42] In Britain, while banks lobbied individually, U.S. banks had no lobbying group at all until 1972, at which point the Bank of England requested that American banks form such an organization so that they could easily ascertain what the American banks wanted in terms of policy.[43]

Bribery. Bribery is an extreme form of lobbying. Although there is no certain way to know whether extensive bank bribery exists, no charges have yet been leveled. Several factors suggest that overt bribery would less likely be initiated by banks than MNCs. Banks provide a service many countries, particularly LDCs, need desperately. Banks usually syndicate loans to governments, which partially diminishes foreign officials' ability to threaten to turn to other funding sources. Sunk bank investment in foreign nations is often small compared to investment by manufacturing or resource-oriented companies, thus minimizing the viability of threatened expropriation. Until recently governments were so eager to borrow internationally that nations could not realistically threaten not to borrow. Finally, banks can legally pay "bribes" by approving loans at favorable rates to officials, which would normally be rejected.

Lobbying Effectiveness. In sum, bank lobbying in the United States has been handicapped by a number of factors. Banks cannot agree on their goals and the large-small bank division diminishes the effectiveness of lobbying efforts. In addition, banks are politically unpopular; in recent years congressmen charged with watching over bank behavior have been hostile to large banks' aspirations. Throughout the 1960s Wright Patman as Chairman of the House Banking and Currency Committee attacked big banks and tried to force them to keep interest rates low. Banks circumvented his power, but could not push favorable legislative changes through his committee. Current

House and Senate banking chairmen, Henry Reuss and William Proxmire, both from Wisconsin, are among the most economically sophisticated members of Congress.[44] Their suspicion of large banks and of the supposed laxity of regulatory agencies has been fanned by a series of publicized banking problems. The collapse of several large U.S. banks, charges of speculation in the foreign exchange markets, publicized losses on real estate and shipping loans, the banks' involvement with W. T. Grant and New York City, and fears concerning liquidity, capitalization, lending to developing nations and over-lax regulation have stimulated tremendous concern among legislators about the stability and operations of the banking system. Large numbers of bankers have been called to testify before congressional committees. Particularly since 1974 these witnesses have been defensive, sullen, and unable to reverse the negative impression within Congress concerning banks. Under such circumstances it seems unlikely that banks, for all their resources, will successfully lobby in Congress in the near future.[45]

The publicity and politicization which accompanied recent international monetary issues also hindered bank lobbying in the executive branch and in the Federal Reserve. Although many banks have government relations departments to press their point of view and improve their public image, publicity has given bureaucrats greater leeway in dealing with bank lobbying. Officials could always play the demands of the large banks off against the small. Recent notoriety of bank issues also allowed officials to develop new, strong, lobbies with which to combat bank arguments. Public lobbies, such as those spearheaded by Ralph Nader, environmental groups, and church groups, can be rallied against bank positions, allowing the bureaucrats freer choice. Apparently there has also been frequent denigration of commercial bankers and their goals within the U.S. Treasury. It has been reported that several Treasury secretaries did not deal enthusiastically with commercial bankers because, by and large, they found them less interesting and less intelligent than investment bankers and corporate officials.[46]

Thus, while numerous links exist between the public and private sector and occasional victories for bank lobbyists on international questions occur, the balance of the effort seems to be distinctly against large bank lobbying effectiveness. Despite the huge growth in funds at their disposal, and perhaps in part because of the publicized growth, bank lobbying potential has been hurt rather than helped in recent years.

PUBLIC ADVOCACY BY TOP BANKERS

Still, large banks have decided to come out of the closet and publicly advocate their views. The media are always happy to report the statements of David Rockefeller, Walter Wriston, A. W. Clausen, Robert Roosa, and

Gabriel Hauge. Smaller banks do not get such coverage and cannot easily counteract the public views of important bankers. Large banks also influence government monetary policies by insistently repeating policy recommendations in their economic newsletters. Morgan Guaranty, Citibank, and Chase Manhattan newsletters provide information and suggestions to policy-makers who do not receive coherent arguments from other government or business sources. Understandably, many officials are sometimes swayed by the arguments of these banks. However, other factors which hinder quiet lobbying remain. Government officials, particularly middle-level technocrats, do not like being pressured and can stimulate countervailing pressures as needed. Even more damaging, bankers are perceived as wanting direct influence. Any public official appearing to give in to their blandishments, even if the policy makes sense, is likely to be hounded by the press and the public. As a result, sensible statements made in good faith by bankers may actually persuade officials to take the opposite decision rather than appear to be giving in to bank pressure.

Bank of America has been particularly active in advocating policy for the U.S. and singularly ineffective in realizing it. In 1971 the head of its international department suggested that formalized international meetings between government officials and bankers on international monetary issues would help governments adopt sensible policies and deal with problems in the international monetary system.[47] The proposition was ignored. More dramatically, on August 19, 1971 Bank of America advocated a nine-point plan for monetary reform. Despite a banner publication in the prime trade paper, the proposal does not seem to have been reported in the major general newspapers or in the *Wall Street Journal*. Although the final solution closely corresponded to the bank's suggestions, there is no indication that its proposals affected government negotiators. While President Nixon's decisions were probably influenced by his "Wall Street friends," and the general attitudes volubly expressed by bankers in favor of a rapid return to peaceful cooperation, bankers apparently were not influential in determining the terms of the Smithsonian accords.

An even more abrupt instance of the difficulties of direct influence took place at the Nairobi International Monetary Fund Meetings in September 1973. The President of Bank of America called for greater flexibility by the United States in dealing with developing countries. Treasury Secretary Shultz rebuked him immediately for getting involved in governmental affairs.[48] More recently Gabriel Hauge, Chairman of Manufacturers Trust Company, advocated that the IMF and private banks might cofinance international balance of payments loans. Hauge suggested that such an arrangement might help countries suffering from balance of payments problems raise more money on better terms. The following day William Dale, Deputy Managing

Director of the IMF, questioned the feasibility of cofinanced loans and effectively tabled the topic in the short term.[49] Such rebukes may persuade bankers to issue more defensive, reactive statements demonstrating the soundness of their banks, of the banking system, and of the international monetary order.

PERSONNEL MOVEMENT INTO GOVERNMENT

From time to time someone notes that Paul Volcker left Chase Manhattan to enter the Treasury or that David Kennedy was Chairman of Continental Illinois before becoming Treasury Secretary under President Nixon.[50] Are banks running public policy by infiltrating the government? Or have banking attitudes been brought into the government by expatriate bankers? The reverse may be true. Government-trained business and academics helped persuade the Treasury that the dollar's parity needed adjustment. Significantly, there is no evidence that the New York Federal Reserve Bank was subjected to intellectual influence from banks despite its close business community links.

While the personnel flow to the Treasury, particularly at the top, has been heavily spiced with bankers, the flow of individuals between the Federal Reserve and the banks is predominantly in the opposite direction. Many top bank economists and foreign exchange supervisors began their careers with New York Federal Reserve Bank and were lured to the private sector by higher salaries. This personnel flow is greater than the flow between the banks and the Washington bureaucracy and apparently 'cements the relationship between banks and the New York Federal Reserve Bank with firmer mortar than the relationship between the banks and either the Federal Reserve Board or the Treasury. This partly explains why most banks steadfastly supported the New York Federal Reserve Bank and fixed rates until August 1971, even after they became convinced the dollar was overvalued.

Also, although David Kennedy was a banker, he had little impact on the Treasury bureaucracy or on changing U.S. international monetary policies. The devaluation Secretaries came from Texas politics and the University of Chicago, Paul Volcker, as Under Secretary for Monetary Affairs had major impact on U.S. policy and was a chief negotiator in the effort to find a new monetary equilibrium but was not a traditional banker. He moved to Chase Manhattan where he was responsible for planning, not lending from the New York Federal Reserve Bank. His perspective was considerably broader than most bankers.

LENDING DECISIONS AS DIRECT INFLUENCE CHANNELS

The U.S. economy is so vast and complex that decisions by one or a group of banks to lend or not to lend on a certain project has minimal national impact. This is not the case in those developing countries where governments increasingly depend on foreign banks to supply necessary funds for development and balance of payment adjustment. The refusal of banks to lend to a nation, particularly when linked to the refusal of the World Bank and IMF to lend, can lead to catastrophic economic problems. Banks therefore maintain considerable direct influence over LDCs' economic policies.[51]

Does this carry over to developed European nations? Most bankers do not consider the question. Although all have some sort of capsule "international banking policy," these invariably explain how their chosen international structure will meet the needs of their corporate clients.[52] This remains true even though an increasing percentage of banks' international business is conducted with governments and government agencies. It is probably accurate to say that U.S. commercial banks have no more desire to manipulate foreign officials than they do U.S. officials.

In theory, banks can grant or refuse governments loans. In developing countries this may give them influence over some policies, but European nations still are more dominant than banks and can implicitly threaten foreign banks' rights if loans are not provided at attractive rates as needed. Thus, in early 1974 when France, Great Britain, and Italy each borrowed massive sums to ease their balance of payments situations, these loans did not strengthen banks' positions vis-à-vis these governments. In fact, the seeming line of direct influence has been diminished by government borrowing in the Euromarkets. Developed countries were able to demand the best rates in the market. The rush of new banks into the Euromarkets made it difficult for big banks to refuse to do business because alternative sources of funding were available. In addition, the larger banks wanted to be helpful and extended more aid than they sometimes felt prudent because they were captives within borrowing nations. Only once have banks formally taken a political role in relation to a loan. In 1976 Peru needed money to combat its balance of payment problems, but did not want to submit to the terms which would have accompanied IMF aid. It turned to a syndicate of banks to raise the funds, which refused to supply the money without direct assurances of the Peruvian government to work to bolster the domestic economy. Peru did receive the entire loan, but the participating banks were unhappy with their political role and are unlikely to take a similar position in the near future. In sum, there is little evidence that this form of direct influence in the developed world is any more effective than other routes to direct influence over governments and government policy. Although lending decisions can be used to influence developing nation policies, bankers hesitate to be so blatant.

Size and growth may have given bankers the potential to threaten retaliation if governments do not adopt certain programs, but there is no evidence that this ploy has been used. Similarly, the willingness of banks to express their opinions on international monetary topics has been counteracted by the publicity and politicization surrounding these areas. In recent years, problems of banks have further undercut their position because of bad publicity concerning their internal problems. Overall, the efficacy of bank direct influence has not been great.

Bank Attempts at Direct Influence

However, the general ineffectiveness of banks direct influence is not absolute. The limits of their influence are best illustrated by looking briefly at two recent bank attempts to influence U.S. international policy.

DIRECT BANK INFLUENCE AND EXCHANGE REGULATIONS

Banks were unhappy with increasingly stringent exchange regulations of the 1960s and attempted to persuade the U.S. government to remove them. Yet, when constraints were lifted in 1974, most bankers were caught by surprise. Restraints had only recently been relaxed and bankers were not tipped off that they would be abolished before the government's announced target date at the end of 1974. Bankers acknowledge that their attempts to hasten the removal of exchange regulations were ineffective.[53]

The next chapter illustrates that banks circumvented the intent of many of the exchange regulations through their foreign structure and Eurocurrency operations, but these evasions induced the U.S. to pass even more stringent controls. Bank arguments against exchange controls induced policy changes when petitioners could demonstrate that revisions they proposed would not lower the efficiency of existing exchange programs and that discrimination against one group of institutions could be shown. In practice this meant that smaller banks and MNCs only marginally involved with overseas transactions had a better chance to convince policy-makers to alter regulations which hurt their operations. Large banks and MNCs were perceived by officials as more dangerous to the stability of U.S. payments and therefore their claims of unfair treatment were greeted with greater skepticism. Even when these conditions were met, delays in altering the exchange regulations were normal.

Three examples of bank attempts to influence policy-makers on exchange regulations illustrate the process of direct bank influence. First, when the Voluntary Foreign Credit Restraint Program was instituted, foreign bank lending by domestic offices was tied to previous international loan levels. However, even a healthy percentage of nothing is nothing, so smaller banks which had not yet broken into the international markets complained. The government admitted that the regulations as written discriminated in favor of established banks and therefore instituted a second computation method based on assets rather than loans. Officials reasoned that the extra volume of loans this would permit was miniscule compared to the scope of the program as a whole.[54]

Second, tremendous pressure was brought to bear by the banks on various aspects of the Interest Equalization Tax. As originally instituted, the IET did not cover bank loans, but a move was made to give President Johnson stand-by authority to restrict bank loans with maturities over one year. Prompted by New York banks, New York congressional representatives mounted a strong drive to block granting the President this authority. The banks lost. American banks also lobbied the government on the restriction which controlled their lending with maturities of over one year from foreign branches. The banks pointed out that this discrimination against U.S. banks gave unfair advantage to foreigners. Eventually, in early 1967, the government agreed to the banks' arguments and removed this restriction. This was one of the key moves which stimulated tremendous growth of the Eurocurrency market in the late 1960s.

A third bank lobbying effort concerned the imposition under Federal Reserve Regulation M of marginal reserve requirements on loans made by branches of U.S. banks abroad to U.S. entities. Regulation M was instituted in 1969 following bank use of the Eurocurrency market to circumvent tight domestic monetary policy in the United States. Banks began complaining that while they were forced to pay 10 percent in reserve requirements on such loans, foreign banks were exempt because the Federal Reserve had no authority over their foreign activities. Although admitting the discrepancy, the Federal Reserve Board was not overly sympathetic since U.S. banks had undermined American monetary policy by borrowing from their foreign branches. In time, the reserve requirement under Regulation M was raised to 20 percent, then lowered first to 8 percent and in April 1975 to 4 percent. However, it is unclear whether this was a response to massive bank lobbying, to Republican free market beliefs, to diminishing fear of bank circumvention of policy, or to greater problems faced by banks under Regulation M after the termination of exchange restraints.

In these cases bank lobbying was intense, but government reaction was slow and not always to bankers' liking. Bankers were defeated when officials questioned their motives or felt they were likely to undermine government policies. The lobbyists were more successful when they could show that the changes would not materially affect U.S. policy and that they were clearly handicapped vis-à-vis some other group of banks from the United States or abroad.

DIRECT BANK INFLUENCE AND EXCHANGE CRISES

Bank lobbying concerning exchange rates took a different form but was not notably successful. Bankers and businessmen had concluded by 1970 that the dollar was seriously overvalued. This harmed their competitive position outside the United States and led them to complain that parity adjustment was needed. The focus of their complaints was on protection of their competitive position, but underlying this was their belief that the dollar was being propped up for political reasons. Bankers and businessmen lobbied government officials without any real hope that this would lead to a dollar devaluation.[55] Inside the government this lobbying apparently spurred thinking and planning about possible scenarios of dollar devaluations, but the bank and business lobby was not the most important pressure to this end.[56]

It appears that most bankers and businessmen did not expect direct lobbying to prove effective. Instead, they protected themselves in the foreign exchange and Eurocurrency markets as best they could. Whenever events indicated that the dollar might weaken, bank and corporate leads and lags, short- and medium-term borrowings, and foreign exchange conversions put pressure on the dollar and on central banks defending its parity. Eventually this pressure proved decisive. The August 15, 1971 Nixon shocks followed.

It is unclear whether bankers perceived their foreign exchange and Eurocurrency activities as a way of achieving a necessary parity change in the dollar's value. Good business dictated their actions. However, it is likely that some bankers and businessmen realized that they were pressuring the government towards devaluation. Some bankers perceived themselves as the "conscience of the system" and believed that they could not have persuaded the government to devalue except in the way they proceeded.[57] It is possible that a communication gap existed between bankers and Treasury officials which prevented the government from realizing the dollar's predicament until there was little choice except to adjust its parity and the monetary system in the midst of crisis instead of through negotiations.

Summary and Conclusions

Banks' lobbying efforts are intense and of long standing; nevertheless, it appears that, overall, banks have limited direct influence over government policy.[58] When the banking industry unites to oppose increased government regulations, it is a formidable opponent for would-be reformers. However, if the industry is divided, as is often the case, the bank lobby is not generally effective. Banks have become prime targets and scapegoats which can be blamed for problems, played off against other interest groups, or generally vilified. Middle level officials seem to picture themselves as new-style Davids vanquishing corporate Goliaths. As a result, bank direct influence through lobbying, personnel transfer, or public pleas for change have been less effective than during the heyday of the 1920s. The fact that many banks have decided to beef up their lobbying effort in Congress and the executive branch may have been counterproductive to their cases. Morgan Guaranty, for instance, claims that it has been a more effective lobbyist than Citibank despite its smaller effort because it lobbies more selectively. When an issue is vital, it brings in top level officials, knowledgeable about the particular area. Citibank and other retail banks often use the same lobbyists on all major issues. Officials get tired and suspicious of these persistent lobbying efforts.[59]

Some claim that the huge increase in international banks' visibility and publicity in the foreign exchange and Eurocurrency markets have increased direct bank influence. They have concluded that since banks have increased their international clout, they will automatically use that clout to insure favorable government policies. These critics do not explain how bank activities can be translated into effective power over government officials and their policies. It appears, in fact, that these international banking developments have not contributed to the ability of banks to lobby officials in developed countries or to impose their influence on home and host country governments. The substantial influence of banks' economic newsletters is unrelated to banks' foreign expansion.

However, this does not mean that bank activities in the foreign exchange and Eurocurrency markets have had no effect on the international monetary developments of the past decade. What is required is a different perspective of power. Instead of concentrating completely on the ability and desire of banks to influence officials, it is necessary to examine the ways bank activities contribute to international monetary outcomes. Intent is not as important as behavior to such an analysis. The vast number of interconnections between governments and banks that have developed in the past fifteen years perhaps make it impossible for either group to know precisely what impact banks are having on government policies and options on any given issue at a particular time.

The next four chapters investigate the role of banks in affecting outcomes in diverse monetary realms and the pressure these activities place on officials by limiting the range of their choices. Indirect and circumventing influence replace direct power as the focus.

NOTES

1. At the close of 1961 First National City Bank operated 77 foreign branches, Chase Manhattan Bank 24, Bank of America 14, First National Bank of Boston 10, Morgan Guaranty Trust Company 4, Bankers Trust 2, Manufacturers Hanover Trust Company 2, and Chemical Bank 1.

2. Russell G. Smith, speech delivered at a St. Mary's College symposium, January 28, 1959, p. 9. Bank of America Archives, San Francisco.

3. C. M. van Vlierden, "New Era in International Banking," *The Banker* 121 (February 1971): 16.

4. Barnett and Müller, op. cit.: 56.

5. Moore, op. cit.: 14.

6. This figure is somewhat deceptive since branch figures include "shell" branches opened in the Caribbean for tax purposes and to provide a cheap "Eurodollar window." Most often these branches are legal fictions.

7. The Edge Act was passed by Congress in 1919 and became Section 25(a) of the Federal Reserve Act. It authorized the Federal Reserve Board to charter corporations "for the purpose of engaging in international and foreign banking . . . either directly or through the agency, ownership or control of local institutions in foreign countries." A short introduction to Edge Act regulations is Peter Brunsden, "The Edge Act in U.S. banking," *The Banker* 123 (Feburary 1973): 143-152.

8. Rimmer de Vries, "A banker's view of overseas activities of banking organizations and the role of regulations," paper presented at a conference sponsored by the Federal Reserve Bank of Minneapolis, Minneapolis, March 27, 1973: Tables I and II.

9. Thomas Hanley, "United States multinational banking: current and prospective strategies," (New York: Salomon Brothers, June 1976): 3.

10. See, Servan-Schreiber and Levitt, op. cit.

11. John Fayerweather, *The Mercantile Bank Affair* (New York: New York University Press, 1974).

12. See, Fritz Machlup, "Eurodollar creation: a mystery story," *Banca Nazionale Del Lavoro Quarterly Review* 94 (September 1970): 219-260; Paul Einzig, *The Euro-Dollar System: Practice and Theory of International Interest Rates* (New York: St Martin's, 1970); Jane Sneddon Little, *Euro-Dollars: The Money Market Gypsies* (New York: Harper and Row, 1975); and Geoffrey Bell, *The Euro-Dollar Market and the International Financial System* (New York: Macmillan, 1973).

13. Regulation Q, Russians, the U.S. payments deficit, U.S. exchange regulations and other causes have been blamed for the birth and growth of the Eurodollar market. See, U.S. Congress, Joint Economic Committee, *The Euro-Dollar Market and Its Public Policy Implications,* by Ira O. Scott Jr., Economic Policies and Practices Paper No. 12, 91st Cong., 2nd sess., 1970; and Fritz Machlup, "Five errors about the Eurodollar system," *Euromoney* (July, 1972): 8-14.

14. The BIS and Morgan Guaranty periodically publish estimates of the size of the Euromarkets. The BIS figures are generally somewhat higher. See, Milton Gilbert, "The size of the Eurodollar market," *Euromoney* (August 1971): 12-15; and David Ashby, "The $300 billion super-dollar market," *The Banker* 124 (May 1974): 449-454.

15. The Euromarket multiplier has been estimated to range everywhere from 5 to 95 percent. Milton Friedman is on the high side, Fred Klopstock and Jane Little on the low side, and Fritiz Machlup in the middle. It appears that redepositing of Arab petrodollars after the oil price rise in the late 1973 has increased the multiplier.

16. Practitioners usually argue that Euromarkets are stabilizing. See, David Ashby, "The Eurocurrency market: a source of instability?" Speech at a conference on Crises in the Foreign Exchange Markets, London, July 10, 1974; and G. A. Costanzo, "The Eurodollar: villian or victim," *Euromoney* (June 1971): 24-28.

17. Frances Cairncross, "How the BIS works," *Euromoney* (March 1970): 12.

18. Paul Einzig, *Foreign Dollar Loans in Europe* (New York: St. Martin's, 1965): vi-vii.

19. New York rates are made more expensive by the necessity of the borrower keeping a percentage of the loan deposited in the bank as a "compensating balance." As long as banks must deposit reserves with the Federal Reserve, they wish to be assured compensating balances from their depositors. This is not required in the Euromarkets.

20. Marina von N. Whitman, "The current and future role of the dollar: how much symmetry?" *Brookings Papers on Economic Activity* 3, 1974: 562; and Bank for International Settlements, *Forty-Seventh Annual Report*, 1976-77: 103, 105.

21. Bank of England, *Quarterly Bulletin*.

22. Fred Hirsch, "The Bagehot problem," London, March 1975, mimeographed.

23. See, e.g., Costanzo; also Stanislas Yassukovich, "Dilemmas in Euromarket regulation," *The Banker* 123 (April 1973): 368-371. But see also Frederick Heldring, "A curb on the Eurocurrency market," *Euromoney* (March 1973): 42-43.

24. See, e.g., Brimmer, "Multi-national banks."

25. See, e.g., Paul Einzig, *The History of Foreign Exchange* (New York: St. Martin's, 1962).

26. Interviews with representatives of Citibank and Morgan Guaranty, London, October 1974. The dollar's vehicle currency role has been changing since March 1973. It is now possible to shift directly from one European currency to another.

27. Improved communication networks have reduced the size of disparities and the lag time between their appearance. Thus over 200 banks participated in the Society for Worldwide Interbank Financial Telecommunication (SWIFT) which provides a private international network to enable banks to transmit between themselves: international payments, statements, and messages. William Hall, "Swift: the revolution round the corner," *The Banker* 123 (June 1973): 633-639; and "SWIFT to add new speed and security to international banking," *Forbes* (June 1975): 29.

28. U.S. Congress, House, Committee on Banking, Currency and Housing, *Financial Institutions and the Nation's Economy. Compendium of Papers Prepared for the FINE Study*. Book II, 94th Cong., 2nd Sess., 1976, II: 878.

29. Interviews with representatives of Wells Fargo and Bank of America, London, October 1974.

30. Interviews with a representative of Chemical Bank, London, September 1974 and with a representative of Chase Manhattan, New York, July 1974; and *FINE papers*, II: 878.

31. Interview with a representative of a large MNE, New York, July 1974. Interview with a representative of Bank of America, San Francisco, January 1974. Interview with a representative of Marine Midland, London, October 1974.

32. Interview with a representative of the New York Federal Reserve Bank, New York, June 1974.

33. Quoted in *Wall Street Journal*, March 30, 1976.

34. Harold Taylor, "The banking lobby: a papier-mache monster," *Bankers Magazine* 153 (Spring 1970): 75.

35. Robin Pringle, "Why American banks go abroad," *Bankers Magazine* 150 (August 1967): 52.

36. Interview with former treasury official, March 1975. John Odell, during research for his dissertation, "Sources of foreign policy change: The United States in the international monetary system," Ph.D. dissertation, University of Wisconsin, 1976, also received this impression.

37. The advisory group included David Rockefeller (Chase Manhattan), Walter Wriston (Citibank), Henry Fowler (Goldman Sachs, former Treasury Secretary), Gaylord Freeman (First Chicago), Robert Roosa (Brown Brothers, former Treasury Under secretary), the heads of G.E., Caterpiller Tractor, and others.

38. For instance, a group composed of Edward Bernstein (E.M.B. Ltd.), James Burtle (W. R. Grace), Rimmer de Vries (Morgan Guaranty), Peter Kenen (Princeton), Walter Salant (Brookings), Wilson Schmidt (Virginia Polytechnic), Charles Schwartz (IMF), Robert Ulin (Mobil), and Marina V. N. Whitman (Pittsburgh) met with government officials from several agencies and recommended major changes in the reporting structure of statistics related to the U.S. payments position because previous formats were less meaningful under a flexible exchange rate system. See, "Report of the advisory committee on the presentation of balance of payments statistics," *Statistical Reporter*, U.S. Department of Commerce (June 1976): 221-238.

39. Joseph Barr at Harvard Center for International Affairs Seminar, October 15, 1975.

40. *Wall Street Journal*, March 30, 1976.

41. In the early 1970s these included: George Chittenden and Dennis Weatherstone (Morgan Guaranty), John Hawes (Bankers Trust), Robert Leclerc (Continental Illinois), Edward Reichers (Citibank), William Lantz (Chase Manhattan), and Herbert Evers (Marine Midland).

42. William Spencer, *Harvard Business Review* 53 (November-December 1975): 99.

43. Telephone conversation with a representative of Mellon Bank, London, September, 1974.

44. The only Wisconsin bank among the largest 100 in the U.S. is the First Wisconsin Bank. It ranked 33rd by assets at the end of 1976.

45. On December 1, 1975 Senator Proxmire introduced legislation which would restrict bank expansion and concentration within the U.S. New York *Times*, December 2, 1975. For a summary of pending international bank legislation as of mid-1976, see, Robert Russell, "The need for regulation of multinational banking," paper presented to the International Affairs Fellowship Program, May 14, 1976.

46. Interviews with treasury and former treasury officials, Washington, July 1974.

47. C. M. van Vlierden, "International commercial banks: a link between two systems," *Euromoney* (July 1971): 12-14.

48. *Wall Street Journal*, September 25, 1973.

49. *Wall Street Journal*, June 9, 10, 1977.

50. See, Peter Beter, *The Conspiracy Against the Dollar* (New York: George Braziller, 1973).

51. See, Jonathan D. Aronson, "Politics and the international consortium banks," *Stanford Journal of International Studies* (Spring 1976): 59-62. But, see Chapter 6 for the other side of the coin.

52. For a summary of these policies, see the special international banking section in *American Banker*, February 27, 1977.

53. Interviews with representatives from Wells Fargo, First National Bank of Chicago, Bankers Trust, San Francisco, Chicago, New York, 1974.

54. Andrew Brimmer, Seminar at Harvard Center for International Affairs, May 7, 1976.

55. Interviews with representatives of Wells Fargo, First National Bank of Chicago, and Morgan Guaranty, San Francisco, Chicago, New York, 1974.

56. John Odell interviews, 1974.

57. This same phrase was used by representatives from Continental Illinois and Marine Midland.

58. Geoffrey Barraclough has argued that in another area, U.S. policy towards the Middle East, banks have had tremendous direct influence. He claims that the difference between the "hard sell" and "soft sell" towards the Middle East was a difference between Kissinger and the international banking cofraternity led by David Rockefeller and George Ball. Barraclough argues that the softening of State Department policy which appeared on one level to be an OPEC victory was probably

> a victory for the powerful interests in Washington and on Wall Street which are worried sick about the financial consequences of continuing confrontation. Certainly, tug-of-war has been going on in Washington ever since Ball's pronouncement in December [1974], between the hard-liners and . . . the "appeasers," and Kissinger's speeches of May 27 and 28 (1975) seemed a clear sign that—for the moment at least—the latter had won the day.

"Wealth and power: the politics of food and oil," *New York Review of Books* (August 7, 1975): 27.

59. Interview with a representative of Morgan Guaranty, New York, March 1975.

Chapter 4

BANKS AND U.S. EXCHANGE

REGULATIONS, 1963-1974

Banks' international indirect and circumventing influence have increased more rapidly in recent years than direct bank influence. Banks' international activities have induced policy-makers to alter their international monetary policies, have undermined the effectiveness of government programs and policies, and have helped shape international monetary outcomes. In the case of bank influence on U.S. exchange regulations between 1963 and 1974, a classic confrontation developed. U.S. regulations limited the ability of banks and corporations to export capital from the United States, whereas private firms opposed the regulation of their export activities.

In a February 1965 White House meeting President Johnson persuaded private sector leaders to pledge support to measures designed to protect the U.S. payments position, the dollar, and the fixed-rate monetary system. Although the president promised that these measures would be temporary, the Voluntary Foreign Credit Restraint Program which emerged demonstrated a longevity that rankled business leaders. Citibank Vice Chairman G. A. Costanzo echoed the prevalent business perspective in 1969 when he recommended

> that steps should be taken to terminate these controls. . . . Capital controls, instead of being temporary as they were supposed to be, have

proliferated. They have become self-perpetuating, despite their questionable usefulness. They have turned attention away from the underlying causes of our payments problem and lulled us into a false sense of purpose.[1]

Significantly, those opposing regulatory programs labeled them "controls," while regulators persistently referred to them as restraints or constraints since no licensing or approval of individual transactions was required.[2]

Private, direct influence attempts were massive, but largely ineffective, since most Treasury, Federal Reserve, and Commerce officials supported the continuation of existing exchange regulations and could defuse complaints. Governor Brimmer, who administered the VFCR, noted that when bankers protested too loudly, he inquired whether their 1965 White House pledge was no longer in force. This usually smothered the ardor of middle-level bank critics.[3]

It is useful to reiterate here a distinction made in the introduction. Indirect influence is most likely to be successful in instances where government regulations and concern are focused on the market in general rather than on market participants. Indirect influence is more easily undercut by governments which are dictating precisely the limits of what private actors may and may not do. On the other hand, circumventing influence is far more applicable by private actors in coping with regulations focused on them and their activities. It plays little role when government regulators are concerned with markets not actors. Thus, private actors could not effectively overload regulations aimed at them. Indirect bank influence depends on the spillover of pressure between markets and is ineffective when official attention is focused on the private actors. Since the U.S. exchange restraint programs were directed at private actors, compliance with at least the letter of the law was necessary. The use of indirect private influence to topple exchange programs was therefore limited.

Banks and MNCs responded with circumventing influence employing legal loopholes to evade the programs' intent. Banks circumvented U.S. exchange regulations aimed at them and helped their clients get around restraints on their actions whenever possible. However, before more thoroughly examining the implications of private activities on the passage and removal of exchange regulations, on their effectiveness, and on the decision-making possibilities available to government officials concerned with them, a short review of the intent and content of U.S. exchange regulations promulgated during the 1960s is needed.

Exchange Regulations and the
U.S. Balance of Payments

Descriptions of the evolution of U.S. credit restraint programs, available elsewhere, need not be replicated here.[4] A brief recounting of events which preceded the regulations and of relevant sections of programs affecting bank freedom suffice to lay the groundwork necessary to analyze subsequent bank-government interactions.

WHY EXCHANGE REGULATIONS?

In 1961 when John Kennedy took office, the United States had just recorded its largest payments deficit since World War II (as measured on a net liquidity basis). President Kennedy believed that the two major problems facing his new administration were nuclear weapons and the balance of payments deficit. His economic braintrust counted on curing the payments deficit primarily through the implementation of better domestic economic management. To augment domestic programs, measures aimed at curbing foreign outflows were also initiated. These included the founding of the gold pool, the implementation of long-term liquidity measures, and a series of exchange regulations designed to limit long-term capital outflows.

In the early 1960s private U.S. capital outflows increased as markets became more integrated and private familiarity with international market operations grew. Capital became more mobile and responsive to market forces. A spurt of long-term portfolio lending from the United States occurred in 1962 and 1963 as U.S. MNCs became intrigued with foreign expansion. America acquired a large volume of foreign, illiquid investment assets in this period. Necessarily, short-term private and official claims against the United States grew simultaneously, and the U.S. reserve position declined continually.[5]

Since the administration was committed to maintaining the dollar's central role in the Bretton Woods monetary system, U.S. officials felt it necessary to attack the payments problems to maintain international confidence in the dollar's convertibility at its existing gold parity. Although some feared that such programs might injure America's reserve banker role by fostering the development of international capital markets, the risk was perceived as acceptable.[6] U.S. officials were willing to slow New York's growth as a money center even as they stimulated the growth of foreign money markets.

Kennedy and Johnson's economic advisors believed that the U.S. payments position would respond quickly to their prodding so that exchange restraints would be needed only temporarily.[7] Indeed, the Interest Equalization Tax (IET) promulgated in 1963 curbed long-term portfolio lending from the United States and sharply discouraged U.S. issues of foreign securities. Meanwhile, "other capital flows began to accelerate, offsetting much or all of the gains from the IET." Bank loans to foreign borrowers from the United States and direct investment abroad accelerated in 1963 and 1964.[8] This led to the imposition of the Voluntary Foreign Credit Restraint program (VFCR) in early 1965.

There was never an underlying plan supporting the exchange restrictions; they were introduced bit by bit. This was partly because each program or revision had a psychological as well as an economic purpose. U.S. officials, besides believing that a solution was always around the corner, hoped to demonstrate to skeptics at home and abroad "an immediate statistical improvement in the balance of payments to restore international confidence in the dollar."[9]

For a time, administration economists believed they could fine-tune domestic and international economic developments. They were partially successful before 1965 in curbing some of the most serious outflows of funds. Their task, however, was complicated immensely by President Johnson's simultaneous pursuit of the Great Society and the Vietnam War. This led to a degeneration of exchange restriction planning into an exercise in ad-hoc policy-making. Not surprisingly, most private executives perceived proliferating exchange restraints as ineffective, cosmetic attempts to treat a fundamental economic problem. They preferred fewer controls, but learned to cope with existing ones.

What Regulations?

THE INTEREST EQUALIZATION TAX

In the spring of 1963 a decision was taken to impose capital constraints. Poor second-quarter payments figures reinforced administration resolve. Kennedy's July 19, 1963 balance of payments message urged Congress to enact an IET, "which would stem the flood of foreign security sales in our markets" and recommended that this tax should "increase by approximately one percent in the interest cost to foreigners obtaining capital in this country, and thus help equalize the interest rate patterns for longer term financing in the United States and abroad."[10]

The IET increased the cost of foreign borrowing in the United States by placing a tax on the U.S. purchase of foreign long-term securities. Canada was exempted after Canadians pointed out that their traditional reliance on U.S. capital markets meant that the tax would severely disrupt and perhaps seriously injure their business sector. The IET successfully curbed foreign bond issue in the U.S.[11] It appears likely that foreign long-term borrowing would have continued to increase in the absence of the Interest Equalization Tax.

Originally, the IET did not directly affect commercial banks as much as underwriters, although it stimulated growing private interest in European expansion possibilities. Kennedy's advisors felt sure the IET could be dispensed with once foreign capital markets had developed the capacity to handle large security placements. However, continued payments difficulties persuaded White House officials to make the IET applicable to bank loans of one year or more on February 10, 1965. Previously, all bank loans were exempted. President Johnson justified this action by pointing out that foreign bank loans of more than one year increased from $1.5 to $2.5 billion in 1964.[12] The 1964 tax cut and the failure of monetary policy had flooded the banks with money. Lagging domestic loan demand induced greater lending overseas. In essence, bank activities provided President Johnson with a reason to further clamp down on capital outflows. Bank behavior narrowed the scope of choices available to U.S. decision-makers. However, the government's reaction to bank activities further upset private sector officials.

Although not applicable to loans with terms less than one year or to export credits, the additional one percent cost of long-term loans to foreigners increased the real cost of such loans by about 15 percent. In response, banks' long-term claims on foreigners decreased yearly from 1966 to 1970. However, foreign branches of U.S. banks could effectively extend untaxed longer-term credits by automatically rolling over short-term credits, thus circumventing the IET almost at will.

On February 21, 1967 the president waived the IET for U.S. dollars loans with maturities of one year or more made to foreign borrowers by overseas branches of U.S. banks. In effect, this was an admission that loan roll-overs had circumvented the previous restrictions and that the government wanted to constrain but not choke off U.S. foreign commercial bank activity. This ruling extended to dollar loans an exemption which had always applied to foreign currency loans made by foreign branches of U.S. banks. Freed to engage in long-term foreign lending from foreign branches, foreign loan maturities were extended.

The effective rate of the IET was reduced to 3/4 percent a year in April 1969. In February 1973 President Nixon promised to terminate all U.S. exchange restrictions by December 31, 1974, and on December 26, 1973 exchange restraints were sharply reduced. The effective IET rate was reduced to approximately ¼ percent. Then, the administration surprised the private sector by announcing the termination of all exchange restraint programs on January 29, 1974.

The Voluntary Foreign Credit Restraint Program. Although the IET affected bank freedom after 1965, it was never aimed directly at commercial banks. Treasury administrators of the IET focused on underwriters, MNCs, and foreign borrowers. By comparison, the VFCR restricted the flow of bank funds out of the U.S. and was overseen by the Federal Reserve System. It was supervised by Governor J. L. Robertson until mid-1968 when Governor Andrew Brimmer took over. Day-to-day operational programs were handled in each Federal Reserve district by a reserve bank officer. According to Governor Brimmer, the major objective of the VFCR "was to reduce, but not to eliminate the banks' foreign lending. This was to be done without endangering other important national objectives, such as the financing of exports of U.S. goods and services, and meeting the credit needs of the developing countries."[13] Significantly, the VFCR did not limit foreign loans from overseas branches, but only the lending from the United States. This impelled U.S. banks without foreign branches to follow their customers abroad.

Governor Brimmer succintly described the content and development of VFCR restraints between 1965 and 1969:

> The guidelines issued on March 3, 1965, requested the banks to hold loans and other foreign assets covered by the program to 105 percent of the amount of credits outstanding on the base date of December 31, 1964. . . . While the program applied to all banks, only banks with total foreign assets of $500,000 or more were requested to report to the Federal Reserve Banks. . . . During 1965 the reporting banks [approximately 150] increased their holdings of covered assets by $168 million, as compared with an increase in total foreign assets of $2.5 billion in 1964. . . . In December 1965, the Board announced revised guidelines for banks for 1966 which increased the target ceiling to 109 percent of the end-1964 base.[14]

Guidelines for 1966 also corrected inequities discovered in the program. Banks with bases "between $500,000 and $5 million were permitted to adopt a ceiling of base plus $450,000 . . . even though in most cases that exceeded 109 percent of their end-1964 base."[15] In 1967, small bank provisions were liberalized and inequities resulting from large banks' earlier expansion were handled by allowing banks to choose for their 1968 ceiling either their 1967 ceiling or 2 percent of their end-1966 assets, whichever was larger. This provision, even though subject to some qualifications, added about $600 million to the aggregate ceiling.

Following a reappraisal of the U.S. payments situation, LBJ imposed a still more restrictive balance of payments program on January 1, 1968. For the first time banks were asked to reduce their foreign assets outstanding. Ceilings were reduced to 103 percent of the end-1964 base or, for banks electing the "2 percent" calculation, to the 1967 ceiling plus one third of the difference between that amount and 2 percent of total assets as of the end of

1966. Additional 40 percent reductions on some short-term credits were requested later in 1968. On April 4, 1969 banks were permitted to retain existing ceilings or adopt a new ceiling equal to 1½ percent of total assets, raising aggregate ceilings by about $400 million to $10.1 billion. After a lull, export credits were excluded from ceilings while ceilings were further reduced on November 11, 1971.[16] In sum, these changes allowed banks without historical lending bases to establish foreign financing operations.

Although loopholes permitted bank activities to undermine the U.S. payments position while evading the VFCR, banks were forced to abide by the "voluntary" ceilings. Banks overshooting their ceilings were quickly questioned by Federal Reserve officials. Persistent problems led to Governor Brimmer's intervention.

Existing figures reported by the Federal Reserve suggest that the VFCR successfully choked off the growth of foreign lending by American banks from the United States. To monitor capital flows after lifting restrictions, the Board asked for continued data on bank foreign lending and investments. In 1974 foreign assets held by U.S. banks for their own account increased $14 billion to over $31 billion. In 1973 the increase had been only $2.5 billion, mostly in exempted areas such as Canadian assets and export credits. However, the 1974 increase was largely offset by increased bank liabilities to foreigners other than foreign institutions.[17] When the VFCR was dismantled along with other exchange restraints in January 1974, a temporary program which had staggered along for nine years died.

In sum, though the VFCR effectively limited certain types of capital outflows, private actors' coping behavior in regard to these programs had other implications for U.S. and foreign officials. These sequelae were to outlive the exchange restraint programs. Some have argued that while the VFCR was effective in 1966, it lost effectiveness thereafter, but spill-overs from the program harmed the stability of the monetary system. At this juncture, however, it is safe to say only that the VFCR created huge bureaucracies in the Federal Reserve Board (to administer it) and in the large U.S. banks (to circumvent it).

The Foreign Direct Investment Program. In the wake of sterling's November 1967 devaluation and the sharp deterioration of the U.S. capital account, President Johnson chose to reaffirm U.S. support for the dollar and the Bretton Woods system. The FDIP was hurriedly assembled by top Treasury officials in a weekend. Assistant Secretary of Commerce W. H. Shaw was given five days to organize the Office for Foreign Direct Investment to administer the new program.[18]

The OFDI regulations had less impact on banks than the IET or VFCR. However, the new program forced MNCs to rely more on foreign sources of funds, which propelled another wave of international bank expansion.[19] The FDIP restrained direct investment through imposition of "annual limits on net capital outflow plus reinvested earnings and, in some areas, mandatory repatriation of a prescribed share of total earnings."[20]

MNCs were required to raise a higher proportion of their international financing requirements abroad and were even forced to raise money abroad to repatriate to the United States. Since the financing link of many foreign MNC outlets was severed by the FDIP, U.S. banks wanting to maintain their corporate customers needed to open foreign facilities. Some regional banks feared that large, money-center banks would steal both the international and domestic business of their MNC clients unless they opened foreign branches. Not surprisingly, foreign corporate borrowing as a percentage of foreign direct investment increased to 30 percent or more in the three years following the introduction of the OFDI regulations although it had not exceeded 12 percent in 1965, 1966, or 1967.[21]

Federal Reserve Regulations D, M, and Q. Three Federal Reserve Regulations (D, M. and Q) allowed banks to cope with restrictions of U.S. authorities to counteract bank responses to exchange restrictions. These frequently revised regulations helped the Federal Reserve control foreign activities of U.S. banks related to monetary policy.

Regulations D and M helped the U.S. choke off banks' headquarters borrowing from foreign branches by imposing reserve requirements on these borrowings. In August 1969 Regulation M was applied against Euroborrowings to halt bank circumvention of tight U.S. monetary policy. Regulation M reserve requirements were raised from their initial level of 10 percent to 20 percent on Eurodollar borrowings in excess of a reserve free base in November 1970 to encourage banks to preserve their bases. The rate was dropped to 8 percent in May 1973 and to 4 percent in April 1975. Regulations D and M caused serious contention between banks and the Federal Reserve, particullarly after certain Regulation M loopholes died with the termination of exchange regulations. Banks claimed that these regulations allowed foreign banks to lend more cheaply to U.S. companies than U.S. banks and that they were therefore discriminatory.

Regulation Q, perhaps the most controversial Federal Reserve Regulation, prohibits member banks from paying interest on deposits with a maturity of less than 30 days. It also allows the Federal Reserve to set maximum interest rates for time deposits of varying denominations with maturities over 29 days. These ceilings, however, are not applicable to deposits from foreign central banks and certain international institutions. At times Regulation Q has also been used to limit the maximum interest rates payable on large denomination certificates of deposit, which created considerable interest differentials between the U.S. and European markets since in the Eurocurrency market banks are free to pay interest on nonresident deposits of any size or maturity.

Regulation Q has bothered small banks less than large ones. Smaller banks typically have more stable sources of funds than larger ones, whose depositors move funds to take advantage of small interest rate differentials, and smaller banks are therefore less threatened by Regulation Q ceilings. Janet Kelly claims that small banks actually "feel threatened by the removal of Regulation Q since they are less able to compete against big banks by offering more attractive rates to lenders and borrowers."[22]

Regulation Q was drastically revised on June 24, 1970, when interest ceilings payable on single maturity time deposits of $100,000 or more with maturities of 30 to 89 days were removed. On May 16, 1973 Regulation Q was further amended by removing limits on the interest banks could pay on CDs in denominations over $100,000 on all maturities over 29 days. Regulation Q ceilings are still suspended.

Although Regulation Q was suspended for domestic reasons, the change probably helped the U.S. payments position by equalizing interest rate differentials between the United States and Europe. While Regulation Q ceilings were in effect, individuals who were never constrained by various exchange restrictions, could move money out of the United States to take advantage of higher foreign interest rates. VFCR contributions to the payments situation were partially offset by low Regulation Q ceilings. Once ceilings were gone, individuals had less incentive to export funds. In theory this should have helped the U.S. payments position.

REGULATIONS, RESTRICTIONS, AND BANK OPERATIONS

How did these regulations and restrictions affect banks' international operations? The IET and VFCR attempted to control the growth of capital flows from U.S. banks which could injure the U.S. payments positions. Eventually, three exchange restraint programs, administered by three different agencies, tried to damp capital flows out of the United States originating from three types of private actors. When private actors evaded these restraints, the government tried to control their behavior by imposing or removing specific regulations.

Bankers believed the restraints harmed their productivity and the welfare of the nation. However, banks of different size, critically concerned with different regulations, largely offset each other's direct influence attempts. Most banks hesitated to fight too strenuously because Andrew Brimmer wore two hats. Although Brimmer separated his duties as VFCR administrator and as judge of bank requests for foreign expansion, banks were afraid to fight him on VFCR and ask him for permission for foreign expansion simultaneously.[23]

Apparently, large banks lost some of their foreign advantages when the VFCR was liberalized to help smaller banks, and smaller banks were somewhat hurt when Regulation Q ceilings were suspended. However, the termination of restrictions in early 1974 seemingly was based on the ideological and philosophical orientation of the Nixon administration and was not tied directly to bank lobbying. Banks were surprised when the Nixon administration chose to end restraints earlier than promised.

The restraint programs also led to a reshaping of the international monetary environment. Banks were forced to develop Euromarket lending. Banks of all sizes also set up "shell" branches in the Caribbean to book overseas loans without opening an expensive overseas branch. Most shells did not accept local deposits and were administered by U.S. headquarters or by Edge Act corporations. No more than a post office box was needed in the Caribbean.

Regulation Q and the credit controls also contributed to the growth and solidification of the Euromarkets. Euromarket evolution was more closely linked to restraints meant to deal with the U.S. payments situation than to outflows of funds from the United States.[24] Regulation Q rates fostered an exodus of funds from America towards less regulated capital markets. The certificate of deposit rates effectively became the lower limit of the Eurodollar deposit rate. Regulation Q also stimulated reliance on foreign funds because banks had difficulty attracting large domestic deposits from corporate clients when domestic interest rates exceeded Regulation Q rates. These limitations together with the foreign push generated by exchange restrictions helped the Euromarkets grow and resulted in subsequent problems facing national monetary authorities.

However, to understand how these mechanisms worked, we must examine the strategies and behaviors employed by banks to elude U.S. restraints, the impact of these activities on choices available to policy-makers, and the outcomes on the international monetary scene.

Potential Channels of Circumventing
Bank Influence

Banks adjusted to the restraint program so that they could continue to serve their multinational customers abroad. These adjustments were largely made by means of increased branch operations abroad and the use by these branches of Eurodollars. Internationalized structure allowed bankers to evade government restraints which could not extend beyond national boundaries. When only eight U.S. banks maintained foreign branches, each could be watched and coaxed towards policies favored by official bureaucracies, but when the number of banks abroad proliferated, supervision became more difficult. In addition, smaller, newer entrants believed that they could take somewhat greater risks on the edges of prudence since their small operations could not upset the system and since they were not as likely to be hounded by regulators.[25]

The use of Eurofunds by foreign branches and subsidiaries confused national monetary policies. The expanding Eurodollar market allowed banks to transfer funds rapidly from bank to bank, from bank to company, from company to company, and from nation to nation. However, since exchange regulations mainly focused on flows of long-term funds, banks' foreign exchange activities are less relevant here. True, leads and lags and the propensity of MNCs to rely on forward hedging affects national payments figures, but these problems were ignored by the exchange restraint programs.

BANK STRUCTURE AND CIRCUMVENTING INFLUENCE

Bankers obey the letter of the law, but sometimes forget its spirit. Some major U.S. banks set up internal units in the late 1960s to identify exchange restraint loopholes which could be used by the banks and their corporate customers to cope with difficulties arising out of the VFCR and OFDI regulations.[26] Sometimes, banks used MNCs or the structure of the market itself to evade bothersome constraints.

For example, one U.S. bank was approached by a state-owned Eastern European company wanting to buy equipment from a Japanese corporation. The Japanese company wanted immediate payment whereas the Eastern European company wished to spread its payments over two years. The U.S. bank served as intermediary. However, the VFCR program restricted the U.S. bank to 103 percent of its 1964 foreign loan base. Sending the funds directly to the Japanese company's headquarters would have put it over its limit. Instead, after checking with the Federal Reserve, the bank loaned funds to an American subsidiary of the Japanese MNC with which it had dealt before. It was recorded as a domestic loan even though the subsidiary immediately repatriated the funds. This legal loophole allowed a short-term outflow of funds from the United States.[27]

Banks also used their international structure to evade the intent of exchange regulations. When customers could not be served from the United States, banks moved overseas. In early 1974 Governor Brimmer argued:

> Basically, the principal motivation behind the opening of foreign branches by most of the U.S. banks which entered the field in recent years was to meet the financial needs of their foreign customers—particularly U.S. multinational firms. [The FDIP] . . . limited the ability

of American corporations to finance their foreign investment with U.S.-source funds. These regulations made it increasingly necessary for these corporations to borrow abroad. Under these circumstances, many U.S. banks essentially followed overseas customers in an attempt to retain their business.[28]

Bankers argued that "controls" increased the demand for dollars abroad for capital investment and short-term borrowing. Since these demands were not met by the increased supply of Eurodollars, the additional funds were provided by dollar outflows from the U.S. which would not have occurred without the increased artificial demand created by the exchange regulations. Bankers felt that the capital restraints distorted money flows without halting them. As world financial integration became more complete, dollars flowed rapidly to where they were needed regardless of official restraints. Closing some pathways only assured increased dollar outflows through channels like "errors and omissions" or "leads and lags."[29]

The U.S. foreign banking system provided bankers with easy, legal ways to meet their own and their customers' financing needs. Foreign expansion also forced banks to begin to consider political implications of their burgeoning contacts with governments and with U.S. and foreign officials.[30] Bankers never wanted to damage the payments situation, but merely to make profits and serve their customers. However, the ability of banks to tap money market funds abroad and the propensity of new branches to draw funds away from the American economy increased tension between the public and private sectors. In an effort to halt unwanted flows of funds, regulators tended "to leapfrog from one category of exchange transactions to another (and from one country to the next)" in a frustrated attempt "to match the flexibility of response of alert company treasurers and bankers." This game of one-upmanship became politically charged where capital markets were most sophisticated.[31] In addition, the exchange restrictions helped create even more efficient, integrated capital markets.

POTENTIAL CIRCUMVENTING INFLUENCE THROUGH THE EUROMARKETS

How might banks circumvent exchange regulations? Did commercial banks' Euromarket activities confuse developed nations' monetary policies? Two distinctions are useful. First, banks evade exchange restrictions both to help themselves and to aid their MNC customers, sometimes simultaneously. Second, evasive activities may or may not have negative, short-term effects on the U.S. payments position. The ultimate implications of circumventing actions for the U.S. economy and for U.S. monetary policy, however, may be unclear even at a later date.

	Minimal, Short-Term Balance of Payments Impact	Negative, Short-Term Balance of Payments Impact
Banks Protecting Their Customers' Interests	Euromarket financing Parallel and triangle loans **1**	Use of the Canadian exemption Loans to U.S. subsidiaries of foreign MNCs **2**
Banks Protecting Their Own Interests	**4** Interbank Euromarket borrowing	**3** Window-dressing Syndicate loans to banks with leeway

Figure 4.1: Methods for Evading Exchange Programs.

Euromarkets were critical to banks' evasive activities. They provided funds for foreign borrowing and helped facilitate interbank transfers. Euromarket lending did not directly injure the U.S. payments position since no direct flows of funds out of the U.S. are involved. Interbank transfers were exempt from exchange regulations thereby allowing unhampered transfers of funds. Some examples, categorized in Figure 4.1 help clarify the mechanisms banks used to evade U.S. constraints.

Banks for Customers: Minimal, Short-Term Payments Impact. The predominant strategies used to cope with exchange restraints relied on the availability of Eurodollars and Eurobonds.[32] The offshore Euromarkets became a recognized source of funds available to MNCs in the mid-1960s. Corporate treasurers no longer needed to borrow funds in New York to send abroad. In the short term, the U.S. payments situation was unaffected by offshore borrowing. Over the longer run, however, the subordination of New York to London in international finance may have hurt U.S. employment, invisible earnings, tax receipts, and perhaps even investment earnings, which might have developed in the absence of exchange regulations. Although it is unclear whether the overall impact of the U.S. restraints on the American payments position was positive or negative, it seems that the overall swing in either direction was not too large. The key factor in the long run may be that the growth of the Euromarkets and the increased competition for international bank profits made crises in the bank-controlled capital markets and in the government-dominated monetary system more likely.

More technical was the growth of parallel and triangle financing. Banks served as middlemen finding customers wanting to borrow funds in each other's national markets. Lending to each other within single countries eliminated short-term payments effects and frequently benefitted both borrowers. For instance, in a publicized case, Raytheon borrowed the equivalent of $4.8 million for its British operations from British Petroleum. BP's U.S. affiliate borrowed a similar sum from Raytheon in the United States. Funds never left either the United States or United Kingdom. Raytheon received a term loan at favorable rates from BP in Britain, while BP escaped a substantial export tax on funds it was going to invest in the United States.[33]

Bank for Customers: Negative Short-Term Payments Impact. When bank manipulations for their customers had negative, short-term impact on the U.S. payments situation, banks usually were relying on loopholes. Different banks varied substantially in the tenacity with which they sought to use these loopholes. The larger banks in particular feared government wrath, and renewed regulatory ardor would follow if bank evasion through loopholes was too blatant. One such loophole, lending to the U.S. subsidiary of a foreign MNC, has already been described.

Another ploy used Canada's exemption from the U.S. constraints. A Canadian bank could sell a certificate of deposit in New York, lend the funds from Toronto to a MNC, which subsequently reexported the dollars to wherever they were needed. U.S. banks had more trouble using this gambit since they have no branches in Canada and only a few banks maintained Canadian subsidiaries. Overall, there seems to have been only moderate use of the Canadian revolving door to move funds abroad.[34]

Perhaps the most important stimulus to outflows from America was the Regulation Q ceilings, which depressed American interest rates substantially below those prevalent abroad. Sophisticated individuals began moving funds out of the United States to take advantage of the interest differential. MNCs also found ways to move money into the higher paying markets. Transfer pricing, leads and lags, and nonrepatriation of some funds were also used. These funds could subsequently be converted into currencies appearing stronger than the dollar. Many believed that these Regulation Q-induced flows, which were stimulated by the weakness of the dollar, created much of the "omissions" in the 1971 U.S. payments situation.

Banks for Selves: Negative Short-Term Payments Impact. Perhaps the simplest loophole in the VFCR was the reporting requirement that each bank inform the Federal Reserve of the total amount of its outstanding foreign loans from headquarters on the last day of each month. This allowed banks to exceed their limits on every other day of the month, as long as maturities were structured to assure that they came due before month-end. Even when this anomaly was pointed out to authorities, no move was made to amend the regulation to cover the average outstanding loans throughout any month. The Federal Reserve simply requested banks not to take advantage of the spirit of the program.[35]

Banks with no lending leeway sometimes still made money and helped their customers. Correspondent banks without international contacts could be given loans for a fee. For example, suppose a large bank had no leeway under the VFCR ceilings and was approached by a French company for a dollar loan. In some instances, it might give a regional bank the loan if it had sufficient leeway. The matchmaking bank would collect a fee for this service. Obviously, such activities did not blatantly twist the VFCR program, but they did maximize the amount of funds which could be loaned from the U.S. given existing ceilings. Similarly, since ceilings were applied by region, banks could trade business with each other.[36] The payments situation would have been marginally improved without the use of window-dressing and syndication techniques to skirt the VFCR program.

Banks for Selves: Minimal, Short-Term Impact. To service the increased Eurolending which developed after the promulgation of the restraint programs, banks were forced to guarantee themselves adequate access to funds. Lending from the Euromarkets required the development of a solid interbank market for funds. Banks with excess funds on a given day lent them to those which needed funds to make loans or to roll them over. The interbank market mechanism which developed resembled the U.S. Federal Funds market in that both allowed banks to balance their overall book. However, while the Federal Funds market deals in one-day money and is monitored by the Federal Reserve, the European interbank market is controlled by the banks and deals with a wide variety of maturities. Banks needing funds not subject to the VFCR and in many cases not subject to domestic reserve requirements could raise the funds in the interbank market.

Bank Impact on Exchange Restraint Policies and Their Efficiency

Banks' Euromarket activities might (1) pressure decision-makers to alter exchange regulations, (2) render exchange regulations ineffective (thus contributing to a deterioration of the payments situation), or (3) indirectly disrupt other government policies without disturbing the balance of payments. These three overlapping possibilities are explored here.

BANK IMPACT ON EXCHANGE RESTRICTION POLICIES

Private executives lobbied against the VFCR and FDIP almost from their first days. Although banks of different size were affected differently by

Regulation Q and the liberalization of VFCR ceilings, bankers united against exchange restrictions. However, although their lobbying was mainly undertaken through the Bankers Association for Foreign Trade, it did not result in material changes in government policy. Similarly, lobbying for the removal of marginal reserve requirements imposed by Regulation M was slow to show results. Private executives' frequent testimony before congressional committees was acknowledged, then ignored. Restraints were relaxed only when ideological supporters of the market mechanism took office in January 1969. Even then, restraints were not lifted in response to direct private pressure.[37]

Circumventing bank behavior was also not successful in pressuring officials to remove restraints, mainly because most such activity did not injure the U.S. payments situation. Indirect bank pressure was ignored. Indeed, effective evasion of restraints, particularly if the U.S. balance of payments was harmed, most often resulted in government counterattacks designed to close loopholes. However, when private actors produced evidence that they were being constrained without helping the economy, officials sometimes relented. Thus, one consideration underlying the 1969 decision to provide leeway under the VFCR for export financing was the drastic shift in emphasis of U.S. bank's international operations towards foreign branches. Fed officials feared that the expansion overseas might result in diminished incentives for American banks to engage in export-promoting activities and therefore liberalized the constraints.[38]

Between 1963 and 1969 stricter regulations were the norm although banks may have prevented even more stringent regulations from being enacted. For while Andrew Brimmer frequently proposed applying reserve requirements against all foreign assets of U.S. banks, this was never adopted.[39] Nonetheless, the general direction was towards strictness despite what the Chairman of Manufacturers Hanover described as "a fair body of opinion amongst bankers and businessmen that the restrictions distort the balance of payments and that their removal would not seriously affect the payments figures."[40]

The main roadblock to potential, indirect bank influence was that the regulations were aimed specifically at the private sector. Officials were trying to control economic system developments by restraining market participants. Private actors could abide by or evade the rules, but publicized circumvention harming the payments situation was more likely to bring government retaliation than relief and indirect overloading of the system was precluded. Only after President Nixon conceded that the dollar was overvalued, did restraint liberalization gain momentum. The first dollar devaluation was a symbolic admission that exchange restrictions had not corrected the underlying problems plaguing the dollar and the U.S. economy.

Paradoxically, potential private pressure against restraints was defused by the unity of opposition within the private sector. After initial pressuring failed to sway officials, private firms concentrated their influence on inducing modification rather than abolition of regulations. Small banks fought for equal access to the Euromarkets. Large banks fought to assure that they would not face foreign banks untouched by constraints. Banks became more concerned about their competitive positions than about the constraints. As long as controls did not discriminate against one group of firms, all could cope with them. After all, bankers knew they could evade the most burdensome exchange constraints.

BANK IMPACT ON EXCHANGE RESTRICTION EFFICIENCY

The IET, VRCR, and FDIP induced many U.S. banks to shift their corporate financing overseas. It has been claimed that Euromarket growth provided banks with numerous new ways to confound government policies and weaken control of the monetary system including the capability to assure that "surviving or restored exchange controls [could] be circumvented more easily" than ever before.[41] What was the impact of such evasion on international monetary policy efficiency? Were U.S. exchange regulations effective in the 1960s and early 1970s or did bank evasion neutralize them?

On a gross level, restrictions discouraged some outflows, perhaps delayed the necessity of devaluing the dollar, but probably did not help improve the balance of payments. Huge one-time flows for equity purchase were certainly discouraged. In the three years after the mandatory program was announced, foreign borrowing, as a percentage of invested funds rose to over 30 percent of the total from less than 13 percent of the total in 1966 and 1967. Simultaneously, the percentage investment derived from reinvested earnings remained stable at about 20 percent.[42] It appears that the IET, VFCR, and FDIP produced some definite success in discouraging the outflow of funds. The issuance of foreign bonds in New York dropped to almost zero after the passage of the IET. Decreased bank loans from U.S. headquarters to foreigners, particularly in 1966 and 1967, indicate that the VFCR created substantial balance of payments savings. In addition, the FDIP pushed MNCs abroad for a more substantial portion of their investment and operating funds.

However, these figures do not convey the entire story. In 1966, the period of greatest improvement from the VFCR, the United States pursued a tight money policy, which attracted funds to the U.S. economy. High interest rates and tight money policy also drew funds to the United States in 1969 and 1970. Many types of flows of funds influenced the impact of exchange regulations and private reactions to the U.S. payments situation. Apparently, savings in some areas which followed the passage of the credit control programs were nearly offset by reversals elsewhere.

Private net investment income (derived from profit repatriation) has been consistently positive and growing since 1960. Only in 1966 and 1969 did it fail to increase when MNCs hoarded their funds in the face of U.S. tight money policy. These inflows were made more dramatic when long-term capital outflows declined after the passage of the VFCR and became positive in the year following the announcement of the mandatory controls. However, as confidence in the dollar sagged, MNCs chose to move funds abroad despite the cost. In 1970 and 1971 long-term private capital flows moved into sharp deficit. In 1973 and 1974 flows were tremendously confused by the floating exchange rate system, which made many balance of payments categories meaningless.[43]

Net liquid private capital outflows and errors and omissions tended to balance each other out. Short-term liquid capital flows were favorable until 1969, moved sharply negative until the first dollar devaluation, and then improved once more. Errors and omissions is a balancing item needed for accounting purposes to assure that a nation's current account (short-term flows) plus its capital account (long-term flows) plus the errors and omissions figure equals zero. These unidentified flows rose to a record $1.8 billion in 1969 following the introduction of the OFDI regulations. That year the Director of OFDI estimated that termination of the exchange restrictions would lead to a deterioration of $3 to $4 billion the following year.[44] Private spokesmen, on the other hand, contended that the capital controls transferred flows from the United States from one category to another but did not materially affect the direction or magnitude of flows. They argued that removal of controls might benefit the U.S. economy and certainly would not harm it. The crude figures seem to support the private sector's conclusion.[45] Although there was apparently a time lag while business firms learned how to effectively circumvent regulations, regulations could become almost useless about a year after they were introduced. Thus, the VFCR was less effective after 1966, and private actors helped build up a record negative errors and omissions figure of $9.8 billion in 1971.

To counteract private circumvention of restrictions, government officials resorted to a multiplicity of measures to defend the increasingly fragile Bretton Woods system. These measures included reserve ratio requirements, penalty or negative interest charges on foreign deposits, which limited the inflow of Eurofunds, two-tier markets to neutralize exchange pressures, and direct and indirect Euromarket intervention by government authorities.[46]

Such measures allowed authorities to close some loopholes and minimize leakage from national economies, and banks and MNCs failed to convince officials to moderate their regulatory ardor. However, the tripartite exchange programs were never integrated into a unified policy, which helped private actors elude regulations.

SPILLOVER IMPLICATIONS OF
CIRCUMVENTING BANK BEHAVIOR

General Costs. Rimmer de Vries, a highly respected international econo-mist at Morgan Guaranty, argued that the shift of bank business abroad caused by exchange regulations hurt the U.S. economy in at least four ways. First, new foreign branches employing nearly 30,000 people almost certainly caused some loss in U.S. employment.[47] Second, the forced reliance of U.S. banks on their overseas branches resulted in substantial tax payments to foreign governments. Third, the rapid expansion of international banking benefited the improvement of the quality and competitiveness of foreign financial markets at the expense of U.S. financial markets. Finally, the shift to the overseas branches, and the growth of the Euromarkets raised con-siderable concern as to the quality of banking practices.[48] Such spillovers probably cost the United States substantial revenues and hurt its payments position. Whether inflows offset the long-term outflow of funds which was slowed by exchange restriction is uncertain. Government officials insist that despite difficulties the programs helped the U.S. payments balance. Private spokesmen contend that constraints only delayed the inevitable and made the transition more difficult.

It is also relevant that U.S. capital restraints accelerated the growth of the Euromarkets and helped them reach unprecedented size. As expected, the termination of restraints did not cause a significant reduction in size of either the Eurodollar or Eurobond markets. However, much of the growth after mid-1974 was related to headquarter funding through Caribbean shell branches.[49] Some critics believe that the huge, efficient, unregulated capital markets which developed in the 1960s could unleash disequilibrating streams of funds which could upset exchange regulations, parity values, and the international monetary system itself. If the U.S. restrictions were responsible for a large portion of the Eurocurrency growth, U.S. authorities perhaps created their own Frankenstein monster. Regardless of intent, the growing availability of Eurofunds provided banks and MNC's with more potential power than at any time in recent memory.

The Disruption of Monetary Policy. Perhaps the most significant Euro-market spillover was the increasing bank capacity to disrupt national mone-tary policies. Euromarket liquidity led to major problems for officials. Swiss central bank President Dr. Edwin Stopper concluded that the existence of the Euromarkets diminished the efficiency of countries' monetary restrictions designed to curb inflation: "As soon as the tight money supply raises the national interest rates above those of the Eurodollar, the inflow of funds from this market begins and counteracts the shortage."[50]

During periods of relative exchange rate calm, the Eurodollar market was the Achilles' heel of U.S. tight money policy. In 1966 the Federal Reserve tightened the money supply to slow the economy. Bankers felt obliged to continue serving their corporate customers even if it meant absorbing heavy capital losses through the liquidation of marketable securities.[51] They used Eurodollars to circumvent and frustrate Federal Reserve policy. Banks simply borrowed dollars in London and relent them in the United States (which helped the U.S. payments position but defeated tight money). U.S. banks' short-term liabilities to their foreign branches and to foreign banks rose. Heavy demand for funds pushed up the Eurodollar rates, but banks were willing to take losses on these loans to assure their customers continued access to funds.

The events of 1966 persuaded some banks that Eurodollar access was necessary to protect customers from future credit squeezes. They moved abroad. When the scenario was replayed in 1969-1970, the same plot was reenacted on a larger scale. On January 1, 1969 U.S. headquarters owed their branches $6.0 billion. On September 24, 1969, American banks listed their liabilities to their overseas branches at $14.4 billion, the bulk of which was accounted for by twenty banks. After monetary conditions eased in early 1970, borrowings, which had pushed three month Eurodollar rates from an average of 7.53 percent in January 1969, to 11.28 percent in June 1969, became extraneous. Borrowings receded to $0.9 billion on December 29, 1971. Three month Eurodollar rates followed the borrowings down and averaged 5.8 percent in December 1971.

This rapid decline in borrowed funds was caused by the easing of U.S. monetary policy and by the imposition of Regulation M reserve requirements in May 1969. In effect, the Federal Reserve drove out foreign borrowings by U.S. headquarters and neutralized the favorable payments contribution they had made. To preserve some of the borrowings, however, the Federal Reserve allowed banks to maintain a minimum base, untaxed.

Not surprisingly, these sudden U.S. moves, taken during a period in which the U.S. economy was booming, upset European government planning. European capital markets were first stripped of available lendable funds and then suffered an equally disruptive return of those funds. They complained vigorously to U.S. authorities about the U.S. market manipulation although they understood its inevitability in light of the U.S. economy's dominant position in the world economy.

After close study of the credit crunches of 1966 and 1969-1970, Governor Brimmer concluded:

> The experience with monetary policy in the United States suggests strongly that the evolution of the commercial banking system has altered the flow of funds, changed the distributional effects of monetary policy, and placed strains on traditional instruments of central

banking. . . . Because of the[se] activities . . . the financial system in the United States has become much more open to influence of foreign financial developments than was the case a decade ago.[52]

Similarly, former Federal Reserve Chairman William McChesney Martin viewed the ability of banks to circumvent Federal Reserve policy as one of the major failures he had experienced in nineteen years running the Federal Reserve System.[53]

Summary and Conclusions

In sum, it appears that although banks did not materially influence governments to remove exchange restrictions, they evaded the brunt of regulations which threatened to disrupt their ability to service their customers' needs. When these alternatives did not directly damage the U.S. payments situation, they were allowed and even encouraged by government authorities. However, leaks still took place from the U.S. economy and the American payments situation continued to deteriorate despite the regulations. The ultimate inefficiency of exchange regulations was demonstrated in 1971 when nearly $10 billion escaped from America through unknown or unrecorded channels.

In the meantime, the U.S. lost some of the benefits associated with being the dominant financial center and increasingly lost control over the effectiveness of their own monetary policy as the Euromarkets grew. In retrospect, it is dubious that exchange restrictions were worth the side effects they caused. The exchange programs did not correct the U.S. economic situation, but fostered unregulated and potentially destabilizing markets for funds while fanning serious dispute between the public and private sectors about their appropriate interrelationship. It became obvious that private actors could be restrained within narrow boundaries by governments working within their own nations or by governments cooperating to control international markets. However, since government cooperation was not forthcoming on whether or how to control the Euromarkets, these markets continued to expand and rise in importance.

It appears that indirect and circumventing bank influence was ineffective in placing pressure on government officials to terminate exchange regulations. Certainly, pressure was exerted, but this pressure was perceived as totally self-interested and was therefore ignored when officials believed that narrow self-interest was moving against larger national goals. Banks and MNCs were also not as upset by exchange restrictions as sometimes claimed, since they could continue to function smoothly with only minor hassles. As a result, their activities in stimulating the Euromarket's growth put temporary pressure on key areas of government control of their domestic and international

Table 4.1: Influence Employed by Banks in the International Monetary System

	Direct Influence	Circumventing Influence	Indirect Influence
Response to:	Existing or proposed policies or legislation.	Policies and legislation aimed at market participants.	Policies and legislation aimed at controlling the economic system.
Channels:	Lobbying Personnel transfer Public appeals Bribery	Capital flows Currency exchanges International structure	Capital flows Currency exchanges International structure
Strategy:	Persuasion	Evasion	Coercion
Impact on:	Policy-making	Policy effectiveness	Economic outcomes
Intent:	Conscious	Conscious at primary level. May have unintentional side effects	Conscious or unintentional at both primary and secondary levels
Influence at work during:			
Exchange Regulations	Persuaded officials to adjust policies to treat all banks fairly. Unable to persuade U.S. to remove constraints.	Learned to evade regulation, making them ineffective. Unintended expansion of banking, Euromarkets was important result.	Little or no indirect influence

monetary policies. Governments, in turn, responded by closing more loopholes instead of removing restrictions. The circumvention of constraints was interpreted as a sound reason for greater vigilance and control of the private sector. Only when ideological, free market advocates gained control of the government did this begin to change. And, even then, the new high officials maintained the restrictions for almost six years after coming to power.

On the other hand, banks were quite effective at altering outcomes for at least short periods of time. They found ways to conduct their business beyond the control of the U.S. government. The process of corporate-government interaction on exchange restrictions was a cat and mouse game. The government would pass a set of regulations; the banks would find the weak spots and exploit them. The governments would respond by closing off loopholes, but would miss some or create new ones in the process. Since government policies were not aligned, they would alternate between policies which helped the balance of payments and those which tried to isolate and make effective domestic monetary policy. More important than any single instance of evasion was the overall success banks enjoyed in creating strategies of evasion which bolstered the size of the Euromarkets. The potential of these markets to overwhelm government policies in several areas with huge flows of funds from one nation to another became the critical problem facing governments in the monetary system in the late 1960s.

In conclusion, Table 4.1 reiterates the format presented earlier. It is clear that banks had only limited direct influence on U.S. policy-making concerning exchange restraints. Their ability to circumvent these regulations aimed at them was considerable and subsequently provoked developments unforeseen by public or private officials. However, while policy was directed at the market participants, they had almost no ability to employ indirect influence to alter monetary outcomes. This type of influence could only be used effectively when regulatory concern was focused on the markets as a whole.

NOTES

1. U.S. Congress, Joint Economic Committee, *A Review of Balance of Payments Policies. Hearings before the Subcommittee on International Exchange and Payments,* 91st Cong., 1st sess., 1969: 187.

2. Interview with Andrew Brimmer, Harvard Business School, May 13, 1976.

3. Ibid.

4. See, John Conybeare, "United States foreign economic policy and the international capital markets: the case of capital export controls 1963-1974," Ph.D. dissertation, Harvard, 1976; the IMF's annual *Reports on Exchange Restrictions*; and Andrew Brimmer's JEC testimony in *Balance of Payments Policies*: 163-166.

5. U.S., President, *Economic Report of the President,* January 1966: 165. Also see, Raymond Vernon, "A skeptic looks at the balance of payments," *Foreign Policy* 5 (Winter 1971-72): 52-65.

6. Henry Aubrey, *The Dollar in World Affairs* (New York: Praeger, 1964): 250.

7. Conybeare, op. cit.: Ch. 4.

8. *Economic Report of the President,* 1966: 165.

9. Gerald Wright and Maureen Appel Molot, "Capital movements and government control," *International Organization* 28 (Autumn 1974): 673.

10. U.S., President, *Public Papers of the Presidents of the United States,* John F. Kennedy, 1963: 580.

11. For figures see, Sir Alex Cairncross, *Control of Long-Term International Capital Movements* (Washington: Brookings Institution, 1973): 33.

12. New York *Times,* February 11, 1965.

13. *Balance of Payments Policies*: 163.

14. Ibid.: 163-164.

15. Ibid.: 164.

16. Board of Governors of the Federal Reserve System, *Annual Report,* 1971: 206-207.

17. Board of Governors of the Federal Reserve System, *Annual Report,* 1974: 231.

18. Conybeare, op. cit.: 96-97.

19. Stuart Robinson, *Multinational Banking* (Leiden, Netherlands: A.W. Sijthoff International Publishing Company, 1972): 265-266.

20. IMF, *Report on Exchange Restrictions,* 1969: 498.

21. U.S., Department of Commerce, *Foreign Direct Investment Program: Selected Statistics,* 1972: 5.

22. Janet Kelly, *Bankers and Borders* (Cambridge, Mass.: Ballinger, 1977).

23. Interview with Andrew Brimmer, May 13, 1976.

24. See, Fritz Machlup, "Five errors."

25. Interviews with representatives of Salomon Brothers, Marine Midland, and Bank of America, London, October 1974.

26. Interviews with representatives of Morgan Guaranty and Citicorp, April 1976.

27. Interview with representative of a U.S. bank, 1974.

28. Andrew Brimmer, "Prospects for commercial banks in international money and capital markets: an American perspective," paper presented before the Conference on World Banking, London, January 17, 1974: 9.

29. See, e.g., G. A. Costanzo's testimony in *Balance of Payments in Policies,* p. 188, and Eugene Birnbaum's testimony in U.S. Congress Joint Economic Committee, *The Balance of Payments Mess: Hearings before the Subcommittee on International Exchange and Payments,* 92nd Cong., 1st sess., 1971: 206.

30. Interviews with top level representatives of Bank of America, Wells Fargo, and First National Bank of Chicago, San Francisco, Chicago, January, April, 1974.

31. Alice Barrass, "Afloat in a sea of controls," *The Banker* 123 (June 1973): 616.

32. For more on longer-term Eurobonds, see, Gunter Dufey, "The Eurobond market: its significance for international financial management," *Journal of International Business Studies* 1 (Spring 1970): 65-81.

33. Sanford Rose, "Capital is something that doesn't love a wall," *Fortune* 83 (February 1971): 110.

34. Interviews with representatives of Chemical Bank and First National Bank of Boston, New York, Boston, July 1976.

35. Interview with a representative of Chemical Bank, July 1976.

36. Ibid.

37. John Odell interviews.

38. Andrew Brimmer, "Capital outflows and the United States balance of payments: review and outlook," paper presented at the Federal Reserve Bank of Dallas, February 11, 1970, p. 18.

39. For a description see, ibid., pp. 23-28.

40. Gabriel Hauge, "Changes in regulations: impact on the markets," *Euromoney* (April 1973): 25.

41. Einzig, *The Euro-Dollar System,* p. 114.

42. U.S. Department of Commerce, *Foreign Direct Investment Program: Selected Statistics,* 1972.

43. *Wall Street Journal,* December 10, 1975.

44. *Balance of Payments Policies,* pp. 197-198.

45. See, *Economic Report of the President,* February 1975: 350-351.

46. Stanislas Yassukovich, "Dilemmas of Euromarket regulations," *The Banker* 123 (April 1973): 369.

47. For a full treatment of the impact on multinational business on U.S. employment, see, U.S. Congress, Senate, Committee on Foreign Relations, *Direct Investment Abroad and the Multinationals: Effects on the U.S. Economy. Report for the Subcommittee on Multinational Corporations.* Prepared by Peggy Musgrave, 94th Cong., 1st sess., 1975.

48. Rimmer de Vries, "Charting a new course in U.S. international banking regulations," *Bankers Magazine* 155 (Autumn 1972): 76-77.

49. See, U.S. Congress, House, Committee on Banking, Currency and Housing, *International Banking: A Supplement to a Compendium of Papers Prepared for the FINE Study,* 94th Cong., 2nd sess., 1976, p. 89; and Andrew Brimmer, "American international banking: recent trends and prospects," remarks before a conference on New York as a World Financial Center, New York, April 30, 1976.

50. Edwin Stopper, "The conflict of monetary and social policies," *Euromoney* (February 1971): 16.

51. Andrew Brimmer, "Monetary policy and the allocation of commercial bank credit," lecture at the Vermont-New Hampshire School of Banking, Dartmouth, Hanover, New Hampshire, September 11, 1966: 13.

52. Andrew Brimmer, "Multi-national banks," p. 54.

53. Seminar by William McChesney Martin, Harvard, November 12, 1975.

Chapter 5

BANKS DURING INTERNATIONAL

MONETARY AND BANKING

CRISES, 1964-1976

The relationships among governments, commercial banks, central banks, and international monetary organizations are constantly shifting and evolving. The changing interactions are encouraged by the public sector's focus on markets and their control rather than on market participants. This chapter examines the evolution of these relationships in the context of British and American monetary and banking crises since 1964. Four separate periods can be distinguished. In the first period, before 1971, governments controlled money markets but were eventually forced by underlying economic conditions to adjust exchange rates. General exchange market conditions presumed fixed rates, and commercial banks could "trigger" crises but had no ability or desire to cause them. The second period, which stretched from the Smithsonian Agreement in December 1971 through March 1973, was characterized by the dominance of general exchange market conditions and the adjustment by market participants to the new market flexibility. Commercial banks were more influential in this period, especially European banks while most governments continued to assume that exchange rates reflected fundamental market factors rather than enhanced private actor influence. In the short third period, which extended until July 1973, governments abdicated to floating rates. Commercial banks, particularly smaller ones, exerted major influence as exchange market conditions became less and less predictable. Finally, the relationships began to stabilize, especially after a serious banking crisis in 1974, and a new balance was struck among commerical banks, central banks, and finance ministries, which allowed for a more predictable flexible exchange rate system.

The shifting interrelationships were made possible by the growth and integration of the Eurocurrency and foreign exchange markets. They were facilitated by the inability of finance ministers and central bankers to concur on what could and should be done to manage rates and introduce monetary reform. European and American opinion was particularly split over the future reserve asset role of the dollar. While this had only secondary interest to private practitioners, it detoured public cooperation away from the flexibility issue and allowed commercial banks to exert greater indirect influence.

Exchange and Monetary
Crises, 1964-1976

Although channels through which banks could influence exchange crises existed well before 1971, these were ineffective or underutilized while governments were determined to defend the Bretton Woods arrangement. Most explanations of exchange crises focus on so-called "underlying causes." It is assumed that speculators trigger crises only when a currency's value is fundamentally out of line. Two questions are central. Did the ability of private actors to trigger exchange crises increase over time? Could microeconomic competition unrelated to underlying economic conditions create "political" exchange crises not dictated by economic necessity.

BANKS AS TRIGGERS: CRISES BEFORE 1971

The processes leading to the 1967 sterling devaluation and the 1971 dollar devaluation were strikingly similar. Both currencies were fundamentally overvalued. Preliminary minicrises were turned aside by the monetary authorities in both cases. Central bankers in both instances opposed devaluation, but were overruled by political leaders.[1] Each government decided to devalue before the main speculative pressure struck. Bank and exchange market speculation did, however, demonstrate to public officials that private power to overthrow exchange regimes was growing swiftly. In neither case is there any firm evidence that bankers speculated improperly and created unjustified crises. The main difference was that the Americans faced the added problem of trying to readjust the value of the system's reserve asset without disrupting the entire monetary order.

The 1967 Sterling Devaluation. What impact did banks exert on monetary crises during the Bretton Woods era? In the case of sterling, the deterioration of the British payments balance was actually more severe in 1964 than 1967. In 1964, the election of the Labour Party stimulated intense uncertainty among City leaders. Prime Minister Wilson believed his "newly elected government . . . was being told . . . by international speculators, that the policies on which [it] had fought the election could not be implemented; that the Government was to be forced into the adoption of Tory policies to which it was fundamentally opposed."[2] Wilson proclaimed his determination to keep sterling strong, threatened to float the pound and call new elections on the issue of "dictation by overseas financiers,"[3] and banned discussion of possible devaluation in Whitehall.[4]

However, when the bank rate was raised on Monday, November 23 rather than on the traditional Thursday, the private sector perceived government panic, rather than firmness, and speculation increased. After a "virtual avalanche of selling developed" on November 24, central bankers saved sterling by arranging a $3 billion credit package which temporarily quieted the markets. Charles Coombs, who arranged the package from New York, saw it as a central bankers' demonstration of faith in the Bank of England and in its Governor rather than in the British government or economy.[5]

Mild crises fueled by speculation recurred in 1965 and 1966 and were countered with stiff new controls. The key blow, which doomed sterling, was the closure of the Suez Canal during the Six Day War. The Labour Government concluded that a devaluation was almost inevitable on November 3,[6] and rejected U.S. credit offers of up to $1.5 billion.[7] On November 16 when Chancellor Callaghan refused to confirm or deny that negotiations on a credit package were underway, the market "knew" a devaluation was imminent and speculation multiplied. Gentlemen to the end, Britain supported the pound on the seventeenth while the government prepared the necessary public statements and notified the IMF and key governments. Finally, on November 18, 1967 the pound was devalued by 14.3 percent from $2.80 to $2.40. Significantly, the bulk of the speculative wave struck after the formal decision to devalue was taken. Once triggered, however, the changed structure of the system encouraged increased speculation against sterling. The magnitude of flows reinforced the government's view that devaluation was required.

Although banks could have profited by speculating against currencies, they distrusted their ability to predict timing and normally minimized their open exposures. While it is true that before 1971 "there was often an incentive to acquire a position in a currency when it was at its ceiling and pressure was clearly upward, or at its floor with pressure clearly downward, and wait for the parity change,"[8] American commercial banks do not seem to have taken this route. As late as October 1967, bankers worried that a new central bank credit package to support sterling might be negotiated, which, given "the grossly oversold position of sterling might have led to massive short covering such as occurred in late 1965 and again in early 1967."[9] To protect their positions, banks hedged their exposure, pushing sterling somewhat higher for a time.

During the 1967 sterling crisis, U.S. banks helped their corporate clients hedge. Since MNCs usually wanted to sell pounds forward, banks acquired a surplus of sterling. They balanced their position by selling spot sterling, mostly to the Bank of England. Overall, most banks retained nearly balanced positions. However, bankers encountered a major roadblock. On spot contracts sellers must deliver the currency within two business days. After the devaluation, American banks needed to acquire large amounts of sterling for settlement, but the London exchange market was closed on the following Monday. The Bank of England, disturbed by what it considered excessive speculation, tried to prevent shorters from obtaining pounds to offset their position and threatened to nullify unsettled contracts, leaving U.S. banks very long in forward sterling. New York bankers protested that their contracts were legitimate, commercial, and nonspeculative. An emergency New York Federal Reserve Bank study confirmed bank contentions. Therefore, after informing a recalcitrant Bank of England, the Federal Reserve lent banks sterling at overnight rates of over 100 percent to allow them to settle their spot contracts.[10]

Much of the private pressure involved long overdue corporate activity. Just before the devaluation, MNCs rushed to hedge previously neglected funds. Corporate leading and lagging of payments contributed substantial pressure. Many MNCs refrained from hedging before 1967 because they could cover themselves between the early warnings of crises and parity changes. However, once excited, they moved rapidly.

Conceivably, if MNCs never hedged, long-run foreign exchange profits and losses would cancel each other out and hedging costs would be saved. Corporate executives, however, fear sharp losses damage shareholder morale while sharp gains create false expectations of future growth. Recent changes in reporting requirements that demand quarterly accounting have spurred these fears. As Euromarkets and foreign exchange markets expanded in the 1960s, corporate hedging, totally indistinguishable from speculation, triggered but did not cause devaluations, including sterling's. In sum, while market growth and pressure eventually led to the abandonment of government hope in further controls and forced a devaluation, the banks were responding to underlying economic conditions. In turn, central banks responded to private actors' behavior and usually were able to maintain control.

The First Dollar Devaluation. As early as 1959 the Treasury and economists such as Robert Triffin warned that the Bretton Woods system must eventually break down because the dollar, the system's reserve asset, could not be subjected to perpetual payments deficits and remain healthy. Until 1967, however, sterling shielded the dollar. Inexorably, the U.S. payments situation deteriorated from 1960 to 1971. Each year the net liquidity balance was negative and reserves fell. American payments deficits mounted in the face of increasing Vietnam spending. Credit restraint restrictions were made mandatory on January 1, 1968. In mid-March 1968 renewed speculative buying of gold forced the adoption of a two-tier gold market. Following George Pompidou's election as President on April 28, 1969, France surprised the financial world by devaluing the franc 11.1 percent against the dollar. A month after Willy Brandt came to power in September 1969, the mark was allowed to float and then revalued by 9.29 percent against the dollar. Not until 1971, however, did the American trade balance become negative.

On December 14, 1970, John Connally was designated by Richard Nixon to succeed former banker David Kennedy, a weak leader, as Secretary of the Treasury. Connally's strength and savvy paid off when pressure on the dollar mounted. In early March 1971, British, French, German, and Japanese reserve positions were improving. When French Finance Minister Giscaird d'Estaing suggested that the gold price be raised to stem the dollar flow and private German economic research groups suggested that the mark be allowed to float, frantic speculative bidding forced the Bundesbank to absorb $1.2 billion on May 4, 1971. The following day the Bundesbank withdrew from the market after absorbing $1 billion in the first forty minutes of trading. European markets closed. The Swiss franc was revalued by 7.07 percent, its first parity change in 35 years, and the Austrian schilling was revalued 5.05 percent. The mark and Dutch guilder were allowed to float upwards. By early May European central banks indicated they did not want to accept more dollars.

Pressure mounted on August 8 when a routine U.S. IMF drawing and gold transfer coincided with a Treasury admission that "serious problems exist" and the issue of a congressional report by Henry Reuss which concluded that the dollar was overvalued. These announcements convinced the private sector that a dollar devaluation was imminent. Within one week, $3.7 billion was converted into stronger currencies. European central banks could not tolerate the pressure.[11] With trepidation and relief Europe accepted President Nixon's August 15, 1971 announcement that the dollar would no longer be directly convertible into gold.

Banks and corporate speculation triggered the crisis, but did not cause it. The triggering mechanism was probably more effective because the Euromarkets and foreign exchange markets were well developed by 1971. Eventual devaluation was probably inevitable, however. Nixon and Connally were not altogether displeased when bankers advised their corporate clients that the dollar's outlook was bleak. Corporate treasurers moved accordingly, the test run in May 1971 convinced key private executives that they could force the needed correction in the dollar's value. When coupled with the withdrawal of the New York Federal Reserve Bank's authority to intervene to defend the dollar as needed, the private sector's dislike for political manipulation of exchange rates sounded the death knell for the dollar.

Bank Impact on Crisis Outcomes Before 1971. Neither crisis was caused by private actors. As the 1960s progressed, the major change in bank role was their increased ability to channel funds through the foreign exchange and Eurocurrency markets into strong currencies. As it began expanding, the Eurodollar market

> was seen as hot money because there was a tendency to feed on itself and create more money. It scared the Hell out of a lot of banks. Between 1960 and 1965 it was felt that it was so volatile that it could disappear overnight. By 1970 this attitude had turned around and the general feeling was that the market worked as a stabilizer during crises.[12]

By mid-1971 *The Banker* could comment editorially that

> the ever-growing Euro-currency pool was the main feature which distinguished the current crisis from its predecessors. . . . [I]t distorted German domestic monetary policy; and it helped to fuel speculation as against the main candidate for revaluation, the D-mark. Both involve the German authorities, who stand accused of the twin counts of refusing to take necessary corrective action on the Euro-dollar borrowings by German companies and contributing to the ease in which such dollars could be borrowed by allowing them to be relent into the market.[13]

At the same time the Governor of the Bank of England noted that "the danger of concentrating attention on the Euromarkets is that it distracts from the real causes of international maladjustment—for any problem that is transmitted must have underlying causes."[14]

Within the foreign exchange markets, techniques remained stable that market size and psychology changed. Foreign exchange markets grew rapidly during the 1960s. Slowly, bankers realized that the traditional view of foreign exchange activities—as a nonprofitable service provided to corporate customers—was outdated. Profitability was perceived as possible. Market participants saw central banks as defending unviable exchange parities which allowed

Banks During International Monetary and Banking Crises, 1964-1976   **[101]**

them to take "one-way bets." If authorities repulsed market pressure, private losses were minimal. When crises forced desirable parity changes, profits could be substantial.

Private actors could have substantial impact on the timing and outcome of crises by pursuing what they perceived as sound, economic policies. Their roles were substantial without ever resorting to direct attempts to influence government policies. While foreign exchange market participants became more tenacious after profit possibilities materialized, there was never any unanimity of approach among banks acting in the foreign exchange markets.

These changes in foreign exchange and Euromarket structure did not augment bank power except concerning crisis timing. Most exchange crises before 1971 were caused by the "failure by governments to adopt prompt and effective deficits or surpluses in their balance of payments accounts."[15] Each crisis up to and including August 1971 was based on "underlying economic conditions that triggered the banks. No one ever attacked a strong currency."[16] Indeed, while banks converted their own and their clients' funds to protect against maladjusted exchange rates, they continued to support the Bretton Woods fixed rate system at least until mid-1971. Most international firms failed to analyze "the impact of a limited increase in exchange rate variability on their trade and investment outlook." Most MNCs had no clear position on the desirability of greater exchange rate flexibility since, to a great extent, commercial banks served as the spokesmen for business on monetary questions.[17]

Bank views and actions are well illustrated by Citibank's famous 1965 foreign exchange gaffe. A Citibank dealer in Brussels made unauthorized purchases of forward sterling in the expectation that the pound would weather its annual crisis. When these contracts were discovered, the trader was fired and the open position was offset at substantial loss. In retrospect, the dealer correctly assessed the outcome. Citibank would have made money by holding the contracts to maturity. However, bank managements are more concerned with avoiding fiascos than in making small killings. The dealer's potential profits were far smaller than his potential losses and were therefore perceived as poor risks.

Even market-makers,* which of necessity must accept some speculative positions, normally attempt to offset their long and short holdings when possible and rarely hold open positions for extended periods. Banks also discourage their customers from speculating during exchange crises. Banks refuse to undertake speculative transactions for individuals and try to discourage their corporate clients from taking noncommercial transactions.[18]

---

*A market-maker will accept open positions (long or short) in currencies to assure that customers can transact their business immediately and to fortify the market. Normally, market-makers will hold open positions for a short time.

Given the attitudes and conservative behavior of the business community, it is hardly surprising that private actors were not at the root of exchange crises prior to 1971. While governments were committed to defending badly maladjusted exchange rates, they could enforce their desires on skeptical market participants. However, when banks became convinced that exchange parities were out of line, any false step or harsh public pronouncement by a governmental official could stimulate substantial flows of short-term funds. As these flows increased in magnitude and frequency, governments realized that their parities were undefensible over the long-term and began planning for adjustment. Thus, bank "power" was of a very limited nature. Banks had no ability or desire to cause crises before 1971, but only the capacity to trigger them. However, as the volume of funds available to private actors increased more rapidly than defensive reserves controlled by national authorities, crises became more likely to end in parity adjustment and monetary system change.[19] Still, there were changes in actor behavior and relative crisis roles before 1971, which are displayed in Table 5.1.

THE EXCHANGE MARKETS DOMINATE:
BACKWASH CRISES OF 1972-1973

The most important change following the first dollar devaluation was perceptual. Private market participants had realized that the dollar was overvalued, had complained that this hurt their ability to export goods and services, but had discounted the possibility of a parity change until mid-1971. Once proven vulnerable, however, the dollar immediately became suspect despite its lower value. From this precarious situation grew backwash crises, crises dominated by the exchange market and exchange market psychology more than by governments and market participants. Backwash crises occur when capital markets transmit massive, short-term capital flows from currency to currency without regard to economic expectations. If these flows become so massive that neither governments nor private actors can turn them aside, parity changes become inevitable. Backwash crises may have underlying economic roots or may be set off by spurious rumors. Two classic backwash crises were the June 1972 sterling crisis and the second dollar devaluation crisis.

The Sterling Float, June 1972. Efforts to resuscitate the fixed rate system through economic wizardry failed. Instead of aggressive monetary reform, a patchwork agreement emerged from the Smithsonian Conference. Although fixed rates were reinstituted with wider margins for fluctuation, the appropriate future role and value of the dollar were uncertain. On March 7, 1972 EEC finance ministers agreed to narrow the margin of fluctuation among their currencies to 2.25 percent by July 1, 1972. Pressures on the Italian lira

Table 5.1: Components of Crisis, 1946—August 1971

Role and Behavior of:	1946 to 1958	1959 to August 1971
Governments:	After 1949, intent to meet crises with controls not parity changes. Politics sometimes allowed to replace economics in parity considerations. Able to stop market runs.	As short-term capital flows increase in size, governments begin to consider parity changes and finally come to prefer them. Central banks continue to fight to defend exchange rates.
The foreign exchange and Eurocurrency markets (as actors):	Euromarkets small and controllable. Foreign exchange markets constrained by nonconvertibility of European currencies. Markets do not create crises.	Both markets grow rapidly. More liquidity is in private hands than central bank reserves after 1969. Major flows of funds can be generated rapidly and efficiently.
Commercial banks:	International business is limited and designed to serve MNC clients. Only 7 large U.S. banks have foreign branches by 1958. U.S. banks have little impact on exchange crises.	IET pushes more banks abroad. Business expands. Profit potential of Euro and FX markets recognized. Perceive in late 1960s that parities are out of line. Can trigger large flows of short-term funds.
Multinational corporations:	Leads and lags and hedging can bring pressure on exchange rates, but after 1949 governments control the eventual outcome of crises.	MNC behavior largely unchanged, but they are losing some bargaining position to the banks. Want stability, funding. MNCs bring but do not manufacture false pressure.
Who controls?	Governments dominate.	Governments create and dominate crises, but private sector can bring increasing pressure to bear.

quickly forced Italy out of this "snake in the tunnel."[20] The British joined the float reluctantly on May 1, 1972 to prove they were good Europeans, but were forced to withdraw less than two months later.

The 1972 sterling crisis was markedly different from earlier attacks on the pound. The short-run British economic situation was healthier than at any recent period. For the first time since 1964 Britain had repaid all loans outstanding to the International Monetary Fund. More important, the British balance of payments was in clear surplus, although the British balance of trade was negative in the first two quarters of 1972.[21] The British had weathered more serious challenges before without flinching.

One key difference between 1967 and 1972 was the government's attitude. Conservative Chancellor of the Exchequer Anthony Barber promised in his February budget message that the U.K. would no longer distort the domestic economy in favor of sterling. This alerted traders to possible new problems. Traders believed that shrinking surpluses, inflation, and the threat of a massive dock strike would eventually provoke a crisis. The key stimulus came from Denis Healy, Labour's shadow Chancellor, who predicted on June 18 that sterling would be devalued by July or August. Despite official denials in London, Paris, Frankfurt, and New York, the Bank of England lost $2.6 billion in reserves in less than a week. Treasury Under Secretary Volcker repeatedly praised the strength of sterling, concluding the day before the float that "surplus countries are in no position to devalue their currencies."[22]

Nonetheless, massive pressure mounted rapidly and before anybody clearly understood what was happening the pound was floating. Chancellor Barber blamed the float on "the weight of international short-term capital movements, which proceeded despite concerted intervention by the Bank of England and other European central banks."[23] The mechanism leading to the float was far more isolated from immediate underlying causes and was similar in roots and process to the second devaluation of the dollar which followed eight months later.

The Second Dollar Devaluation, February 1973. The dollar roamed quietly in the year following the Smithsonian accords. It dipped slowly during the first half of 1972, but recovered after the sterling float. Despite the removal of several mandatory controls and the persistent U.S. payments deficit, the Reuter's currency index indicated on January 18, 1973 that the dollar was stronger than at any time in the previous year.

Trouble struck when Italy, attempting to stem the outflow of lira following the fall of the Andreotti government, introduced a two-tier market modeled on French and Belgian markets on January 22, 1973. The Italian move undercut Swiss banks, which were relying on Italian capital flows to handle a tight Swiss credit squeeze. Slowed lira flows forced Swiss banks to convert some of their dollar holdings into Swiss francs as an alternative source of domestic funds.[24] The Swiss central bank absorbed about $200 million to keep the dollar from plunging. However, when efforts to freeze all Swiss francs acquired for dollars below a specific point failed, the Swiss franc was floated the day after the Italian move.

To this point, the dollar was the victim, not the focus of speculation. The dollar was battered because of its reserve asset position; all transactions went through dollars, which were no longer considered "safe" for holding. On January 24, a week after the dollar peaked, the United States announced a larger trade deficit than expected. Favorable German trade figure announcements followed. Trader confidence was shaken, and the dollar fell. Rumors and public statements stoked the fire. Newspapers incorrectly reported that the United States had asked the Germans to float and that Germany was considering a two-tier market. House Ways and Means Comittee chairman Wilbur Mills proclaimed that "the exchange relationships between the dollar and other major currencies will have to be realigned some more,"[25] and Henry Reuss suggested that the United States ask Germany to "let the mark float."[26] After almost $6 billion had been expended during the first week in February to defend the dollar, it was again devalued on February 12, 1973, this time by 10 percent against the SDR and gold. Europeans, tired of continual problems and convinced by experience that they could cope with a devalued dollar, urged the United States to devalue by more than the Treasury expected or thought necessary.[27]

The official American explanation of the crisis was that the first devaluation was too small, which prevented the American trade balance from improving.[28] In late February Treasury Under Secretary Volcker testified:

I suppose speculative situations affected the timing. We would not be proposing a devaluation if we did not think this was desirable in terms of the underlying situation, the underlying imbalance. We are not devaluing because of the speculation problem although the disturbance in the exchange market certainly affected the timing of it.[19]

On the other hand, the *Wall Street Journal* commented, "Oddly it is a crisis caused more by fear than by fundamentals."[30] A New York bank economist mused, "It really snuck up on us. There's no reason for it, except that most foreign exchange dealers are manic-depressive by nature."[31] In the aftermath of the devaluation, Robert Shaffer, Bank of America's senior London economist, expressed it differently, noting that "It's hard to believe that the dollar isn't already undervalued, but it may be more undervalued soon."[32]

Although government and private officials concurred that the second dollar devaluation was more than sufficient to reverse U.S. payments position, rumors that the European nations planned to reinstitute a joint float fueled another attack on the dollar on March 1, 1973. The Bundesbank was smothered by an additional $3 billion. All European markets closed, and government officials realized that they had no alternative except to allow exchange rates to float. The Europeans reopened their exchange markets on March 19, 1973 to a new, more flexible era. Yet, the question remains, what role did banks play in instigating the sterling float, the second dollar devaluation, and the March 1, 1973 deluge?

Bank Roles in Backwash Crises. Between August 15 and December 18, 1971 foreign exchange rates floated. By the time the Smithsonian Agreement restored fixed rates, bankers realized they could cope with flexibility. Although losses became more probable, dealers confidently predicted that they would make money in a floating environment. When fixed rates were restored, many top bankers remained fascinated by potential foreign exchange profits and redoubled their pressure on dealers to produce profits.

Simultaneously, dealers' market perspectives changed. While dealers expected successful defense of the dollar, they used the dollar as a "safe" haven, confident that it would maintain its value against gold. After 1971, dealers became wary. Many believed that the first devaluation was insufficient. New criteria ordered dealers' perceptions and behavior. Their time frames shortened noticeably, and they began reacting more to news flashes than to economic analyses of medium-term prospects.[33] Unsure of their prospects, many MNCs attempted to hedge their entire foreign currency positions, thereby increasing market transaction volume. This market shift persuaded some traders, particularly at smaller European banks, that if the central banks and the equilibrating, large bank market-makers refrained from intervening, they could influence daily exchange market movements.[34]

These developments had noticeable impact. During the Bretton Woods era, parity changes helped improve payments stability. Devaluations discouraged imports and encouraged exports. Revaluations usually had the opposite effect. Although adjustment was sometimes delayed by inelastic import and export orders, payments flows eventually equilibrated. After August 1971, however, dealer skepticism, corporate and government portfolio diversification, collapsed trader time frames, and top management pressure for profits contributed to market unpredictability and a classic bandwagon mentality.[35] Exchange rate adjustments were as likely to lead to a deterioration of the payments situation as to its improvement.

During backwash crises, bank perception of outcomes was extremely unclear. Some U.S. banks were completely surprised by the second dollar devaluation.[36] At least one major bank had recently borrowed Swiss francs near their ceiling because it expected that official support of the franc made it more likely that its value would fall than rise. This bank suffered substantial losses when the franc floated through its ceiling and stayed there.[37] Similarly, Swiss banks apparently fared poorly in 1973. Martin Mayer contends that they usually "hold more foreign currency than most banks, because the Swiss government has always kept interest rates on the franc below those available elsewhere, and as a result they took a beating widely believed to have been in the hundreds of millions of dollars on the unexpected devaluation of February, 1973."[38] Even those correctly predicting the dollar's debacle hesitated to openly provoke its downfall. For instance, Clyde Farnsworth of the New York *Times* noted on February 20, 1973, that

> a multinational bank in Belgium [which] last week received a substantial supply of marks from a second multinational bank ... actually paid 4 percent to take the deposit because the second bank did not want the marks on its books. It was afraid of arousing the wrath of the German authorities who were trying to clamp down on speculation. When the 10 percent devaluation came, the second bank quietly got its 6 percent.[39]

The market's fluid structure allowed jittery banks quickly to reverse their dollar bullishness in January 1973. Since many MNCs had already hedged when the crisis arose, the second devaluation apparently was fueled by a somewhat different group of speculators than the first. Most market members believe the critical pressure in 1973 came from the European banking sector.[40] Table 5.2 provides some evidence for this belief by summarizing the role of private capital transactions in the U.S. balance of payments for 1972 and the first quarter of 1973. This data indicates that banks were a huge drain on the American payments situation in the first quarter of 1973 after contributing to a better balance in the final quarter of 1972. This supports the view that banks were more important in 1973 than MNCs and that the decision to attack the dollar was sudden. There is also some indication that foreign banks may have been more responsible than their U.S. counterparts for the bulk of this speculation. The relationship between U.S. bank loans to foreign banks and the dollar exchange rate around the period of the second devaluation shows a nearly perfect inverse relationship. Between December 1972 and March 1973 bank loans to foreign banks climbed from zero to about $2 billion while the dollar's effective exchange rate dropped by 10 percent.[41] Apparently, foreign banks fueled their needs partly by borrowing from American banks. They built up a dollar debt which would be cheaper to repay in case of devaluation and found a source of funds to convert into stronger currencies in the spot markets. The most forthright indictment of Europe bankers was made by Sieghardt Rometsch of the Chase Manhattan Bank in Frankfurt/Main.

Table 5.2: Private Capital Transactions in the U.S. Balance of Payments 1972 and First Quarter 1973 (in $ millions seasonally adjusted)

	1972				1973
	I	II	III	IV	I
U.S. Corporations					
Direct investment	−1,302	−183	−1,148	−771	−2,139
Other assets	−179	−118	−289	−341	−658
Liabilities	289	1,081	626	840	513
Foreign direct investment in the U.S.	−361	185	178	160	247
	−1,553	965	−633	−112	−2,037
Banks					
U.S. assets, Total	−1,401	106	−894	−1,317	−3,346
U.S. liabilities, Total	714	1,430	344	2,437	−1,750
Total Flow of Funds	−687	1,536	−550	1,120	−5,096

SOURCE: U.S. Congress, Senate, Committee on Finance, **The International Financial Crisis. Hearings before the Subcommittee on International Finance and Resources.** 93d Cong., 1st sess., 1973. p. 136.

I may remind you again of the first 10 days in February this year. But this wave of speculation again demonstrated—this time with particular clarity—that it is not the multinational corporations that are mainly involved in these upheavals in the monetary system. One should, rather, direct one's attention to the balances (running into billions) of foreign banks and other foreign account holders with German credit institutions, since the source of speculation is to be found there rather than among multinationals.[42]

The large U.S. banks were more noticeable for their lack of speculation than for speculation against the dollar in 1973. One key to understanding the interdevaluation period is to focus on the markets. Governments and their central banks lost control of the Eurocurrency and foreign exchange markets. Multinational corporations ran for cover. Large banks refused to take control of the market once central banks were forced to abdicate. Small banks may have helped build up pressure on exchange rates, but they could never have done this successfully had major equilibrating speculators been active. In a sense, these backwash crises developed from vague and misunderstood underlying phenomena, and were brought into the limelight by the functioning of the capital markets. Had the markets been smaller or more firmly controlled, it is probable that the February 12 crisis and the March 1 fiasco would have been avoided. Table 5.3 summarizes the development and roles of various

Table 5.3: Components of Crisis, December 1971–March 1973

Role and Behavior of:	Smithsonian to March 1, 1973
Governments:	Stung by devaluations and unable to agree on sweeping international monetary reform, governments are cautious about supporting new exchange rates. They admit their confusion concerning proper parity levels and lose their will to mount spirited defenses of their currencies. Finance ministries recognize the political importance of these developments and increasingly replace central banks as the key governmental actors and negotiators.
The foreign exchange and Eurocurrency markets (as actors):	Both markets continue to grow. Neither governments nor the private sector move in to forcefully take control. As a result the short-term perceptions and rumors which circulate among dealers can propel the market to move for or against currencies without much regard to their medium or long-term economic outlook.
Commercial banks:	Banks squeezed in Euromarkets resort to high volume to keep profits high. Large banks make major foreign exchange profits because of the rise in demand for MNC cover. Banks and their dealers develop a predilection for crises and lose their fear of flexibility. Large banks probably speculate less than in pre-1971 period. Small banks probably speculate more, but this is not equilibrating in nature. European banks with short-run perspectives do seem to have some impact on the creation of monetary turmoil, but only because there is no balancing force in the markets.
Multinational corporations:	MNCs drastically increase their stock of hedged contracts. They attempt to be covered at all times and no longer believe they can predict the timing and direction of parity changes with sufficient accuracy to justify waiting until the last moment. As a result flows of funds generated by MNCs during backwash crises is probably less than in the late 1960s.
Who controls?	Nobody controls, markets once pushed in a direction can create and intensify crises.

actors from December 1971 through March 1973 using the format introduced in Table 5.1.

BANK DOMINATION, 1973-1974

As the economic debate over the optimal level of exchange rate flexibility intensified in the late 1960s, Treasury and Federal Reserve Board officials sympathetic to floating began to dominate U.S. monetary policy-making. However, European officials were not convinced of the efficiency of free markets. Indicative of this split was free floater George Shultz's 1972 compromise proposal for a "crawling peg" system, which was rejected by French-led European officials. Had the February 1973 devaluation been avoided, floating might not have emerged. However, confidence was shattered by the unexpected February 12 move and confusion reigned after March 1, when European and American officials became convinced that only floating might calm the storm. They could not figure out any other alternative strategy. In essence, central bankers and finance ministers ceded the control of the international monetary system to the private sector operating the capital markets. Government officials conceded they could no longer manage the system.

The Aftermath of the British Float. In terms of dollars, the pound floated from $2.59 on June 16, 1972 down to $2.44 in late June. It rested there until late October and then dipped to about $2.34. It automatically gained ground when the dollar was devalued in February. Partly because of Britain's reduced role in the world economy, sterling's downward float produced no major backlash and turmoil. In late November, the Bank of England was forced to compensate holders of roughly £3 billion of devaluation-guaranteed sterling balances. The British further demonstrated their resolve to remain floating by obtaining EEC permission to continue to float through April 1973.[43]

The most intriguing of sterling's vacillations was its rapid fall starting in late September. Through July, according to the Bank of England, "News which might normally have affected confidence had little effect on the rate."[44] In early September dealers' concern with inflation increased, but sterling was protected by purchasers of spot funds covering their June forward commitments. Then, false rumors of a new parity setting triggered the heavy sterling sales which drove sterling to $2.40. Heavy overseas sales forced sterling down further. William Batt, a senior international executive at National Westminster Bank, placed the blame more explicitly:

> The speculators over the past two years have been major banks. We all know of rings. . . . We are aware that various banks got together in the past and have taken positions—we can go back to October/November [sic] 1972 when sterling suddenly went from 2.44 down to 2.32 be-

cause seven banks decided to sell sterling and they took up a position of one billion sterling short.[45]

These banks explicitly manipulated exchange rates and confounded British exchange policy until the Bank of England stepped forcefully into the fray near the end of the year. These distortions in the floating markets indicated that floating might not work as smoothly as some economists supposed.[46]

The Floating Rate System, 1973-1974. When the system began floating in March 1973, it was natural to ask whether floating exchange rates eliminated crises. Milton Friedman responded with accustomed panache in congressional testimony in June 1973:

> Like the Sherlock Holmes clue of the non-barking dog, the most important development of the past several months in the international monetary area is what did not happen. Despite unprecedented gyrations in the market for gold, despite stories day after day about a "crisis" in international money markets, there were no headlines reading, "German Reichsbank Takes in Billions of Dollars of Hot Money in a Single Day," no announcements of hastily called meetings of central bankers . . . to do something about the international crisis, or emergency trips by Chairman Burns and Secretary Shultz to Paris or Basle . . . that would have happened if it had not been for the existence of floating exchange rates.[47]

Friedman was met on the conceptual battlefield by Ricardo Arriazu, an alternate IMF executive director, who argued that for lesser developed countries in particular, the new system was not a panacea. He noted that floating had changed crisis characteristics, not avoided crises. Instead of massive movements of reserves, there were huge exchange rate movements.[48] Data supports Arrizu's complaint. From March 19, 1973 through mid-July, 1973, exchange markets floated with minimal central bank intervention. Market volatility, however, persuaded central bankers to return to the fray in a limited way in the summer of 1973, when intervention steadied the fluctuations of the three strongest currencies used as safety valves by hedgers and speculators.[49]

Volatility continued. Currencies varied by as much as 2 percent a day and ten percent a week throughout 1973 and 1974. More important, dealers could not estimate the proper values for currencies. As late as July 1974, a leading London investment banker expressed befuddlement when he queried:

> Why has the U.S. dollar, which everyone agrees should be bought, which has practically the highest domestic interest rate and the most determined Governor of a Central Bank fighting inflation, been a weak

currency in the exchange markets in recent weeks? The reverse question can be asked about the pound sterling. . . . The old rule of lending or being long in hard currencies can hardly operate since there is no market certainty to the hard currency.[50]

Since those who risked money to equilibrate the system lost money, banks and MNCs became extremely hesitant to follow their own reasoning.

Bank Impact and Policy During the Float. When governments withdrew from exchange markets, private activities, no longer constrained, began determining market developments. Banks, confident that they could make profits and that relative exchange rate calm would be restored, welcomed the floating system. MNC treasurers were less certain of the new system, but were assured by the bankers that it would prove workable.

Most MNCs chose to hedge their transactions under the emerging floating system.[51] Large banks were also hesitant to take large open positions. Yet, according to Geoffrey Bell, "there can be no argument: by any economic criteria the dollar did fall too sharply subsequent to the second dollar devaluation."[52] Why? In late June 1973 Authur Burns expressed surprise at the dollar's continued deterioration and noted, "I think exchange dealers are influenced unduly by day-to-day developments."[53] Treasury Secretary Shultz was also confused by the dollar's failure to recover.[54] Others pointed to portfolio diversification and Watergate as the culprits.[55]

Initially, large banks were extremely pleased by the float. Large profits became more likely; possibilities of large losses were discounted. The head of Bank of America's London exchange operation explained:

> Lending and foreign exchange operations during the float are more treacherous because you cannot specify as easily your downside risk. Before, you could be sure that if a currency fell to its parity floor, a central bank would intervene and support it, thus limiting your possible losses. But now, in the float, the central bank may or may not intervene. You can suffer losses on a $10 million transaction now that would have been possible only on a $100 million transaction before.[56]

As mentioned previously, most large banks' profits were made on increased transaction volume and on wider spreads on contracts rather than by taking larger open positions. Prior to floating, market-makers accepted sizeable maturity gaps, thereby taking views on currency movements. Sometimes they refrained from matching small retail jobs until they built large positions to handle at wholesale prices. These policies were loosely regulated by top management since risks were low. The floating rate system, however, created two new risks which minimized large-scale, large bank speculating. First, the market's complexity increased, making it difficult to keep track of the banks' exposure and thus discouraging wild risks. Second, the fear that counter-parties might not fulfill their contracts because of bookkeeping errors increased.[57]

Smaller international banks did not have the advantage of large contract volume. To compensate, many took chances. The rise in the relative percentage of interbank contracts compared to commercial contracts suggests that many banks began speculating to make profits. This was not new. The Basle subsidiary of the United California Bank attempted to reap large profits by investing its own funds in volatile cocoa futures in 1970. The subsidiary collapsed amidst embarrassment, losses, and scandal.[58]

In essence, foreign exchange markets acted like bank-dominated commodity markets during floating. Banks needing profits to offset losses in other parts of their business gambled on foreign exchange. Banks confident of their prescience, or greedy, or determined to manipulate markets profitably also started speculating. Simultaneously, equilibrating speculators vanished, large banks cut back their open positions, and markets became more vulnerable to manipulation. These market changes were important since the foreign exchange market, like a commodity market, requires both hedgers and speculators to function.

In late 1974 an anonymous article in the *International Currency Review* asserted that exchange markets were rife with illegalities. Continental dealers, it claimed, frequently accepted gifts and entertainment from clients. Dealers were poorly monitored and sometimes moved exchange rates on a whim. Traders also dealt for themselves as well as for their banks.[59] Although most bankers thought the article exaggerated the malfeasance, some admitted that irregularities occurred and added that sometimes when positions soured, the losses "belonged" to the bank but when they made money, the dealer sometimes kept them.[60] All agreed, however, that such activities were far more common on the Continent than in London and New York. In the same vein, a British banker claimed that a major component in the dollar's early 1974 weakness was an open position of $5 billion dollars maintained by a large German bank. He noted that in thin markets existing at that time, this single position depressed the dollar in relation to the mark.[61]

While MNC speculators existed, the most spectacular manipulation involved the so-called "rings" which have already been mentioned in connection with the decline of sterling in late 1972. One banker described "ring" operations as a "kind of pooling operation, where they suddenly flood the market with orders, driving the price of, say, the German mark a few points—and there is no way you can go against it.[62] Apparently, most ring activity was conducted through a single German broker.[63] The participating banks coordinated their signals in the morning and moved in one direction. In thin markets no bank acting alone could counteract speculators so traders in large banks reinforced rather than mooted small banks' speculative activities. When a wave formed, the speculators simultaneously reversed their position, while the rest of the market rushed on. Most "ring" speculating seems to have taken place in the spot markets using this "bigger fool" mechanism. In mid-1974, Robert LeClerc, the head of the foreign exchange dealers association, commented as the ring phenomena was waning that "the speculating banks were taking large enough positions to artificially influence exchange rates."[64] This speculation by banks acting alone or in unison was one factor contributing to the volatility and the lack of predictability on the markets between 1973 and 1974. It gave banks tremendous influence over the markets because the largest banks and the central banks were reluctant to oppose them wholeheartedly.

After the volatility of the March-June 1973, Arthur Burns reluctantly concluded that renewed central bank intervention was necessary to calm the exchange markets. Corporations which had had their planning upset were relieved by this renewed intervention, but most banks believed it was premature. Bankers argued that it took time for exchange rates to find their appropriate economic level and therefore a learning period was inevitable. Besides, banks, being concerned about profits, could hardly fault a development which had allowed most of them to make foreign exchange profits and had not then shackled any bank with large losses. Indeed, Table 5.4, which lists banks' announced foreign exchange profits since 1969, shows a massive upswing in bank profits as flexibility increased in the early 1970s.

In sum, during the floating period, banks became the international monetary system's chief regulators. The international monetary regime was no more, but was replaced by a system in which governments articulated their unwillingness to intervene. Large banks were usually above-board in their

Table 5.4: Foreign Exchange Trading Revenue of Reporting Banks, 1969–1976 (in $ millions)

Bank	1969	1970	1971	1972	1973	1974	1975	1976
Bank of America	n.a.	n.a.	n.a.	n.a.	n.a.	64.2	50.4	61.9
Bankers Trust	0.7	1.9	4.4	6.4	1.8	17.5	16.9	15.2
Chase Manhattan	n.a.	n.a.	n.a.	n.a.	36.5	49.5	45.0	47.4
Chemical Bank	n.a.	n.a.	n.a.	n.a.	n.a.	8.9	7.0	6.0
Citibank	19.8	22.9	23.7	3.08	70.6	79.7	26.2	17.8
Manufactures Hanover	n.a.	n.a.	n.a.	n.a.	n.a.	10.1	7.7	8.1
Morgan Guaranty	3.3	4.1	10.7	19.7	42.3	40.2	32.5	33.8

SOURCES: Annual Reports, Thomas Hanley (for Saloman Brothers), "U.S. Multinational Banks," 1976, p. 37.

dealings and would have preferred to stabilize the markets, prove that government fears and controls were unnecessary, and allow the free enterprise system to operate globally. However, their power over the market and over governments was evanescent. Unfortunately, as Polanyi suggested more than thirty years earlier, the market system free from regulation proved unstable.[65] Some banks hoped to make windfall profits; others could not effectively mute their actions. Even after central banks reentered the fray in July 1973, markets remained volatile. Some banks continued speculating.

Volatility from mid-1973 through mid-1974 was approximately as great as during the first three months of free floating.[66] The exact causes of this are impossible to determine. Banks had some impact, but the double digit inflation, Watergate, rising commodity prices, the oil embargo and subsequent quadrupling of oil prices, and the uncertainty of governments as to exactly what could be done contributed to the confusion and helped cultivate exchange rate volatility. Table 5.5 summarizes these developments.

THE REEMERGENCE OF GOVERNMENT AUTHORITY
AFTER HERSTATT

The foreign exchange markets remained extremely volatile through mid-1974. Once governments ceded their power over the markets, they had difficulty reestablishing their control. Eventually, they regained some influence, but only after a series of bank losses and failures convinced large banks to re assert their authority over smaller banks, MNCs, and the markets themselves. In a sense, the events described below allowed governments to take the helm once again and sharply limited the influence of smaller banks to upset exchange markets while searching for short-term profits. However, since government attempts to control the monetary system are focused on the market, not market participants, the potential for bank indirect influence remains.

The Banking Crisis of 1974: Sequence of Events. The most publicized banking crisis since 1931 was precipitated by the collapse of the Bankhaus Herstatt of Cologne on June 26, 1974. There had been warning signals. Early in 1973, following problems at the Scottish Co-operative Bank, almost thirty London fringe banks suffered severe liquidity problems, making it virtually impossible for them to borrow any money. Some were allowed to fail; others were rescued when the Bank of England "asked" the London clearing banks to prevent their ruin.[67] About the same time, mismanagement and fraud prompted the U.S. Comptroller of the Currency to close the U.S. National Bank of San Diego and sell its assets. Several European banks faced substantial losses on what they had considered conventional interbank loans. These potential losses focused global bank attention on the quality and safety of

Table 5.5: Components of Crisis, March 19, 1973—June 1974

Role and Behavior of:	From Floating to Herstatt
Governments:	After three months of nearly clean floating, volatility forces sparing market intervention. Central banks no longer attempt to defend exchange rates but rather attempt to smooth and patrol them. Still, rampaging inflation, rising commodity costs, and uncertainty as to what the proper economic levels of currencies should be prevents firm action. Governments relinquish control over the markets to the private sector and are hesitant to simply take them over again by fiat.
The foreign exchange and Eurocurrency markets (as actors):	Markets continue to grow despite the termination of U.S. exchange restrictions in January 1974. Government intervention is minimal. Neither central banks nor large banks are playing the role of equilibrating speculator. Small banks or other market participants therefore have the ability to substantially move the market by taking large open positions. Other large banks follow along since they have no apparent risk because their books are basically balanced. The markets still carry tremendous inertia, which can move rates on the basis even of spurious rumors, but they are also being steered by market participants.
Commercial banks:	Bank profits are being squeezed in the Euromarkets as margins fall. Volume of transactions in both the Euromarkets and foreign exchange markets rise. Large banks no longer willing to make markets except in a few major currencies in the spot or near forward markets. Large banks make profits, but lose control over the Euromarkets. Smaller banks begin taking open positions either individually or in rings. Percentage of interbank transactions in foreign exchange and Euromarkets increases. Euroloans grow more risky.
Multinational corporations:	MNCs fearing volatility increase their hedging activity. Demand for Euromarket credits increases. Stock of contracts up, but flow of exchange contracts down. Complaints are heard about lack of forward cover. MNCs become generally reactive, trying to protect themselves.
Who controls?	Governments, central banks, MNCs and most large banks retreat from risk. Smaller banks and individual speculators play key role.

interbank lending and severely injured bankers' confidence in the word of their counterparts.

Although confidence was further shaken when the state controlled Hessische Landesbank Girozentrale announced huge loan losses in early 1974, foreign exchange speculation continued until the Westdeutsche Landesbank Girozentrale lost over $100 million in foreign exchange, the Union Bank of Switzerland suffered exchange losses totaling more than $150 million, and the Franklin National Bank was taken over by the Comptroller's office after announcing substantial losses in foreign exchange and other areas.

The *banking* (not monetary) crisis peaked when the Bundesbank closed the Bankhaus Herstatt at 4:00 P.M. German time on June 26, 1974. Foreign exchange losses were initially estimated at $160 million. Since the New York market was still open, several banks, including Morgan Guaranty, were caught halfway through spot transactions with Herstatt, i.e., they had paid Herstatt dollars, but had not received their mark counterpayment when Herstatt was closed. Fear of similar interbank losses immediately spread through the market. The next day large banks would not lend money to banks with less than $4 billion in assets.[68] The volume of exchange transactions dropped to 10 to 20 percent of its mid-June level and the average transaction size diminished correspondingly. Interbank exchange transactions nearly disappeared and commercial transactions declined markedly. Market-makers refused to take open positions and served only as brokers. In New York, the New York Clearing House took the unprecedented step of allowing banks to recall payments until 10:00 A.M. the following morning to protect against counterparty insolvency. Market participants were terrified.

Bankers even began referring to the pre- and post-Herstatt eras. Some feared a new Kreditanstalt, leading to the collapse of the world banking system, and were further frightened when several small German, Phillippine, and Israeli banks failed within two weeks of Herstatt. Problems continued. On September 3, 1974, unauthorized exchange dealings resulted in a £33 million loss at the Lugano, Switzerland, branch of Lloyds Bank International. Three days later, the Western American Bank (Europe), once the largest of the consortium banks, announced that its American, British, and Japanese parents had provided considerable support to stave off major losses. WAB's problems prompted new fears that consortia and subsidiaries might not be supported by their parents in troubled times and stimulated a Bank of England request that consortia shareholders provide the central bank with "letters of comfort" spelling out their obligations.

Even after central bank-spawned "liquidity banks" emerged to assure solvency to well-managed institutions, small and large banks continued suffering losses. On October 2, Chase Manhattan announced that it had mistakenly overvalued its bond portfolio by $34 million. In mid-October, the Banque de

Bruxelles announced substantial post-Herstatt foreign exchange losses, which quashed market hopes that speculation had ceased after June 26 and stimulated new fears.

There was concern about even the soundest banks. Reportedly, fully owned subsidiaries of Bank of America and Citibank had some difficulty raising money in the interbank markets.[69] Although other banks trusted that the parents would try to honor any losses the subsidiaries might suffer, they feared that courts and stockholders might prevent repayment. This dread grew from a stockholder suit filed against the United California Bank in connection with the 1970 Basle losses. UCB covered losses greater than its equity investment to protect its reputation. Stockholder sued, claiming undue dilution of earnings.[70] Some bankers feared that if the stockholders won, subsidiaries would become extinct.[71]

Changes in Euromarket Behavior and Bank Power. Behavioral changes after Herstatt effectively halted most foreign exchange speculation by smaller banks. Rings vanished from the market, aiding central banks' stabilization efforts. Although Herstatt was not involved in the Euromarkets, bankers realized that similar problems might strike there and moved the market to a more conservative posture. In the go-go 1960s, regional banks entering the Euromarkets were treated almost identically to prime name banks. Small banks could usually obtain funds for within 1/32 percent of the largest banks. Although these smaller banks were more likely to fail, no one cried wolf. Large banks did not create a tiered interbank interest rate system, in part because the new entrants took portions of Euroloans from large bank syndicators when funding demands prevented any single prime lender from monopolizing most loans.

By the end of 1973 the proliferation of low margin balance of payments loans to developed nations worried syndicators. William Low, a leading London financial journalist, analyzed over 250 1972 and 1973 loan syndicates and found that the "typical medium-term credit arranged in 1973 totaled $67.5 million, had a final maturity of 8.6 years, and carried a spread of 0.94 percent. During 1972, the comparable figures were $38.6 million; 6.67 years; and 1.18 percent."[72] In May 1974, more than a month *before* Herstatt's collapse, the *Financial Times* reported that the London Interbank Offer Rate (LIBOR), the rate at which banks lend to each other, had become tiered. Large banks, assured of central bank support in case of a liquidity squeeze, could borrow funds at or below LIBOR. Others paid more. This tiering was reinforced by conservative OPEC investors, who used only a few of the largest banks. As long as large banks were sure of their smaller brethren, they distributed excess funds on the interbank market. However, once confidence faded, placing money became far trickier. Some favored banks, therefore, refused to accept short-term Arab deposits.[73] Herstatt cemented the new order. OPEC nations became even less willing to provide medium-size banks with funds. Overnight, banks active in the Euromarkets fell from over 200 to less than 40. Large banks were back in firm control.

Assessing bank motivations is extremely difficult. Higher spreads to smaller banks were economically justifiable, but were pursued so dilligently that at least some top bankers probably hoped to squeeze out smaller banks. Fear of falling dominoes was also a factor, but few bankers expected more major failures or an exodus of smaller banks from London. They expected large banks to control the markets more tightly and smaller banks to rethink and curtail some of their foreign activities.[74]

Reginald Barham, Morgan Guaranty's chief London dealer, commented two weeks after Herstatt that "the day of the large speculator is over, which is no bad thing."[75] To reassert their position and to foster their long-term profit potential, large banks began policing the markets. Established Western banks began squeezing Italian and Japanese banks. The Italians were ostracized because they were state-controlled at a time when the Italian economy was nearly bankrupt. Large Italian banks were forced to pay large premiums to attract any interbank funds to service their loans.

The Japanese banks were disciplined for overlending. Significantly, nobody believed the Japanese banks were unsound even as they were being charged crippling interbank rates. The Japanese were "punished" for special governmental advantages that they received in the early 1970's when the Japanese government lent these ostensibly private institutions huge sums of money rather than declaring them as governmental reserves. As reserves, they would have instigated others to pressure for a yen revaluation. The Japanese banks received approximately $10 billion in short-term funds, which were relent in the Euromarkets at longer maturities. From a minimal 1970 base, the Japanese became a major market force by 1973. The oil embargo hurt the Japanese payments balance and forced the government to recall its short-term loans. The banks replaced these funds with interbank borrowings. This acceptable and practical solution backfired in mid-1974 when prime banks cut their interbank lines, leaving Japanese banks over the new self-imposed management lending limits. During July and August 1974, Japanese banks were forced to pay as much as 2 percent over LIBOR to fund commitments on which they were earning less than 1 percent over LIBOR. Other banks profited. Top executives applauded the reduction of interbank credit lines and cheered the reemergence of large bank market dominance.[76] In the Euromarkets spreads widened, maturities fell, and loan quality improved as loans were increasingly tied to projects with predictable cash flow-generating capacity.

As larger banks regained market control, central banks redoubled their efforts to regain initiative by supporting problem banks. In September central bankers guaranteed their support for banks caught in liquidity problems beyond their managements' control, and the Bundesbank announced that it would start its own liquidity bank to aid troubled German institutions. Bankers, frightened by Herstatt, began hounding market speculators and softened their opposition to foreign exchange and Euromarket controls, allowing central banks to reassert their authority.

Still, banks indirectly influenced the markets even as they took safer, more conservative liquidity positions. The world economy is so tied to the banking system that bank actions proved counterproductive to fighting the wave of worldwide recession. A London investment banker commented that

> The necessities of microeconomic analysis preclude the banks doing the kinds of things they should be doing right now. What we are doing is countereconomic to getting things going again. That is, we are holding large amounts of cash, trying to remain very liquid, not investing in instruments that would get economies moving. Since everybody wants to protect themselves, the effect is to hurt the economy as a whole.[77]

In retrospect, however, most commercial and central bankers believed that the Herstatt scare was beneficial. Central banks were able to reassert loose control over exchange market fluctuation and most speculative practices vanished from international exchange markets. While exchange rates continued to fluctuate, volatility decreased.

The tracing of the behavioral impact of diverse actors on the exchange rate system since 1958 is completed by Tables 5.6 and 5.7. Table 5.6 plots the changes which allowed the partial reassertion of central bank authority. Table 5.7 summarizes the sweep of bank-government interplay within the foreign exchange and Eurocurrency markets since 1958.

In sum, it is clear that banks of all sizes played sometimes significant roles in the development and resolution of international monetary crises in the postwar era. Until 1971, MNCs and large commercial banks used international markets to maximize the predictability of their operating environments and to insure their continued profitability. Decisive government action deflected market perceptions concerning parity changes, although as market activity increased, it became harder and harder for central banks to organize opposition to exchange rate adjustments. Banks and MNCs were important in these crises as reflectors of underlying maladjustment among currencies. The economic wisdom of the market eventually triumphed over politically motivated support of parity values. Only after 1971 is there evidence that private actors helped create crises without economic justification.

After the Smithsonian Agreement, large banks speculated too little, not too much. Between the dollar devaluations, conservative bankers felt that the

Table 5.6: Components of Crisis: Herstatt to the Present

Role and Behavior of:	Herstatt Onwards
Governments:	Central banks return aggressively to the business of intervening to protect exchange rates. Volume of intervention equals that in the pre-1971 era. Economic conditions settle somewhat, small bank speculators cease manipulating the markets, and the Jamaica accords in early 1976 institutionalize the central banks' new market role. Although unwilling to protect exchange rates with unlimited vigor, they regain considerable power over the market and are able to eliminate most major fluctuations which do not have an underlying economic reason.
The foreign exchange and Eurocurrency markets (as actors):	Market growth stops for several months after Herstatt, then resumes. Foreign exchange volume declines, particularly the number of interbank exchange transactions. New foreign exchange reporting requirements are imposed by many central banks. Fluctuation declines sharply between mid-1974 and early 1976 but increases after the Jamaica accords. Although still sizeable, the markets are no longer completely out of control mainly because of renewed confidence that the central banks will act consistently.
Commercial banks:	Small bank foreign exchange and Euromarket activity is sharply curtailed for a time. Rings break up or become inactive. Speculation for own book nearly vanishes. Slowly, large bank market-makers begin to return to the markets. Large banks reimpose conservative policies. While profits from foreign exchange continue high, the 1975 returns are lower than those in 1974. None of the banks complain about the crop. When Jamaica does not completely revamp the system, banks move to bring currencies to their perceived economic value, bringing on major volatility in 1976.
Multinational corporations:	MNCs strongly advocate a return to greater stability, though not to fixed rates. Some still are unable to raise necessary financing and have trouble getting reasonably priced forward market cover. Hedging volume remains high, but seems to slip slightly.
Who controls?	The governments and central banks resume control of exchange markets, but with more reasonable aims. Small banks have little power over crisis developments, and larger banks and MNCs do not even try to gain such power.

[121]

Table 5.7: Contribution of Various Actors to Supporting Stable Exchange Rates: Bretton Woods to the Present[a]

Actors	1946-1958	1959-1967	1968-8/1971	8/1971-12/1971	1/1972-2/1973	3/1973-6/1973	7/1973-6/1974	Post-Herstatt
Governments	+++	+++	+++	+	+	0	+	++
MNCs	-	--	--	-	0	0	0	0
Large banks	+	+	-	0	0	0	0	0
Small banks	0	0	-	-	--	---	---	0
Extraneous economic factors	+	0	0	+	0	-	-	0
"Sum"	++++	++	-	0	-	----	---	++
Interpretation	Govt. control	Govt. control but slipping	Govt. defend but not control	Wait and see	Nobody controls, market determines	Small banks manipulate	Small banks rebuff weak govt. efforts	Govts. regain moderate control
Bank power	None	Minimal	Trigger	Learning	Moderate	Major	Major	Minimal

a. The determinations of these ratings was necessarily subjective. Since accurate measurement is impossible and weighting of each actor's influence is also difficult, the "Sum" should be interpreted only as an approximation of where power lay.

dollar's value was too high but were hesitant to speculate against it and there-fore took few open positions. The dollar's reserve asset role and market un-certainty concerning its stability left smaller banks free to cause currency fluctuation on minimal information. Small, mostly European banks also seemingly took open positions to profit from currency volatility. These banks did not create crises, but in the absence of resolute government support of currencies they generated more pressure than might have been expected given the existing economic conditions.

Small bank power over exchange volatility between March 1973 and June 1974 was the most potent example of bank influence discovered. Small banks, working alone or in groups, believed that regulators would not notice their activities as they manipulated capital markets for profits. They wrongly felt that they would not be noticed in their actions. However, in the absence of equilibrating speculators, the funds pumped through the exchange markets by small institutions caused large fluctuations. Their "power" rested on government and large bank inactivity, but was very real while major actors were sidelined. They could, on occasion, create crises with no roots in the underlying economic situation of the currencies affected.

Still, the capacity of smaller banks to control volatility and make profits was severely limited. Once central banks reentered the fray, their potential profitability grew poorer. After the rash of foreign exchange losses by banks public and private regulators moved to vanquish small bank market control. Once large banks reduced their credit lines to smaller banks, speculative, de-stabilizing small bank activity was curtailed.

The difference in bank power potential in this and the previous chapter are marked. Table 5.8 summarizes the distinction and effectiveness of bank indirect influence and the importance for exchange crises as opposed to bank circumventing influence in relation to exchange regulations.

Bank Influence on
Government Decision-Making

Clearly, certain banks influenced, intentionally or unintentionally, the timing, scope, and outcomes of exchange crises. The question remains: Did banks indirectly influence government decision-makers as well as crisis de-velopments? In addition, did government officials react to and learn from changing bank behavior in international capital markets, and how did this influence their policies? Firm answers to these queries are not possible on the basis of present research. Yet it is clear that a strict power explanation within the framework presented here suggests interesting possibilities. It is in that spirit that these concluding speculations are offered.

Table 5.8: Influence Employed by Banks in the International Monetary System

	Direct Influence	Circumventing Influence	Indirect Influence
Response to:	Existing or proposed policies or legislation.	Policies and legislation aimed at market participants.	Policies and legislation aimed at controlling the economic system.
Channels:	Lobbying Personnel transfer Public appeals	Capital flows Currency exchanges International structure	Capital flows Currency exchanges International structure
Strategy:	Persuasion	Evasion	Coercion
Impact on:	Policy-making	Policy effectiveness	Economic outcomes
Intent:	Conscious	Conscious at primary level. May have unintentional side effects.	Conscious or unintentional at both primary and secondary levels.
Influence at work during:			
Exchange Regulations	Persuaded officials to adjust policies to treat all banks fairly. Unable to persuade U.S. to remove constraints.	Learned to evade regulation, making them ineffective. Unintended expansion of banking, Euromarkets was important result.	Little or no indirect influence
Exchange Crises	Gave advice which was largely ignored.	"Tools" created by evading exchange restraints used to wield indirect power.	Major impact on the development of crises, their timing, and resolution, particularly when low government will.

GOVERNMENT LEARNING

Monetary officials learned to cope with the growing waves of short-term capital flows. From 1949 through 1967 European officials maintained parity values by imposing various exchange constraints. After the sterling devaluation, monetary officials realized that exchange restraints would no longer sufficiently guard exchange rates and within two years the French devalued and the Germans revalued their currencies. All three of these parity changes were fostered by the realization that it would be impossible to repulse indefinitely the short-term capital flows which grew larger with each crisis.[78]

U.S. officials, concerned with the dollar's key currency role, were slower to accept the importance of growing capital flows. They regarded exchange market developments as accurate reflections of underlying economic conditions and concluded that improved U.S. economic conditions would calm the capital markets. Two key factors dissuaded U.S. officials from seriously considering devaluation until 1971. First, New York Fed officials who were responsible for the defense of the dollar believed that the dollar was not overvalued and should be defended at all costs. Only after Arthur Burns became Chairman of the Federal Reserve Board was the New York Federal Reserve Bank seriously restrained by Washington. Second, American officials would not risk undercutting the dollar's reserve asset position and destroying the Bretton Woods system unless they were positive that no other course was available. Most Treasury officials remained convinced that the dollar could be saved until July 8, 1971, when disastrous second quarter trade figures became known. Even when the decision to devalue was taken, U.S. officials apparently did not seriously consider the impact of the market and market-makers on their policy. Similarly, European and Japanese officials apparently never believed that private actors' behavior could impel the U.S. to alter its policy choices.[79]

After 1971 American officials conceded that markets (not market participants) could influence crisis timing. They worried about the magnitude of short-term capital flows, but perceived such flows as indications of fundamental economic imbalances. Therefore, it was not considered necessary to disaggregate market activities and examine the actions of specific sectors or individual actors.

European officials were less monetarist in outlook than their American counterparts and favored tight U.S. exchange regulations to support the dollar. They feared floating and were wary of market manipulators. Since central bankers still controlled more liquidity than speculators, when the decision was made to move back into the market, central bankers were able to vanquish manipulators who were attacking currencies without economic justification. It would have been far more difficult for them to defeat flows of funds stimulated by genuine economic conditions.

U.S. officials outside the New York Federal Reserve Bank failed to distinguish in practice between the market and market participants. George Shultz and Arthur Burns, for instance, expected the second devaluation to calm exchange markets and ignored the warnings of Charles Coombs that market participants would not perceive the devaluation so favorably.[80] When pressure resumed on March 1, 1973, U.S. officials had no alternative but to acquiesce to floating rates. Shultz, who favored floating, expected that the markets would quickly adjust and work smoothly.[81] It appears that except in New York U.S. officials were so focused on the reserve asset role of the dollar that they failed to seriously consider whether market participants were distorting exchange market operations. Even the decision to resume intervention in July 1973 was justified in terms of exogenous factors which disrupted market equilibrating tendencies. In summary, it appears that European officials were more willing to learn about changes in market structure and to entertain new ideas about the roles of private actors during exchange crises.

BANK IMPACT ON GOVERNMENT POLICY

Although American officials may have failed to learn the lessons of the market as well as their British counterparts, the key question remains: Would U.S. monetary policy have been greatly different had learning taken place? While this is an exercise in second guessing, some indications come through.

The pre-August 1971 period is clearest. Government officials downgraded market signals to the rank of temporary problems. U.S. officials , not recognizing that the dollar might be overvalued and determined to support its key currency role, began to "benignly neglect" the dollar's support.[82] European officials took comparable steps to control valid market pressures. Better vision might have allowed officials to make earlier exchange rate adjustments thus encouraging more effective equilibration, but the final outcomes probably would not have varied substantially. If for political reasons, governments had delayed adjustments even more, destabilizing impact on effected economies might have been worse. The net impact of private actors' market activities was probably to speed necessary adjustments thereby contributing to the industrialized world's economic prosperity.

Bank impact on policy in early 1973 is more problematic. Charles Coombs and his associates warned that a second devaluation might upset rather than calm exchange rates and markets because dealers would interpret the move as a sign of weakness undermining the dollar.[83] Coombs advocated pressuring the Japanese and Germans to revalue their currencies.[84] In Washington Coombs was ignored by officials convinced that the overvalued dollar must once again be readjusted. They opted for a policy decision which Coombs considered "the greatest mistake in foreign economic policy in the history of the republic."[85]

Markets and market participants reacted as Coombs had feared. The violence of their reaction doomed any semblance of fixed rates. Had market reactions been accurately predicted, completely free floating might have proved unnecessary. Revaluations would have been less destabilizing. The key problem was to reestablish the dollar, the system's reserve asset, as a safe refuge from market torments. When this possibility evaporated, trader uncertainty increased, transaction volume skyrocketed, and regulation of exchange movements became impossible to contemplate.

In time, market and bank behavior also convinced government officials that free floating was unacceptable. Continued volatility under floating rates convinced officals to seek a return to the markets. The unexpected continued deterioration of the dollar in the second quarter of 1973 forced finance ministries to allow the resumption of limited central bank market intervention. U S officials took this step reluctantly, expressing hope that they could soon withdraw once more. Apparently, the Treasury never fully accepted the political aspects of market activities which undermined the floating system.

European officials were relieved to resume intervention. Canada and Japan had never completely stopped. Europeans immediately set out to repulse privately instigated market distortions. Reportedly, the Bank of England reaped substantial foreign exchange profits in late 1973 and early 1974 while combating the actions of speculating European private bankers.[86] The Bank of England turned the tables on these private speculators while recognizing that they could no longer fight the valid corrective forces at work in the exchange markets. This lesson was sometimes still forgotten. In 1976 the Bank of England intervened massively and ineffectively to support sterling after major monetary reform failed to materialize at the Rambouillet-Jamaica meetings.

DIFFERENCES IN GOVERNMENT LEARNING

Why have American and European officials reacted so differently with regard to exchange and capital market activities? Much of the difference may be related to the monetarist economic predisposition of most American decision-makers. In retrospect, European speculators might not have become so powerful if U.S. officials had been more sensitive to their activities. Yet from 1959 through 1971, American and European officials maintained static, opposite views concerning the causes of monetary crises. Why were government officials so slow to learn the lessons of previous crises? Why did U.S. and European officials interpret crisis situations so differently? Existing fragmentary evidence suggests answers to these questions.

In 1964 and 1967 Prime Minister Wilson and his Labour colleagues blamed the attack on sterling on international speculators. The Bank of England was so enraged by supposed speculation that after the sterling devaluation it attempted to punish the speculators. Conversely, in the United States monetary officials denied that private activities directly or indirectly influenced either crisis outcomes or government crisis policies.[87] While President Nixon did rail that "speculators have been waging all-out war on the American dollar" in 1971 and chided speculators again in 1973, this was apparently more rhetoric than conviction. The Treasury apparently prepared a much blander August 15 speech for Nixon, which included no references to undue speculation. Nixon and Connally discarded this draft when they chose to claim the suspension of convertibility as a U.S. victory.[88]

Although critics smirk that Nixon's free market rhetoric abounded while his Administration pursued active, Keynesian-inspired market manipulation, we may ask what are the roots of the American romance with free market as compared to European and Japanese concern with market participants? Several plausible explanations exist.

The smaller European and Japanese economies are more vulnerable to massive capital inflows and outflows than is the U.S. economy. European and Japanese officials may therefore be more sensitive than their American counterparts to the instigators of such flows. However, this does not explain the failure of U.S. officials to recognize speculation after 1971 or the abundant, often misplaced, blamed heaped on speculators in Europe before 1971.

A more bureaucratic perspective on government misperception of private influence emerges on examining the communication links between banks, markets, and government officials. The basic flows of information within the monetary bureaucracies seems to have largely shaped government perceptions. In the U.S., key commercial bank decision-makers are the senior vice presidents in charge of the foreign exchange and Eurocurrency operations. They follow the exchanges more closely than others and are responsible for communicating relevant news to top management. These New York senior vice-presidents regularly talked with Charles Coombs at the New York Federal Reserve Bank, and subordinates communicated and cooperated with New York Federal Reserve Bank officials. Occasionally, the senior vice presidents talked with Paul Volcker at Treasury or Alfred Hayes, the New York Federal Reserve Bank's President, but for the most part they worked through Coombs. Senior commercial bank officials talked regularly with Hayes, Shultz, and Burns, but their conversations were usually more general than at lower levels.[89]

The key communication bottleneck was in New York. Alfred Hayes was seen as peripheral to developments by Washington officials. Coombs, the best informed government official, talked frequently with Volcker, Burns, and the Federal Open Market Committee, but was considered an extremist and an alarmist in Washington.[90] Coombs favored staunchly defending the dollar in 1971, but his exhortations were ignored and his policy recommendations discounted. It is unclear whether Coombs' policy recommendations were workable, but apparently his extremeness prevented Shultz and Burns from fully accepting the market information he conveyed to them in 1973.

The physical separation of the New York Bank and the exchange markets from the Federal Reserve Board and the Treasury meant that important monetary officials in Washington were somewhat out of touch with market developments. The lack of confidence in Coombs in Washington tended to isolate officials who might otherwise have directed their attention at discrete market developments. Top bankers in communication with top U.S. officials were hesitant to point too critical a finger at their compatriots. Coombs was not taken seriously. In addition, European central bankers and finance ministry officials could not easily communicate their views on market developments as forcefully as they wished to Shultz. The normal communication lines flowed through New York, and U.S. Treasury officials were perceived more as adversaries than friends. The close bond among central bankers, cemented by monthly Bank for International Settlement's meetings, did not exist among finance ministry officials in Europe, Japan, and the United States.

Perhaps the most important reason why Treasury officials failed to learn from crises after 1971 was their previous success in assessing the monetary climate. Before the dollar devaluations, markets admirably reflected what needed to be done. Operations of specific banks and MNCs did not need to be segregated to be understood. The message was clear. There was no reason to expect distortions created by individual speculators to affect the exchange markets. As mentioned earlier, Burns and Shultz were perplexed by the March 1, 1973 rampage of funds. They believed that appropriate adjustments should foster a return to market tranquility. Paul Volcker, who was resolved not to cave in to market pressures after March 1, remembers no mention of speculative bank rings while he was Under Secretary for monetary affairs at the Treasury.[91]

The anomaly of the deterioration of the dollar after March 1, 1973 has been widely studied. It remains unclear how factors including Watergate, portfolio diversification, inflation, and bank speculation affected the outcome. However, the U.S. position favoring floating exchange rates never seems to have considered the possibility that a small number of speculators created undue market distortions. Policy proposals were based on the assumption of market rationality, even after March 1973. Scapegoats, extraneous to the exchange markets, were blamed for causing volatility, never market imperfection.

Bureaucratic communication channels also help explain the British fear of speculators. The structure of information flows on monetary matters in Great Britain differs substantially from the U.S. situation. London, unlike New York, has been the traditional focus of exchange crises. For well over one hundred years the London foreign exchange market was the largest and most important in the world. More recently, London has also served as the center of the Eurocurrency market. The Bank of England is run by a technocrat while the British Treasury is led by a politician, the Chancellor of the Exchequer. Traditionally, British governments have authorized the Bank of England to protect sterling without much political interference. In addition, the central bank is not segmented geographically. When crises arise, the Governor of the Bank of England has a direct line to the Prime Minister and the opportunity to garner all relevant market information. When crises strike, the market is at hand and, at least until 1976, communication between the central bank and the market was smooth and steady. The Bank of England may actually have become overly engrossed in the intricacy of indirectly controlling market developments and lost sight of the possibility that the market might transmit proper economic warnings.

At least four factors predispose the Bank of England to focus on speculation more than its U.S. counterpart. (1) The British economy is more vulnerable to short-term capital flows than the U.S. economy. Smaller flows may create severe problems. (2) The contacts between the Bank of England and London banks is more informal, but also more complex than in New York. In the 1950s the Bank of England discouraged leads and lags and became expert at dealing in the market. The Federal Reserve Bank of New York rarely intervened actively in exchange markets during crises since they centered in Europe. (3) More funds were needed to defend currencies in Europe than in America since the crises arose outside the United States. (4) The proximity of the Prime Minister and the Bank of England and the central banks close and long-standing concern with currency fluctuations related to flows of funds provoked greater fear of speculators in London than in New York and Washington.

Summary

Under specific conditions some banks affected the development and timing of exchange crises through their Eurocurrency and foreign exchange activities. However, the ability of these institutions, mostly smaller banks, to control the monetary system was mostly accidental and minor. Their influence was related to inaction and indecision by governments and large banks and not to their own expertise and foresight. However, despite the impact of banks on monetary crises, there is little evidence that their actions impinged on the perceptions and policy decisions of government officials. Overall, the misperception of the role of large and small banks may have contributed to the misunderstanding between monetary officials in various nations seeking monetary reform and market stability, but probably had less impact on day-to-day international monetary policy and practices. The problem was not that banks were uncontrollable, but that few realized the necessity of controlling them.

NOTES

1. Interviews with senior representatives of the Federal Reserve Bank of New York, Bank of England, and John Odell interviews.

2. Harold Wilson, *A Personal Record: The Labour Government 1964-1970* (Boston: Little, Brown, 1971): 37.

3. Ibid.: 38.

4. "How did we ever get here? a banker's diary, 1964-1973," *The Banker* 123 (September 1973): 1005.

5. Charles Coombs,

6. Wilson, op. cit.: 451.

7. Minutes of the Federal Reserve Open Market Committee Meeting, November 14, 1967: 3.

8. U.S. Congress, Joint Economic Committee, Subcommittee on International Economics, *Hearings on How Well Are Fluctuating Exchange Rates Working?* 93d Cong., 1st sess., 1973, Testimony by Alan Teck, Vice President Chemical Bank: 72.

9. Charles Coombs, "Interview," *The Banker* 117 (November 1966) and interviews with representatives of the New York Federal Reserve Bank, June 1974.

10. Minutes of the Federal Reserve Open Market Committee Meeting, November 27, 1967: 20-21.

11. New York is several hours behind the more active European markets. Therefore the bulk of the dollar's support was undertaken by European central banks. Complaints sometimes surfaced when after steady European support of the dollar was completed for the day, the New York Federal Reserve Bank would allow the dollar's value to slip.

12. Interview with a retired high level representative of Bank of America, San Francisco, February 1974.

13. "The currency crisis: Germany and the Euro-currency pool," *The Banker* 121 (June 1971): 584.

14. Sir Leslie O'Brien, "The Eurodollar market: controls are not the answer," *Euromoney* (June 1971): 10.

15. Robert Russell, "Crisis management in the international monetary system, 1960-1973," paper presented at the meeting of the International Studies Association, New York, March 16, 1973:6.

16. Interview with a senior representative in a British clearing bank, London, October 1974.

17. John Watts, "The business view of proposals for international monetary reform," in George Halm (ed.) *Approaches to Greater Flexibility of Exchange Rates: The Burgenstock Papers* (Princeton, N.J.: Princeton University Press, 1970): 167.

18. Interviews with numerous American bankers, a British consortium banker, the treasurer of a *Fortune 500* manufacturing firm, and from conversation with James Burtle, Vice President for Business Economics for W. R. Grace.

19. Particularly after 1969 the growth of the Eurocurrency market as traced by Morgan Guaranty and the Bank for International Settlements far outdistanced the growth of foreign exchange reserves of industrialized nations. Swap agreements among central banks which increased steadily after 1961 also lagged far behind the growth of funds available to the private sector in the Euromarkets.

20. The snake requires participating central banks to hold their currencies together, but allows them to float against other currencies. In the wider bands prevailing after Smithsonian Agreement, the visual rendering of the snake looked something like this:

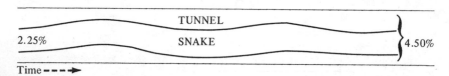

21. Bank of England *Quarterly Bulletins,* various issues.

22. Paul Volcker, Testimony, U.S. Congress, Senate, Committee on Banking Housing and Urban Affairs, *Hearings on Whether to Amend the Par Value Modification Act,* 93d Cong., 1st sess., 1973: 91.

23. Quoted in the *Financial Times,* June 23, 1972.

24. *American Banker,* January 31, 1973.

25. *Wall Street Journal,* February 8, 1973.

26. Ibid.

27. Interviews with high Treasury and New York Federal Reserve Bank representatives.

28. Jack Bennett, Testimony, U.S. Congress, Senate Finance Committee, *Hearings before the Subcommittee on International Finance and Resources on the International Financial Crisis.* 93d Cong., 1st sess., 1973: 121.

29. Volcker, *Par Value Modification Act Hearings,* p. 39.

30. *Wall Street Journal,* February 12, 1973.

31. Ibid.

32. Ibid., March 2, 1973.

33. Interviews with foreign exchange managers for Bankers Trust, First National Bank of Chicago, and Continental Illinois.

34. Interviews with a senior British banker, two representatives from Continental Illinois, and a representative of Wells Fargo Bank, London, October, 1974.

35. Interviews with a senior British consortium manager and a representative from First National Bank of Chicago, London, October 1974.

36. Interviews with two representatives of Bank of America officials and a representative of Bankers Trust, San Francisco, New York, 1974.

37. Interviews with two representatives of the bank suffering the loss.

38. Martin Mayer, *The Bankers* (New York: Weybright and Talley, 1974): 445.

39. New York *Times,* February 20, 1973.

40. Numerous bankers at various levels of authority agreed that banks, usually European ones, were the main speculators in 1973 but not in 1971. However, the fact that so many institutions and individuals are accused of being the culprits forces caution in assigning blame. For instance, dealers for Morgan Guaranty in London dissented from this general view and held that bank speculators may have been more important in 1971 than in 1973.

41. See the graph compiled by Henry Kaufman of Salomon Brothers and reprinted in U.S. Congress, Senate Multinational Corporations Subcommittee, Staff Report on

Multinational Corporations in the Dollar Devaluation Crisis: Report on a Questionnaire, 94th Cong., 1st sess., 1975: 92.

42. Sieghardt Rometsch, "Multinational corporations and national monetary and financial policy," paper presented at the SUERF colloquium, Nottingham, England, April 10-13, 1973, quoted in ibid.: 87.

43. "Uncertainties surrounding UK economy lead to a continuing float of the pound," *Business Europe* (December 1, 1972): 377.

44. Bank of England *Quarterly Bulletin* 12 (December 1972): 439.

45. In response to the question: "Who are the major speculators in foreign exchange dealing and how can they be curbed?" Transcript of a conference on "Crises in the foreign exchange markets," London, July 10, 1974: 29.

46. Substantial research has been conducted on this question using the Canadian dollar float as a point of departure. This, however, has dealt with the case where one currency floats while the rest remained fixed among themselves. See, Paul Wonnacott, *The Canadian Dollar: 1948-1962* (Toronto: University of Toronto Press, 1965).

47. *How Well Are Fluctuating Rates Working?*, p. 115.

48. Ibid., p. 108.

49. Samuel Katz, "The emerging exchange-rate system [Early 1974]," *Finance Discussion Papers* 46, Washington: Federal Reserve Board of Governors, Division of International Finance, May 23, 1974: Table III.

50. David Mann, "Crises in the foreign exchange markets," pp. 3-4.

51. Interviews with two Treasury officials. This was confirmed in discussion with Rita Rodriquez of Harvard Business School who is conducting research on corporate foreign exchange behavior, February 1976.

52. Geoffrey Bell quoted in *The Economist,* March 23-29, 1974.

53. *How Well Are Fluctuating Exchange Rates Working?*, p. 197.

54. John Odell interviews.

55. See particularly, Walter Salant, "The post-devaluation weakness of the dollar," *Brookings Papers on Economic Activity* (1973: 2): 481-497.

56. Paul Verburgt, Senior Vice President Bank of America, San Francisco, January 1974.

57. John Cooper, "How foreign exchange operations can go wrong," *Euromoney* (May 1974): 7.

58. See, Adam Smith, *Supermoney* (New York: Popular Library, 1972): 111-165.

59. "Imprudence and over-prudence in foreign exchange," *International Currency Review* 6 (July-August 1974): 5-13.

60. Interviews with two representatives of Wells Fargo, London, October 1974.

61. Interview with a representative of a British clearing bank.

62. *Wall Street Journal,* April 11, 1974.

63. Interviews with a representative of a British bank, two representatives of Continental Illinois, and a representative of Wells Fargo.

64. *Wall Street Journal,* April 11, 1974.

65. Karl Polanyi, *The Great Transformation* (Boston: Beacon Press, 1957): 3-19.

66. Richard Blackhurst, "Spot markets under floating rates," *The Banker* 126 (January 1976): 30.

67. See, "Those bank failures and losses," *The Banker* 124 (August 1974): 905-909.

68. The figure seems to have been set at about $4 billion because that was the size of the main Philadelphia banks, one of which, Girard, lost money when Herstatt collapsed.

69. Interview with a representative of Bankers Trust, London, October 1974.

70. *Blumenthal* v. *King,* No. 702861; 71811 WPG U.S. District Court for Central District of California. The case was settled in June 1975 for $700,000.

71. Interviews with representatives of two London consortium banks, September, 1974.

72. William Low, "Euro-study: a review of the Euro-money and Euro-capital Market," (London: International Insider, 1974): 64.

73. According to interviewees, Manufacturers Hanover, Bankers Trust, Chemical Bank, Chase Manhattan, and other either would not accept short-term Arab deposits or did so only at extremely low interest rates for a time. Morgan Guaranty and Citibank, on the other hand, apparently accepted all funds offered by reputable clients. As bankers persuaded OPEC depositors to invest in longer maturities, the deposits were welcomed again.

74. Interviews with representatives of Bank of America and Citibank, London, October, 1974.

75. Reginald Barham in "Crisis in the foreign exchange markets," p. 17.

76. Interviews with representatives of Bank of America, Morgan Guaranty, and Continental Illinois, London, October 1974.

77. Interview with a representative of Salomon Brothers, London, September 1974.

78. Interviews with two representatives of Bank of America and one of Bishops International, London, October, 1974.

79. Interviews with an IMF representative, Washington, June 1974, and with a representative of Bankers Trust, London, October 1974.

80. John Odell interviews.

81. John Odell interviews.

82. There is some debate on whether there ever truly existed a policy of benign neglect. Paul Volcker claimed in a session at the Harvard Center for International Affairs in late 1975 that no such policy was formulated. He stated that the dollar was allowed to fall because nobody in Treasury could figure out what actions to take to defend it. Hendrik Houthakker, on the other hand, argued at the same forum two weeks later that a conscious policy of benign neglect was adopted by the Nixon Administration with regard to defending the dollar.

83. Interviews with two representatives of the New York Federal Reserve Bank, June 1974; and John Odell interviews.

84. Ibid.

85. John Odell interviews.

86. Interview with a representative of a British clearing bank, London, October, 1974.

87. Volcker, *Par Value Modification Hearings*, p. 39.

88. William Safire, *Before the Fall* (Garden City, N.Y.: Doubleday, 1975): 517.

89. Interviews with senior representatives of Wells Fargo, Bank of America, First National Bank of Chicago, and John Odell interviews.

90. Interview with a high New York Federal Reserve Bank official, a high Treasury official; and John Odell interviews.

91. Conversation with Paul Volcker, Princeton, March, 1975.

Chapter 6

THE PRIVATE SECTOR AND

MONETARY REFORM, 1961-1976

The creation of a stable international monetary regime for the late 1970s and 1980s depends on devising realistic rules compatible with the preferences and behavior of concerned public and private bureaucracies. In the past decade, economists and statesmen advocated numerous, contradictory visions of appropriate monetary reforms.[1] International organizations, central banks, finance ministries, multinational corporations, and multinational banks in various nations preferred different plans and clung to them with varying tenacity. The changing coalitions, sometimes conflicting, sometimes reinforcing, dominated the negotiating process and circumscribed the prospects for monetary regime creation. Few analysts, however, have considered the impact of private actors on monetary reform negotiations or analyzed their role in determining final settlements.[2] In fact, an analysis of the interactions among and preferences of actors operating internationally sheds some predictive light on possibilities for future monetary reform.

The impact of banks and MNCs on monetary reform is more subtle than their influence on exchange regulations and crises. Private actors have willingly remained outside the negotiations to reform the monetary system. Private actors indirectly influence monetary reform through government officials in the United States and abroad. In particular, it appears the growth of foreign exchange and Euromarkets has increased the effectiveness of private sector's activities, which channel government reform efforts by shaping official perceptions of viable alternatives.

After analyzing potential private sector influence on monetary reform negotiations, this chapter examines the formation, aggregation, and evolution of public and private sector preferences towards monetary reform. Using this background, we shall examine private influence over government decision-making during (1) the attempt to revitalize the monetary regime between August and December 1971, (2) the emergence of flexible exchange rates in March 1973, and (3) the evolution and institutionalization of managed flexibility after July 1973.

In 1944 finance and foreign affairs ministries, not bankers and central bankers, dominated the construction of the Bretton Woods regime. Private bankers, however, accepted and supported the fixed-rate monetary system once it proved viable. During all exchange crises before 1972, banks pressed for parity changes, not system reform. Occasionally a leading banker called for some reform or a group of executives rubber-stamped a Treasury initiative, but this was rare and did not twist policy-makers from their preferred paths.[3] Nonetheless, as the continued survival of the monetary regime became intertwined with the foreign exchange and Eurocurrency markets, the market activities of banks and MNCs became crucial. The pressure generated by bank and MNC actions was not usually intentional. Private actors merely attempted to make profits in relatively predictable environments.

The size, growth, unregulated nature, and complexity of the Eurocurrency markets worked against government decision-makers during monetary crises. The knowledge that private sector activities could trigger a crisis kept monetary negotiations within definable bounds after August 1971. However, private actors were concerned with achieving an economically sensible set of exchange rates conducive to prosperity and predictability not with designing a monetary regime.

The ease with which private actors could pressure for certain reforms rested on the nature of the Bretton Woods system. The dollar served as the key currency for monetary intervention and was the critical reserve asset in the monetary system. Although the parities of other currencies could be adjusted against the dollar without disturbing the system, the dollar could be repegged only against gold.[4] During the 1960s the growth of central bank-controlled dollars was matched by the growth of foreign-held, privately controlled dollars. Once the dollar, the system's *numeraire,* was proved vulnerable, it became imperative to reestablish confidence in it or to create a new monetary order which did not depend so completely on it,[5] otherwise the machinations of corporate treasurers and bank traders attempting to protect their positions could generate currency and system crises.

After August 1971 the persistent exchange crises bedeviling the dollar began affecting the problem of monetary reform as well. Reforms, perceived as stabilizing were supported by the private sector. Moves which bankers and businessmen did not believe would stabilize the dollar's role and value were followed by furious activity in the foreign exchange and Euromarkets. Since officials in governments and international organizations were slowly learning to respond to private sector behavior, policy was influenced by existing private sector goals.

The threat of volatility generated through foreign exchange markets complements the pressure emanating from Euromarket operations. The threat of speculative foreign exchange movements may shut off certain avenues of reform. Chapter four suggested that speculative flows frequently orginated in smaller banks and MNCs. Large and medium-sized organizations were sometimes forced to alter their policies to cope with the uncertainty and volatility created by smaller competitors. Sometimes this led to grumbling among the larger institutions concerning acceptable market behavior and system structure. Apparently, when larger banks act as market-makers and equilibrating speculators or when they decide to discipline their smaller rivals, their indirect influence on decision-makers is large. However, when the large banks withdraw to safety in thin markets and allow the smaller banks free reign, the smaller banks' preferences have greater indirect influence.

To understand the extent of private influence over monetary reform outcomes it is necessary to study the changing goals and preferences of private executives. Private actors' implicit capacity to shatter the monetary system and alter exchange rates with which they are dissatisfied can only be analyzed from that perspective.

Private Preferences Concerning the Structure of the Monetary Regime

THE AGGREGATION AND MEASUREMENT OF PREFERENCES

In the complex international system of the 1960s and 1970s, it is impossible to separate the interactive effects of individual banks, MNCs and government agencies, so aggregation is necessary. Here, the preferences of MNCs, commercial banks, and central banks are each aggregated and estimated. Despite differences in size, U.S. MNCs operating abroad attempted to minimize risk of translation and conversion exchange losses and maximize their planning capabilities. Although some corporate treasurers speculated for or against currencies when parity changes seemed probable and their direction seemed predictable, most returned to straight hedging strategies when volatility became endemic after August 1971. Thereafter, corporate treasurers, while disagreeing on the appropriate level of the dollar, were united in their search for a monetary order compatible with planning for the future and finding adequate forward cover to assure it.

Measurement of aggregated preferences is a crude process. At best, a sense of each group's relative positions over time and compared to other groups' positions emerges. Although monetary systems can be classified according to several dimensions, only the degree of flexibility of exchange rates strongly concern private officials because it has important implications for their operations. Other dimensions of monetary reform are less important to private officials and are left to politicians.[6]

Determining the preferences of commercial banks is more difficult. The business of banks is money, and various firms accept different levels of speculative risk to make money. Bank foreign exchange strategies reflect these genuine variations in bank orientation. For instance, Citibank was the first to call for floating exchange rates. Its free market orientation has made it consistently more strident in calling for free floating than the rest of the industry. Morgan Guaranty, a market-maker, seems to believe that while governments frequently botch their attempts to regulate the value of currencies, some government regulation is useful and necessary. In addition, traders, economists, and isolated top executives in banks retain their perspective of foreign exchange as a service sector and prefer some government intervention to stabilize rates.[7] Nonetheless, the impact of certain bank groups is dominant at various times. If the remaining banks continue to make profits, their preferences concerning the proper degree of flexibility will not substantially differ from the initiating group of banks. Only when there is a shift from one dominant group to another is severe difference in opinions about flexibility found.[8]

Central banks, unlike their superiors in finance ministries, work together on a close, cooperative basis. Frequently, the gap separating central bank opinion is narrower than the gap between central banks and their own finance ministries. This is largely a product of day-to-day cooperation on fundamental mechanics of the monetary system. Top central bankers meet monthly at the Bank for International Settlements to discuss international monetary developments. To avoid publicity, finance ministry officials are banned. Close cooperation on daily operations, frequent gatherings, and long tenures of central bank governors and officials combine to make central bankers sympathetic to each others' problems. Throughout the 1960s and even during the debates between finance ministries over reform in the 1970s, central bankers were remarkably united in their views about monetary reform. To a large extent, operations forced on unwilling central banks by finance ministries can be separated from activities advocated by central banks. Throughout, the operations and preferences of the Bank of England and the New York Federal

Reserve Bank are used as proxies for other central banks' operations.[9] While this is not entirely accurate, it is acceptably close for the purposes of this analysis.

The preferences of finance ministries at various times on all the dimensions of monetary reform can be described and analyzed but not aggregated. The political debate over monetary reform is articulated and negotiated at this level. On the dimension of flexibility, the two almost constant antagonists were the French and the Americans. The French doggedly insisted on the efficiency of fixed rates while the Americans advocated floating exchange rates. The preferences of other OECD industrial nations' finance ministries were arrayed between these two extremes. The Germans and British were usually closer to the American position, while the Japanese generally sided with the French. For the purposes of this analysis, however, almost all of the attention will be focused on the extreme U.S. and French positions since without some semblance of agreement between these two, no lasting monetary reform is possible.[10]

Although the International Monetary Fund has reentered the monetary reform process with substantial force since 1976, it had little impact on the shape of reform between 1958 and 1975. The epitome of powerlessness was displayed in 1971 when Treasury Secretary John Connally invited the IMF's Managing Director to his office to view Nixon's August 15 speech without informing him of its contents. The IMF and the BIS served as forums through which governments acted, but demonstrated no initiating power themselves. The United States in particular carefully deprived the IMF Secretariat of any meaningful participation in the monetary reform debate. As a result, the IMF, BIS, and other international organizations occasionally involved in international monetary relations are treated only in passing here.[11]

THE UNDERPINNINGS OF PREFERENCES

In the early 1960s all the major actors supported and were comfortable with the fixed rate Bretton Woods system. A dozen years later acrimonious debate concerning a new system raged. The reasons for support of the Bretton Woods system varied widely. The goals of the actors changed over time. When experience proved to some participants that floating was workable, their fixed rate preoccupation vanished.

MNCs in the 1950s and 1960s approved of the fixed rate system for straightforward reasons. The monetary regime provided them with a stable environment in which they could pursue their individual opportunities with minimal concern for international financial disruption. Corporate planners could be fairly certain after 1958 that the francs, or marks, or guilders that they earned abroad could be converted into dollars without loss. Similarly,

MNCs could cheaply and easily protect their projected flows of international credits and debits through forward market transactions when fearful of a parity change.

As long as MNCs believed that economically viable exchange rates would be maintained, they were quite content with fixed rates. Indeed, they should have been. Their expansion and prosperity abroad was unmatched in history. The fixed rate aspect of the system did not harm MNCs in any way, and the reserve asset role of the dollar helped make U.S. MNCs welcome investors in most parts of the world. Until the French began complaining that American MNCs were buying up the productive capacity of the world at bargain prices, the dollars brought in by MNCs under the fixed rate monetary system were better than gold.[12]

The prosperity of MNCs aborad, when coupled with the imposition of American regulations against the outflow of funds, propelled American banks into the global arena. Bank profits came from serving multinational customers throughout the world. In the early 1960s as business expanded, banks made healthy returns from their foreign financing of MNCs and began developing ties with foreign governments and foreign businessmen.

None of this depended on fixed or floating rates. Under the Bretton Woods system, foreign exchange profits were minimal except during major exchange crises. Foreign exchange business was perceived as a service center rather than as a profit center by banks. Since profits from other areas of foreign business flourished and since most traders in banks were content with the general adjustability of exchange rates, there was little desire to shift to a more flexible exchange rate system. The fixed rate system was profitable, workable, and even more important, known. Anybody could predict but nobody could know that greater flexibility would result in continued prosperity and consistently larger profits. Therefore bankers demonstrated no predilection to abandon fixed rates.

Central bankers did not have the profit-motivated justification for supporting fixed rates. Their fears of change were grounded in a view of the international monetary system as an international public good which benefited all. In retrospect it is frequently forgotten that government officials of all stripes who had lived through the depression of the 1930s were genuinely fearful that greater flexibility of exchange rates might lead to a repetition of the "beggar-thy-neighbor" policies of the depression.[13] On another level, central bankers enjoyed being at the center of the action. Over time they took over most of the day-to-day responsibility for the management of exchange rates and for the defense of the monetary system.

Sherman Maisel, a former Federal Reserve Board Governor, cites six reasons why central banks and finance ministries were hesitant to abandon fixed exchange rates: (1) National pride associated exchange rate change with defeat in international politics. (2) Fixed exchange rates were an outside pressure which pushed political leaders toward better internal economic policy. (3) Fixed rates helped maximize the advantages of international trade and investment. (4) Keeping New York as an international financial center was profitable for the U.S. (5) Prosperity had been achieved with fixed rates, so why take a chance on some other system. (6) No country wants to give up control over exchange rates when shifts in exchange rates "alter the relationship between jobs in the export and import industries."[14]

Inevitably, there were differences between central bankers concerning the necessity of reform. In New York, Charles Coombs and his associates cast suspicious glances at Special Drawing Rights, the IMF-created reserve asset, and their explicit tie to gold. Coombs would have preferred formally "crowning" the dollar as the key international currency.[15] European central bankers were less eager to enshrine the dollar. On the fixed-floating dimension, however, while Otmar Emminger of the Bundesbank sometimes took a more flexible stance, general agreement among central bankers was maintained without interruption. They feared flexibility, thought the fixed rate system was workable and defensible, and believed it preposterous for other nations or for market speculators to force sovereign nations to devalue their currencies. During his tenure in New York, Charles Coombs apparently never favored a devaluation of the dollar or any other currency. Ideally, he favored voluntary adjustment through revaluation by surplus nations, particularly Japan and Germany.[16]

In the early 1960s the U.S. Treasury and the New York Federal Reserve Bank had no major disagreements concerning either the importance of maintaining the system or of the methods necessary to accomplish that. The dollar's role as the key reserve asset was appreciated and defended. Treasury officials supported the fixed exchange rates for the same reasons as central bankers. In 1965, however, the Treasury, reacting to continued balance of payments deficits, criticisms of the system introduced by Robert Triffin and other academic economists, and French threats to convert dollars into gold, began exploring the possibility of creating a new reserve asset.[17] The SDR which emerged was linked to gold and never fully supported by most central bankers. However, on the flexibility dimension, the U.S. Treasury and New York Federal Reserve Bank remained in agreement through 1967.

The French, led by Charles de Gaulle and Jacques Rueff, opposed the key role of the dollar in the international monetary system. In their quest for monetary and political autonomy, the French attacked the credit worthiness of the dollar. In 1963 French Finance Minister Valery Giscard d'Estaing called for a new credit reserve unit to displace the dollar from the center of the international monetary system. Later the French abandoned this position and returned to the advocacy of gold as the central reserve asset on which the monetary system should be based.[18]

Despite their continuing differences with American authorities, the desire for monetary autonomy led the French to firm support of a fixed rate system even while devaluing the franc four times after 1947. Their attack against the dollar sprang from their fear of others dictating their fate. Although U.S. authorities supported fixed rates for numerous reasons, the French were dominated by the fear of losing control of their exchange rate. This still underlies the French insistence on returning to a more or less fixed rate system.

In short, banks and MNCs were tied to fixed rates because it helped them prosper. Central banks feared politicians and a return to the 1930s and they enjoyed running the system. The U.S. Treasury saw no reason to abandon a workable system which allowed them to lead the Western world to economic recovery. The French under de Gaulle, wishing to reassert their national pride and autonomy, were opposed to any system which might take control away from France. As the system began to break down, the key actors were differently affected.

CHANGES IN FLEXIBILITY PREFERENCES

The keys to the changing actor preferences towards fixed rates were the increasing frequency of exchange crises and the growing suspicion that the dollar was seriously overvalued. Many private executives became convinced that governments were manipulating the Bretton Woods regime for political purposes and that economic adjustments would not or could not be made. Corporate treasurers found it increasingly difficult to compete abroad because of the dollar's inflated value. In the face of stringent transaction controls which restricted their operations, corporate treasurers became more sympathetic to greater flexibility. Planning predictability and profit growth were endangered by government exchange regulations and by the frequency with which crises struck after the mid-1960s. In June 1969, an informal poll of participants at the Bürgenstock meeting, which brought together a cross-section of academics and practitioners to discuss international monetary problems, indicated that businessmen were becoming more willing to consider flexible exchange rates. Flexibility was perceived as a lesser evil than stepped-up government regulatory constraints.[19]

Similarly, R. B. Fitzsimons reported in 1971 that officials from almost 100 U.S. MNCs had reluctantly moved toward accepting more flexible exchange rates because of "the rising cost of dealing with recurring monetary crises and a growing complex of exchange controls." Many financial executives traced their difficulties to government efforts to support unrealistic exchange rates for their currencies.[20]

Once MNCs began experiencing difficulties under fixed rates, banks also began rethinking their positions. The 1967 sterling crisis demonstrated to bankers that exchange crises could be extremely profitable. In addition, the credit squeeze of 1966 pushed new entrants into the Euromarkets. To establish themselves, they undercut the larger, more established institutions, forcing down the margins on Euroloans. Newcomers also sought new profit centers to hold them over until their Eurocurrency and local business became profitable. Large banks, pressed by the invaders, decided to diversify their profit seeking. Since many bankers believed that the dollar was overvalued, the foreign exchange markets offered them a nearly foolproof profit arena. During crises before 1973, the timing might be missed, but the direction of possible parity changes was always obvious.

Commercial banks began to consider foreign exchange as a potential profit center. Top management started pressuring exchange traders to produce profits.[21] Under a fixed rate regime, large profits could only be generated during crises. Thus, although the articulated policy of most banks steadfastly supported fixed rates, traders began developing an often unconscious predisposition to greater flexibility.

Reluctant to give up a system which had served them well, many bankers still concluded that greater flexibility of exchange rates was preferable to ever-burgeoning numbers of exchange and transaction controls. In part they were persuaded by academic economists who claimed that greater flexibility would help correct the dollar's problems and would prove profitable to the private sector as well. Although only Citibank among the large banks publicly announced a preference for flexibility before August 1971, other banks were mulling the problems and were not adverse to moving slowly towards greater flexibility.

Central bankers, who did not need to make profits but did not want to suffer large losses, were not persuaded that the Bretton Woods order was moribund or that flexible exchange rates were necessary. Their day-to-day preoccupation with the maintenance of the system and the defense of exchange rates did not dispose them to take a broader view. Efforts at monetary reform were undertaken, not by the central bankers, but by finance ministries and were perceived as political more than as economic necessity. Two main reasons slowed central bank moves towards greater flexibility. Central bankers were haunted by the 1930s. In addition, they firmly believed that the imposition of flexible rates would take control of domestic economies away from national decision-makers, who should control the currencies. A third, unspoken and perhaps unconscious, reason central bankers resisted extensive reform was that proposed changes would have drawn power away from them. Years of experience in managing exchange rates had convinced central bankers that their management was necessary to prevent disaster. Otherwise, why had they spent all those years working so hard to control exchange rates?

Robert Russell has traced the multidimensional reform preferences of various finance ministries.[22] He argues that particularly on the flexibility dimension, the influence of academic economists was substantial. With the election of Richard Nixon in November 1968, committed interventionists were replaced by officials more sympathetic to free markets and flexible exchange rates. The Republican party, traditionally the party of business, was committed to the phasing out of government controls over the economy, including over exchange rates and were cheered when large numbers of academic economists advocated the introduction of greater freedom into the monetary system. The appointment of Arthur Burns as head of the Federal Reserve Board foreshadowed a decline in interventionary discretion in New York. Similarly, at the Treasury, Nixon appointees were less concerned with defending the Bretton Woods system than with assuring the prosperity of U.S. business.

In addition, Treasury officials were bedeviled by balance of payments problems which they could not vanquish. Brave remarks of the mid-1960s predicting the imminent reversal of American payments trends proved wrong. Vietnam War spending increased the balance of payments outflow and required greater and greater attention to the international position of the dollar. Slowly, Treasury officials simply withdrew support of the dollar and forced the Europeans to maintain its value. The so-called policy of "benign neglect" began to pervade American monetary operations. Since the Nixon administration's main economic advisors did not believe that flexibility inevitably meant a return to the 1930s, and since they were plagued by international economic problems, they pondered extensive reform.

In France domestic policy autonomy remained at the center of the perspective on monetary reform. Only the troubles surrounding the French franc in 1968 persuaded the French to accept the SDR. Rather than forfeit control of their own exchange rate, the French preferred to try extensive transaction controls to mitigate their balance of payments flows. Finance officials remained rooted in the lessons of the depression and admirably reflected the French bias toward hoarding gold. Stability and fixed exchange rates linked to gold remained the ideal French policy sought.

Despite changes in policy preferences, little was articulated except by finance ministries, until the system was shaken by the suspension of convertibility of the dollar on August 15, 1971. In cathartic fashion, those who had come to question the monetary structure and rules saw possibilities for other arrangements and reoriented their public positions. Once these predispositions towards fixed rates had evaporated, actors' preferences evolved swiftly. The interaction of these actors, particularly of the public and private sectors, delimited the possibilities of the new monetary system especially on the flexibility dimension. In essence, developments in the monetary system in the late 1960s taught each group of actors lessons related to their own aims. This made possible a rapid divergence of preferences of actors concerning needed monetary reforms.

The Role of the Private Sector
During Monetary Reform

THE PATCHWORK OF THE SMITHSONIAN AGREEMENT

On August 15, 1971 President Nixon suspended the convertibility of the dollar, imposed a 10 percent surcharge on all imports, enacted a 10 percent cut in foreign aid, promised to cut Federal expenditures, and imposed a 90-day freeze on wages, prices, and dividends. These measures were designed to improve the U.S. economic position and to force Japan and European surplus nations to relax what U.S. officials perceived as unfair trade and currency practices. On December 19, 1971 the Group of Ten produced the Smithsonian Agreement. The U.S. import surcharge was removed, and the dollar was devalued by 8.57 percent. Subsequently, the United States promised to recommend a devaluation of the dollar against gold from $35 to $38 per ounce in return for trade concessions from the EEC, Canada, and Japan. How did this reform emerge? What was its importance? What role did the various actors play? What outcomes would they ideally have preferred?

The Sequence of Events, August 15-December 18, 1971. From August 16 to August 20 European exchange markets were closed. Japan and European nations protested the imposition of the import surcharge, but most of the American banking and business community were cheered by the U.S. actions. Quickly France moved to a two-tier market; Italy, Sweden, Denmark, and Norway allowed their currencies to float; and the Benelux nations opted for a joint float. The Japanese had hoped to avoid revaluation but were swamped by dollars and forced to float the yen on August 28.

On September 13, the EEC ministers agreed to demand the elimination of the U.S. import surcharge and a rise in the price of gold as the price of their revaluation. The EEC sought a return to fixed parities with the dollar's reserve asset role diminished. Three days later Treasury Secretary Connally demanded a $13 billion turnaround in the U.S. payments position, substantial revaluations of the yen and European currencies, greater sharing of defense burdens, and the removal of trade restrictions. While the Group of Ten debated, the Senate Finance Committee strengthened Nixon and Connally's hand by voting, on November 4, the President wide authority to impose import quotas if the U.S. international economic position was found to be threatened. Connally then flew to Japan to present terms, but no agreement could be found, and Connally threatened to leave the import surcharge on indefinitely. This frightened Peter Peterson and others in the Administration who saw the surcharge as a bargaining tool and not as a political measure. Peterson went to Kissinger to get him to persuade Nixon to overrule Connally.[23] Kissinger's success in this venture allowed a softening of the U.S. position.

At the Rome meeting of the Group of Ten in early December, the U.S. dropped its demand for a package of currency, trade, defense, and other measures and proposed a 10 percent dollar devaluation against gold and an 11 percent depreciation against major currencies. After two days of meetings between President Pompidou and Chancellor Brandt to coordinate positions within Europe, compromise was almost at hand. As a prelude to agreement, Nixon and Pompidou met in the Azores and agreed to devalue the dollar and revalue other currencies. They also agreed that while the resulting system would remain fixed, currencies would be allowed to fluctuate within margins. Three days after the Smithsonian Agreement Nixon met Prime Minister Heath in Bermuda and institutionalized the agreement from the Anglo-American side.

Changing Actor Views, August-December 1971. Businessmen and bankers, already sympathetic to the prospect of greater flexibility, enthusiastically supported the President's August 1971 moves. Robert Abboud of the First National Bank of Chicago reflected many bankers' views when he called the dollar's float "a great step" and "one that had to be done." He did not expect the dollar to float indefinitely but predicted that a system would eventually emerge in which currencies would float over a wider spectrum by as much as 5 percent.[24] The Thursday after the President's speech, Bank of America proposed a nine point reform program which would have meant a smaller international role for the dollar. It suggested that in the immediate future a return to fixed parities was desirable, though with wider bands and more frequent and smaller parity changes.[25] In late October David Rockefeller and Walter Wriston endorsed a modest change in the price of gold.

Between August and December 1971, while exchange rates were floating, banks made large foreign exchange profits and realized that they could prosper under a floating regime. MNCs, relieved at the more realistic value of the dollar, were also pleasantly surprised that flexibility did not initially damage their operations or planning. Although neither bankers nor corporate treasurers favored a free-floating regime, they supported the Nixon moves toward greater flexibility. Had the Smithsonian accords attempted merely to reestablish the Bretton Woods regime with the dollar readjusted, it is likely that private sector transfer of funds would have sparked another monetary crisis. In this atmosphere, finance ministers negotiated.

Even central bankers who fought to avoid the change in the dollar's parity, breathed a sigh of relief when the crisis abated. The Bundesbank, in particular, had been deluged by massive capital flows and opposed the imposition of more exchange controls on its economy and the revaluation of the mark. Officials in New York were upset and bitter but powerless. They believed the speculation could have been turned back, favored German and Japanese revaluations, and disapproved of greater flexibility.[26] However, during and after the Smithsonian negotiations, they had little direct role and were instructed in their actions by Treasury officials.

The French saw flexibility as a means to escape short-term problems but as an unacceptable long-term solution. The U.S. Treasury, on the other hand, became a stronger supporter of greater flexibility than even the private sector. Treasury officials became convinced that fixed rates imposed an intolerable burden on the prosperity of the American business community, hindered U.S. balance of payments adjustment, and that greater flexibility would not set off a series of competitive devaluations or damage world trade expansion. Nixon and Connally realized that this shock could be painted as an American victory,[27] understood that devaluation would help American business competitiveness, and were tired of bending to surplus nations' monetary constraints.

The private sector played a substantial role in determining the outcome of reforms at the Smithsonian. Government officials responded to private entreaties to aid business' competitive position and to indirect threats of renewed short-term capital movements. The Smithsonian Agreement was a patchwork job in which the U.S. settled for a smaller adjustment than desired. Increased band width was accepted, but most underlying difficulties which plagued Bretton Woods remained. However, American negotiators were generally pleased and admitted that it was impossible to calculate exactly the amount of necessary parity changes. Bankers' predictions and U.S. Treasury preferences had nearly coincided and were borne out by the shape of the accords.

On a fixed-float specturm the main actors considered here were aligned something like this as 1972 dawned:

```
FIXED    FR                    MNB  MNC  US                    FLOAT
         CB

         FR — French finance ministry    MNB — Multinational banks
         US — U.S. Treasury              MNC — Multinational corporations
         CB — Central banks
```

THE EMERGENCE OF FLOATING EXCHANGE RATES, MARCH 1973

The Smithsonian Agreement did not resolve French and U.S. differences. Each side compromised, but neither was overjoyed with the extent of readjustment of rates or of the system. On the fundamental issue of distribution of responsibility for the adjustment of international liquidity, no accord was reached.

Events Leading to the Floating System, March 1973. Less than a week after an inflow of $3.6 billion into the Bundesbank forced the closure of the markets on March 1, 1973, the EEC governments agreed to a "catalogue of suggestions" to present to the U.S. After another week European governments agreed on a joint float with sterling and the lira floating independently. Germany also agreed to revalue the mark by an additional 3 percent. On March 16 agreement was reached in Paris on "the basis for an operational approach toward exchange markets in the near future" with each "prepared to intervene at its initiative in its own market, when necessary and desirable, acting in a flexible manner."[28] When the foreign exchange markets reopened on March 19, free-floating exchange rate system was in force. Neither the Europeans nor the Americans had completely given in, but each recognized that temporary floating was the only basis on which markets could be reopened.

Changing Actor Views, January 1972-March 1973. During the period of moderate flexibility between the two dollar devaluations, American MNCs discovered that they could prosper in such an environment. Many MNCs hedged a larger percentage of their flows of funds than under fixed rates, but banks willingly accommodated them at only marginally higher prices than before. As a result, the stock of MNCs hedged contracts rose after 1971, but the flow of contracts during crises diminished.

Many MNC treasurers perceived that the dollar's value was still too high, damaging their export prospects. Apparently the aggregate corporate feeling towards flexibility became slightly more favorable after the Smithsonian. In addition, MNCs accepted greater flexibility because their bankers assured them that even free floating would be workable.

American multinational banks discovered the profitability of floating between August and December 1971. Many young and inexperienced traders announced the dawning of a new, profitable age in which banks would speculate for themselves in foreign exchange. While older traders were more cautious, the less experienced traders trained to handle the more volatile foreign exchange movements soon triumphed. As profits continued to grow without reported losses, traders and senior management began favoring even greater flexibility in the emerging monetary system.

Central bank motivations remained unchanged. They were upset by the volatility and by their loss of control over the monetary system. Admitting in retrospect that some adjustment in the dollar's value might have been needed, they still underscored confidence problems which emerged after the dollar's devaluation. Coombs, in particular, feared that the dollar would become more vulnerable to any speculative capital flight regardless of whether sound economic reason was underlying the devaluation.[29] All this occurred while the dollar's nonconvertibility enthroned it at the center of the transitional monetary regime.[30] Central bankers were caught in a dilemma. They would have preferred moving back towards fixed rates, but, being realistic, they realized that moving the system towards fixity was impossible over the opposition of the U.S. Treasury and the business community. Therefore, they chose the path of least resistance and followed finance ministries' directives.

On a theoretical level the French maintained their opposition to flexible exchange rates. On a practical level, in common with other European nations, they wanted to solve the problems facing them on February 12. Under Secretary Volcker was surprised during his February 1973 tour of Europe and Japan to discover finance ministers urging a larger devaluation than the U.S. expected it could get or thought was necessary.[31] Although the Europeans decided that the dollar might be less bothersome if it were slightly undervalued, few expected the March 1 aftermath.

During 1972 the preferred American position moved further towards acceptance of greater flexibility. George Shultz, a free floater, replaced Connally at Treasury in May 1972. The success of limited flexibility encouraged academic economists, who in turn stepped up their pressure for a further liberalization of exchange rate flexibility. Since both businessmen and bankers continued to support flexibility, the government had little reason to question the direction its policy was drifting.

An important sidelight was that after August 15 the traditional liaison between the New York Federal Reserve Bank and the large commercial banks became strained. Bank and corporate preferences conformed much more closely to the policies being espoused in Washington than those being defended in New York. Although it is impossible to measure the impact of this switch, it appears that Treasury officials were cheered by the support for their views from the private sector and redoubled their efforts to find a system acceptable to the private sector and to its potential prosperity.

By late 1972 preferences of a fixed-float spectrum were portrayed as follows:

FIXED FR		MNC US MNB		FLOAT
CB				

Private Pressures and the Emergence of Floating. Most American businessmen welcomed the second devaluation as a boon to their export efforts. Bankers were less certain. Although the decline was steeper than many expected, one Frankfurt foreign exchange dealer declared, "This gives rise to fears." Some traders, he said, "are expecting the dollar to decline again over the next few days," and they are already conjuring up images of another dollar realignment.[32] By February 21, however, speculators cashing their profits had driven the dollar to its new ceiling and allowed the Bundesbank to dispose of about $1 billion of the $6 billion it took in defending the dollar. Simultaneously, Chairman Burns and Under Secretary Volcker publicly promised that the dollar would not be devalued again.

Nonetheless, on Friday, February 23, the dollar was subjected to a downward speculative thrust fueled by rumors that the EEC was preparing a joint float. A Swiss Credit Bank exchange dealer explained, "It was pure panic. People were selling dollars against everything." Speculators "made a good profit on the dollar's devaluation, and that enables them to speculate again."[33] When markets were swamped on March 1, bankers predicted that governments could not avoid moving to a general currency float. Indeed, the markets would not have tolerated anything else.

The net effect of private activities between February 12 and March 1 was to veto as unreasonable a continued reliance on central bank intervention to maintain exchange rates. However, private actors did not move as a unitary body. Traders and corporate treasurers were unsure of the future after February 12 and protected themselves accordingly. Some market-makers refused to participate in equilibrating speculation. Others continued to sell dollars in the hope of greater profits. Still others were swept along against their better judgment in the wake of market uncertainty and less than confident statements by Shultz and German Finance Minister Helmut Schmidt.

The floating exchange rate system was what most bankers predicted and desired. MNCs, tired of uncertainty, and hopeful that floating would work, supported the move, though less enthusiastically. Partly to quell French, Swiss and Japanese reservations, the new system was to be temporary. Most private executives, however, did not expect, and would not have allowed, a rapid return to fixed rates. In fact, the run on the dollar on March 1 was the private sector's definitive statement on flexibility, not on the value of the dollar. Bankers and businessmen expected that floating would bring stability and prosperity after a short learning period.

In retrospect, the February 12 to March 1 interlude is of great interest. Central bankers and finance ministry officials concluded that the dollar was no longer overvalued. Bankers and business executives concurred. Market psychology, however, was adverse. Traders insisted that the devaluation was too easy, and handsome profits presuaded some to go for double or nothing. In addition, traders, fearing that others would take advantage of the dollar's vulnerable position, protected themselves by moving against the dollar. The pressure increased because investors with assets still denominated in dollars began diversifying into stronger currencies.[34] While remaining publicly mute on exchange rate arrangements, private sector preferences and behavior fueled by rumor and uncertainty doomed the Smithsonian rules.

THE LONG ROAD TO REFORM,
MARCH 1973-JANUARY 1976

Pundits predicted exchange rates would stabilize quickly at new equilbria. However, a rapid, unexpected shift in attitude invaded banks' dealing rooms. Aware of the sudden loss potential inherent in a floating system and buttressed by increasing contract volume, many traders substantially shortened their time frames. Instead of judging the medium-term outlook for a country's currency and economy and acting accordingly, they reacted to the news of the moment and rumors of the street. Some banks consciously manipulated exchange rates for their own profit. Everyone was astonished when the dollar continued to plummet.

Events Leading to the Rambouillet-Jamaica Accords. The major sequence of events leading to Herstatt has already been reviewed. In mid-July 1973 the U.S. Treasury, responding to unacceptable volatility, authorized New York to resume minor market intervention to smooth exchange rates. Other central banks also returned to the market.[35] Unfortunately, the move to calmer markets took almost a year and was only really successful after the Herstatt scare. Volatility between July 1973 and June 1974 was as great as during the first six months of 1973. However, the year starting in July 1974 showed considerably less volatility.[36] The emergence of a new articulated monetary regime was delayed until January 1976, by which time conditions had changed noticeably, and this was reflected in actor preferences. Only then could the ad hoc system which had been working since mid-1974 be institutionalized.

Changing Actor Views, March 1973-January 1976. MNCs' preferences, as rooted to their individual prosperity and planning capabilities, underwent a dramatic shift during 1973. Despite bankers assurances, MNCs found free floating unacceptable. The volatility associated with floating rates made planning almost impossible even though world trade did not suffer. Top companies such as International Harvester, Singer, IT&T, and Xerox suffered foreign exchange losses after the move to greater flexibility.[37] "There has been a burst of transactions coverage" in the two years following the emergence of flexibility.[38]

However, as volatility increased and its predictability vanished, large banks refused to provide inexpensive forward cover. Some companies had difficulty getting cover they wanted and raising funds in the Euromarket except in dollars.[39] As a result, by the third quarter of 1973 the aggregate MNC preference concerning flexibility had swung away from floating. It did not return to a fixed perspective since the corporate executives realized that a return to a Bretton Woods-type system was impractical and undesirable, but led to a call for greater "confidence" to be instilled in the markets by central bank intervention. Preferences of central bankers who realized they had been shunted to the background by their insistence on fixed rates evolved slowly after March 1973. Their low point came in July 1973 when they watched helplessly as volatility played havoc with the exchange markets. After they were allowed to reenter the market, they accepted their new mission quickly. Their aim was to smooth market volatility and not to defend exchange rates at all costs. Central banks "leaned into the wind," but when stiff market resistance developed, they withdrew. Since their intervention points and strategy were now secret, central bankers slowly regained some control over the market. Over time, they accepted their new, limited mission of patrolling rather than defending rates, while remaining opposed to free floating.

U.S. Treasury officials, after initial doubts about floating in early 1973, became convinced that it was viable in the wake of the oil embargo and four-fold oil price rise in late 1973. The banking system successfully redistributed petrodollars. Treasury officials and academic economists asserted, but never proved, that the old fixed rate system would have broken down under the weight of such capital movements.

The U.S. Treasury position was fortified by local support from commercial bankers who were pleased by their rising foreign exchange profits. No major bank losses from foreign exchange were reported in 1973. While realizing that the "one-way bet" was finished and that large losses were possible, most banks felt confident in their own dealers. Large banks controlled their risks by speculating *less*. Rising MNC demand for cover allowed Citibank and others to make massive profits by matching buy and sell orders and taking a slice from the middle.

Some smaller banks without volume or service fee advantages chose to compete by speculating for profit. Estimates place the ratio of interbank to commercial transactions during this period in Europe as high as nine to one.[40] Before bank exchange losses began appearing, banks, unlike MNCs, continued to promise the U.S. Treasury that stability would soon reemerge. Their assurances may have helped persuade Treasury negotiators that the market was with them and their position was viable.

In late 1973 the French and American finance ministries remained unalterably divided in their public conception of reform. The French perceived international monetary system developments as unique and transitory and insisted that over the long-term fixed rates and a gold base would be best for the system. The so-called "dirty float," depending on frequent central bank intervention, became the operational regime.[41] Nonetheless, in negotiations and preferences the various actors could be arrayed on the following spectrum:

FIXED   FR   CB MNC   US   FLOAT
                                                     MNB

Bankers' confidence in floating began to erode when a rash of foreign exchange losses were reported in early 1974. The collapse of Herstatt under the weight of foreign exchange losses on June 26 was the final blow. Bankers immediately reverted to more conservative strategies and concluded that free floating was not such a good idea after all.[42] Some even reversed their opposition to regulation of the Eurocurrency and foreign exchange markets and mildly supported such government action.[43] Leading dealers proclaimed the end of overt bank speculation.

Although Citibank and a few others continued to extoll the virtues of floating, many bankers began siding with corporate treasurers and central bankers in advocating a compromise solution on central bank intervention. In effect, bankers abandoned their new friends in Treasury and reunited with central bank opinion. After three years of reinforcing U.S. Treasury predilections, they moved again into opposition. By late 1974 the preferred flexibility of key actors looked like this:

FIXED   FR   CB MNC MNB   US   FLOAT

Operationally, the monetary system rolled along utilizing substantial central bank intervention while America and France debated the merits of new monetary rules.

Simultaneously, corporate opposition to uncontrolled flexibility was hardened by another series of losses and by the passage of new accounting rules forcing them to report all unrealized gains and losses from foreign balance sheet transactions as part of current income each quarter. MNCs feared that this rule would result in larger fluctuations in quarterly earnings, more top management and investor interest in the value of the dollar, and a possible drop in price-earnings multiples for many corporations.[44] Not surprisingly, MNCs howled about the new accounting rules. When this failed to sway government opinion, they insisted that the U.S. government at least assure greater stability of the dollar in exchange markets.

Private Pressure and the Jamaica Accords. The Rambouillet-Jamaica accords legitimized the ad hoc international monetary system which had developed since mid-1973. Except for some limited concessions to developing nations, Jamaica routinized what already existed and did not alter the operating rules of the system which emerged after mid-1973. It is too soon to know what prompted France and the United States to compromise. The resignation of Jack Bennett, a believer in free markets, and the promotion of the less ideological Edwin Yeo to the post of Under Secretary of Treasury for Monetary Affairs probably allowed greater flexibility in the U.S. position. On the surface, France conceded more for the accrued prestige derived from negotiating bilaterally with the United States. The central banks certainly gained the most. They were told to strengthen their links to the market and their cooperative efforts of the previous year and a half were legitimized. On a day-to-day level central banks were trying to depoliticize and stabilize exchange markets. However, chief executives and finance ministers also promised to deal with special, politically salient questions as they arose.

Banks and MNCs were pleased with the agreement but disappointed that it went no further. Central banks were authorized to smooth exchange rate movements not grounded in underlying economic developments, but were sternly barred from intervening when adjustment was economically necessary. This allowed dealers to return slowly to a more viable perspective concerning currency values. Yet, this adjustment resulted in severe falls in the value of sterling and the lira which responded to market opinion concerning British and Italian economic and political prospects. However, as the volume of cover increased, MNCs could deal more effectively with system volatility.

Bank and MNC roles in the process of monetary reform and system creation remain problematic. Bankers and corporate executives do not wish to participate directly in monetary system reform and have no direct power over government negotiators. It is suggestive, however, that each major shift in the system has coincided with the general preferences of the business community, which seemingly have influenced the scope of decisions open to governments.

Businessmen and bankers vocally reject a return to fixed rates. Predictions of the dire consequences of such a move abound. At the same time, many private executives are unsure that exchange rates will stabilize without government intervention and fear "yo-yo" profits could damage their companies by inflaming shareholder anger and uncertainty.[45] Although unconcerned by the nature of the reserve asset, the automaticity of government intervention, or the level of internationalization of control of the monetary regime, private officials want flexibility without floating to triumph. Their wish has been granted.

However, the new system stabilized more than a year after central banks and private actors opted for a middle position, and government officials, concerned with all dimensions of reform, were slow to respond to these messages. In 1971, 1973, and 1976 governments did not bow to the will of the private sector (indeed the private sector often did not know its own will) but to the structure and behavior of markets and market participants.

Summary and Conclusions

In summary, the analysis of the flexibility preferences of various actors through time helped predict the direction of monetary reform. The evolution of these preferences in the past decade is traced in Figure 6.1. In 1925 and 1944 the preferences of one or two groups and several individuals could help predict the outcome of international monetary negotiations. Today, the interactive network comprising numerous public and private actors must be examined before drawing conclusions concerning the future of monetary reform.

June 1965	FIXED CB*MNC FR MNB US			FLOAT
March 1972	FIXED CB	* MNB MNC US		FLOAT
April 1973	FIXED CB FR	MNC US/MNB	*	FLOAT
November 1973	FIXED FR	CB * MNC	US MNB	FLOAT
September 1974	FIXED FR	CB MNB * MNC	US	FLOAT
January 1976	FIXED	FR CB MNB * US MNC		FLOAT

CB: Central banks (assumed to act more or less together).

FR: French finance ministry. (Japanese would be in a similar position.)

US: U.S. Treasury. (Other OECD finance ministries are usually located somewhere between the U.S. and French extremes.)

MNC: Multinational corporations (assumed to be relatively unitary in their preferences).

MNB: Multinational banks (assumed to be more unitary here than is actually the case. After June 1974 some banks remained in favor of floating exchange rates).

*   Approximate amount of flexibility of monetary system during selected months.

Figure 6.1: The Shifting Positions of Major Actors on a Fixed-Float Preference Concerning Exchange Rates, 1965-1976

Apparently, banks and MNCs are particularly crucial in channeling government negotiators towards monetary reforms. Although their participation in the negotiation process is minimal, their increasing power to destabilize exchange rates and monetary regimes through the capital markets leads negotiators to certain solutions. Private pressure cannot force agreement. Private officials did not speed the reform process between mid-1974 and early 1976. However, they hold an effective veto over articulated reform plans. In February 1973, when governments attempted to retreat to a fixed rate system, which the private sector believed unworkable, banks and MNCs vetoed the system. Similarly, had negotiators decided on free floating or fixed rates after Herstatt, the reforms would have collapsed under the weight of private actions.

This private sector role is strikingly different from those examined earlier. Bank behavior played an important part in determining the success or failure of exchange regulations, but banks were unable to exert effective pressure on decision-makers to move towards a system of controls desired by the banks. While banks circumvented some restraints, they could not nullify those directed at them. Indeed, the more they circumvented regulations, the more government officials imposed new, more stringent restrictions on bank activities.

Potential bank power was also effective in pressuring officials and affecting crisis outcomes when government officials relaxed their will and vigil. While the potential for indirect power during monetary crises remains considerable, the power of banks could be short-circuited by firm government resolve or by threats to the stability of the international banking system. Nonetheless, bank and corporate indirect influence played an important role in the search for monetary reform. Table 6.1 places bank influence in the context of previous chapters.

In this chapter private indirect power was purest since it was independent of participation in reform negotiations. Private power was based not on intent but one behavior motivated by microeconomic goals. Since the preferences of public and private participants in the international monetary realm which relate to the desired level of exchange rate flexibility were grounded in different considerations, experience taught each group different lessons. Given the potential to disrupt the monetary system and individual exchange parities, private actors' preferences became critical to any consideration of viable monetary reform.

Table 6.1: Influence Employed by Banks in the International Monetary System

	Direct Influence	Circumventing Influence	Indirect Influence
Response to:	Existing or proposed policies or legislation.	Policies and legislation aimed at market participants.	Policies and legislation aimed at controlling the economic system.
Channels:	Lobbying Personnel transfer Public appeals Bribery	Capital flows Currency exchanges International structure	Capital flows Currency exchanges International structure
Strategy:	Persuasion	Evasion	Coercion
Impact on:	Policy-making	Policy effectiveness	Economic outcomes
Intent:	Conscious	Conscious at primary level. May have unintentional side effects.	Conscious or unintentional at both primary and secondary levels.
Influence at work during:			
Exchange Regulations	Persuaded officials to adjust policies to treat all banks fairly. Unable to persuade U.S. to remove constraints.	Learned to evade regulation, making them ineffective. Unintended expansion of banking, Euromarkets was important result.	Little or no indirect influence.
Exchange Crises	Gave advice which was largely ignored.	"Tools" created by evading exchange restraints used to wield indirect power.	Major impact on the development of crises, their timing, and resolution, particularly when low government will.
Monetary Reform	Gave advice which was largely ignored.	Little or no circumventing influence.	Along with MNCs, shaped the dimension of possible monetary reform with implicit threat to transfer funds.

NOTES

1. These include: Milton Friedman, "The case for flexible exchange rates," in *Essays for Positive Economics* (Chicago: University of Chicago Press, 1953): 157-203; Charles Kindleberger, "The benefits of international money," *Journal of International Economics* 2 (September 1972): 425-442; and George Halm, "Toward limited flexibility of exchange rates," in George Halm (ed.) *The Bürgenstock Papers*: 3-26.

2. Stephen Cohen, *International Monetary Reform, 1964-1969: The Political Dimension* (New York: Praeger, 1970) attempts to apply strategic concepts to questions of monetary reform but does not consider either the private sector or bureaucratic politics in his analysis. Robert Russell, "Toward explaining the politics of international monetary reform," revision of a paper presented to the American Political Science Association, New Orleans, September 3, 1973, takes the important steps of discriminating between agencies of each government's bureaucracy and contains some analysis of the role of the academic economist and business community. Ken Oye, "Bargaining, belief-systems, and bullion," Harvard Ph.D. dissertation, 1977, examines the 1933 World Economic Conference using a similar, though more complex, framework.

3. John Odell interviews.

4. See, Robert Triffin, *Gold and the Dollar Crisis* (New Haven, Conn.: Yale University Press, 1961).

5. An intriguing suggestion to "crown" the dollar is: Emile Despres, Charles Kindleberger, and Walter Salant, "The dollar and world liquidity: a minority view," *The Economist* (February 5, 1966): 526-529.

6. To plot MNC flexibility preferences, executives' public and interview statements were examined. These were classified according to their relative desire for flexibility. Remarkable agreement emerged among various sources. The changes in preferences were confirmed in interviews with Professor Rita Rodriguez of Harvard Business School and James Burtle of W. R. Grace during February 1976.

7. Interviews with representatives from Morgan Guaranty and Brown Brothers Harriman, New York, June 1974, and a representative of Bankers Trust, London, October 1974.

8. To determine the direction of change of bank opinion on flexibility in the monetary system, public and interview statements of bankers were examined. Although individuals disagreed as to the desirable degree of flexibility, every interviewee concurred on general industry changes in preferences concerning flexibility. While impossible to fine tune this measurement, the general timing and direction of bank flexibility preferences were unmistakeable.

9. Judgment concerning central bank positions and preferences was based on information from interviews and from explanations of central bank policies reported in the Bank of England *Quarterly Bulletin* and the New York Federal Reserve Bank *Monthly Review*.

10. Russell, "Toward explaining," has already classified finance ministry preferences over time.

11. See, Robert Russell, "Transgovernmental interaction in the international monetary system," *International Organization* 27 (Autumn 1973): 431-464.

12. While confidence in the dollar was high, central banks earned interest on their dollar reserves, but not on gold reserves.

13. John Odell interviews.

14. Sherman Maisel, *Managing the Dollar* (New York: W. W. Norton, 1973): 217-221.

15. Charles Coombs, *The Arena of International Finance* (New York: John Wiley, 1976): 210.

16. Ibid.

17. See, John Odell, "Sources of foreign policy change," Chapter 3.

18. Stephen Cohen, op. cit.: 53.

19. Russell, "Toward explaining": 33.

20. Robert Fitzsimons, "Who are the 'currency speculators'?" *The Banker* 121 (November 1971): 1277-1281.

21. Managers of foreign exchange operations for Chemical Bank, First National Bank of Chicago, Bankers Trust, and Wells Fargo Bank all concurred in this view.

22. Russell, "Toward Explaining."

23. Conversation with Peter Peterson at Harvard Business School, January 21, 1976.

24. *American Banker,* August 17, 1971.

25. *American Banker,* August 20, 1971.

26. Interviews with three representatives of the New York Federal Reserve Bank, June 1974.

27. Interview with a former high Treasury official, March 1976.

28. New York *Times,* March 17, 1973.

29. Coombs, op. cit.: 219-229.

30. C. Fred Bergsten, *Reforming the Dollar: An International Monetary Policy for the United States* (New York: Council on Foreign Relations, 1972): 7.

31. Paul Volcker, Seminar at the Center for International Affairs, Harvard, January 16, 1976.

32. *Wall Street Journal,* February 15, 1973.

33. *Wall Street Journal,* February 26, 1973.

34. See, Salant, op. cit.

35. According to one former New York Federal Reserve Bank representative interviewed in June, 1974, the only developed nations which had their central banks intervening in exchange markets between March 19 and July 9, 1973 were Canada and Japan.

36. Richard Blackhurst, "Spot markets under floating rates," *The Banker* 124 (January 1976): 30.

37. *Business Week,* January 26, 1976: 52.

38. Ibid.: 48.

39. Interviews with a former Treasury representative and with the Treasurer of a major MNC. Also see, Interview with Hans Oei of Unilever, *The Banker* 124 (August 1974): 337-390.

40. Interviews with a representative of the New York Federal Reserve Bank, June 1974 and with a representative of National Westminster Bank, London, October, 1974.

41. John Williamson has argued that central bank intervention after March 1973 was as frequent and as massive as in preceding periods. In the three months following the Jamaica Accords, the central banks were forced into massive, record intervention. New York *Times,* May 1976.

42. Interviews with representatives of Morgan Guaranty, Bankers Trust, and Chemical Bank, London, October 1974.

43. Interviews with representatives of Bankers Trust, Bishops International, and the International Commercial Bank, London, October, 1974.

44. Interview with James Burtle, W. R. Grace, February 1975.

45. See, Robert Abboud's testimony in *How Well are Fluctuating Rates Working?* p. 92.

Chapter 7

BANK LENDING TO NON-OIL

DEVELOPING NATIONS, 1970-1977

International borrowing by non-OPEC developing nations increased substantially during the 1970s to fund ambitious development projects and to relieve balance of payments tensions provoked by the 1973 quadrupling of petroleum prices. Medium- and long-term indebtedness of non-OPEC developing countries rose from $90 billion at the end of 1974 to $145 billion at the end of 1976. Debt service payments reached $21 billion in 1976, a 75 percent increase over 1973. Approximately one half of new non-OPEC LDC debt since 1975 came from private sources, a relatively new phenomenon. As a result, by mid-1977 about 40 percent of non-OPEC LDC debt was held by the private sector, mostly on terms less generous than those granted by official lending institutions.[1] American banks alone were owed about $45 billion by non-OPEC developing nations by mid-1976.[2]

This chapter examines the expanding importance of private banks for relations between industrialized and developing nations. Has increased private lending to non-oil LDCs resulted in the emergence of commercial banks as central political actors in the negotiations surrounding the proposed New International Economic Order? If so, what are the dimensions of private banks' influence over relations between industrialized and developing nations? Conversely, has the new abundance of petrodollars allowed OPEC nations to manipulate commercial bankers in their interactions with industrialized nations? As before, the focus remains on the political effect of commercial banks on relations among nations, not on bankers' influence over national politics and policies. Others are beginning to explore that realm.[3]

Private Lending to National Governments

The proliferation of overseas U.S. banking ventures in the 1960s was provoked by American exchange restrictions and corporate clients' borrowing needs, not by the lure of lucrative loans to national governments. While sovereigns and states have long borrowed from private bankers, their repayment record is mixed. U.S. bankers were active throughout the 1920s during the heyday of dollar diplomacy, but retreated at the outset of the global depression. In the 1950s and 1960s American bankers funded loans to foreign governments from their domestic headquarters without wandering the globe. However, interbank competition for corporate clients stiffened as the potential of the burgeoning Eurocurrency markets became clear and U.S. bankers began contemplating new loans to developed country governments.

European nations sought to stabilize their economies in the wake of energy price increases by supplementing IMF drawings with balance of payments loans from international banking syndicates. Great Britain, France, and Italy all borrowed heavily from private sources. Commercial banks, flushed with newly deposited petrodollars and pressed by deteriorating profit margins in their commercial lending, were delighted to lend stable, developed democracies almost unlimited funds at favorable interest rates. However, in the "borrower's market" of the early 1970s, loan margins for industrialized nations plummetted to as little as 3/8 of 1 percent over the cost of money to the lending institutions. Lending risks increased as bankers made profits on loan volume rather than on loan margins. Bankers began searching for new profitable activities.

Hungry non-oil LDCs were obvious potential borrowers. The great attraction of LDC loans to banks were the high, front-end service fees collected by managers and the relatively large spread LDC borrowers would pay for funds. Although lending to non-oil LDCs was perceived as riskier than lending to industrialized nations, banks' bargaining positions were better and therefore their profits were higher in the developing world. David Rockefeller acknowledged the changing texture of international banking when he wrote, "Multinational finance service corporations were called upon not only to expand their traditional activities, but also to take on important new responsibilities as well."[4]

Table 7.1 reproduces IBRD and Citibank estimates of the magnitude of bank claims on selected non-oil developing nations at the end of 1976. Mexico

Table 7.1: Total Long-Term Public and Publicly Guaranteed External Debts of Selected Developing Countries[a] (billions of U.S. dollars)

Non-OPEC LDCs	End-1973		End-1974		End-1975		End-1976
	Total Debt	Owed Banks	Total Debt	Owed Banks	Total Debt	Owed Banks	Total Debt
Latin America							
Argentina	2.89	.66	3.35	.63	3.16	.52	4.20
Brazil	6.92	2.60	9.30	4.40	11.50	5.80	15.00
Chile	3.04	.51	3.73	.55	4.00	.50	4.20
Colombia	1.94	.22	2.12	.20	2.36	.37	2.70
Mexico	5.42	2.36	8.08	4.24	11.25	6.66	14.00
Peru	1.44	.56	2.07	.95	2.67	1.34	3.30
Asia							
Korea	3.20	.31	3.98	.64	5.23	1.00	6.20
India	10.40	.03	11.24	.01	11.88	.02	12.20
Pakistan	4.30	.06	4.52	.08	4.89	.11	5.50
Philippines	.81	.22	1.03	.28	1.28	.32	1.80
Taiwan	.96	.05	1.16	.14	1.69	.42	1.90
Thailand	.44	.01	.51	.02	.62	.05	.80
Africa							
Egypt	1.73	.19	3.89	1.08	6.31	1.21	7.30
Tanzania	.46	.02	.61	.02	.79	.01	.96
Zaire	.89	.41	1.31	.66	1.68	.89	1.90
Zambia	.57	.23	.68	.21	.95	.35	1.20
Total above	45.41	8.44	57.58	14.17	70.26	19.57	83.66
Others	11.89	1.21	15.82	3.03	20.24	4.53	26.34
Total, 77 non-OPEC LDCs	57.30	9.65	73.40	17.20	90.50	24.10	110.00

SOURCE: World Bank and Citibank estimates as cited by Harold van B. Cleveland and W.H. Bruce Brittain, "Are the LDCs in Over Their Heads?" **Foreign Affairs** 55 (July 1977): 734.

a. Debt contracted by the public sector of the borrowing country or by a private borrower with the guarantee of the public sector with an original or extended maturity of more than one year, repayable in foreign currency, goods or services. Such debt encompasses the bulk of a country's external debt, but not all of it. By definition, it excludes all short-term credits and all long-term nonguaranteed private borrowings. Adding these credits to long-term external public debt brings the total debt of 71 non-oil LDCs outstanding at the end of 1976 to somewhere around $160 billion. Data on public and publicly guaranteed debt is collected and published by the World Bank. Unfortunately, the data on the other types of debt is neither as reliable nor as comprehensive as that of the World Bank and is therefore of only limited value.

and Brazil had borrowed more than five times as much from U.S. banks as other non-oil LDCs. South Korea, Argentina, Peru, Taiwan, and the Philippines were also major non-OPEC borrowers. All these nations relied heavily on private, foreign borrowing when their economic growth sputtered after 1973. Their borrowing demands outstripped the ability and willingness of international organizations and industrialized governments to provide loans and aid on favorable terms.

Even after commercial banks were rocked by foreign exchange fiascos in 1974, their lending to the wealthier developing nations increased. Bankers saw these loans as a semisafe alternative to foreign exchange activities and to real estate and tanker lending, and not as part of an interdependent banking system. Risks surrounding LDC lending were perceived as real, but acceptable. Even then, richer LDCs were forced to borrow from more expensive Eurocurrency markets while most industrialized nations could borrow fixed rate, long-term funds from the Eurobond market. Commercial bankers never seriously considered heavy Eurocurrency lending to extremely poor nations unable to generate sufficient cash flows to repay their borrowing. Throughout, Citibank, which made 40 percent of their 1974 profits in developing nations, served as a model for commercial lenders.[5] However, only Citibank, Chase Manhattan, and Bank of America among U.S. banks possess sufficient international diversity of operations to weather a major default in a large LDC. Smaller commercial banks with international operations concentrated in several nations are potentially more vulnerable to a single major loss in one of those nations.

Lending to non-oil LDCs has several attractions for commercial banks. First, banks can earn higher rates of returns by lending to LDCs rather than to prime customers, because loan margins and service fees are usually higher on LDC deals. Second, banks believe that LDC lending insures their continuing participation in these nations' economic future. If commercial bankers feel they can avoid major defaults and rescheduling problems by splitting risks, they eagerly enter nations which show potential for economic development.[6] Bankers stress and LDCs realize that defaults destroy a nation's credit-worthiness worldwide. Therefore, until recently, bankers felt relatively safe since LDC's international financing needs were pressing. Third, bankers can often minimize their direct exposure to default and expropriation by lending funds deposited in an overseas branch to borrowers in that nation. Citibank's Cuban experience is illustrative. Castro's expropriation of Citibank's assets and liabilities cancelled each other out, leaving Citibank with a small profit on the transaction.[7] Although Eurocurrency lending often makes such balancing impossible, bankers believe that their risks are manageable.

By the mid-1970s bankers eagerly lent to LDCs as well as to shaky MNCs and industrialized nations. David Harum's classic definition of banking as "lending money and getting it back" was no longer accurate. Today, contrary to popular belief, bankers don't want to be repaid. They want to feel confident that they could be repaid. Bankers prefer borrowers which dutifully repay the interest on their loans while maintaining steady or slightly increasing borrowings. If a large loan is repaid, bankers must relend the funds or allow them to idle in less profitable investments. In an economy where loan demand is slack, banks must maintain existing loan levels or face declining profits and edgy stockholders.[8] Formerly, a renewable loan to General Motors was ideal for banks. At present a profitable loan to Mexico is perceived as an even better use of funds. Indeed, the current slack in loan demand coupled with tremendous petrodollar liquidity strongly impels international banks to maintain their international lending to non-oil LDCs. Even if world liquidity dries up, the profitability of LDC loans predisposes banks to continue to deal with developing nations.

Even before the oil embargo, commercial banks stepped up their lending to non-oil LDCs because official institutions could or would not meet existing loan demand. The World Bank's lending policies were questioned. Critics argued that IBRD loans should go to the neediest and not to the most likely to repay.[9] While LDCs prefer soft, official loans over private loans, most growing LDCs wish to supplement available official capital.

During the Vietnam War, congressional disillusionment with U.S. foreign aid efforts resulted in severe cutbacks. Even the Export-Import Bank, an export promoting institution which lends money to buyers of U.S. goods, fell on hard times.[10] While European nations approached U.N. foreign aid goals, available funds were insufficient to match LDC demand.[11] Increased OPEC aid was concentrated in nations with large Moslem populations and did not offset the energy financing needs created by rising energy costs. Indeed, despite OPEC promises to redistribute their petroleum earnings, the quadrupling of oil prices hurt non-oil developing nations most. The State Department estimates that two thirds of the balance of payments deterioration among non-oil LDCs since 1973 were caused by rising energy costs.[12] This situation forced both LDCs and industrial nations to turn to commercial banks to finance a portion of their balance of payments deficits.

Commercial banks were ideal sources for LDCs searching for funds. Banks had petrodollars and were willing to lend them. Since outstanding private debt to developing nations was manageable, banks could build substantial portfolio positions before reaching their self-imposed country lending limits. Until early 1975 few private bankers believed that some LDCs might be saturated with funds and potentially insolvent. Privately, bankers admit that their liquidity-laden institutions over-lent to LDCs unable to demonstrate their capacity to repay loans. They cringe but admit that LDC charges of over-lending are substantially valid.[13]

Such overoptimism was epitomized by the financing of $670 million pipeline which raised Peru's external debt by 20 percent. Unfortunately, despite early encouraging signs, insufficient oil was discovered to allow the pipeline to pay for itself. Although it would have been sensible to ship recovered oil through Brazil, private bankers financed the pipeline without proof of its feasibility.[14]

Private lenders are approaching their lending limits even where LDCs have religiously serviced their debts. Mexico, Brazil, and other developing nations cannot and will not continue to increase their borrowing at the present rate. In essence, private loans to LDCs are made to the country and not to individual institutions. Most bankers believe that since LDC governments guarantee most loans, in case default, all of a nation's international debts would sour and not just some proportion of them. As a result, bank prospectuses for new LDC loans are based more on national outlooks than on the potential of the individual borrowers.[15] Many economists conclude that some LDCs may be unable to generate sufficient cash flows to repay the interest on their loans, much less the principal.[16] Some bankers predict that major reschedulings and defaults on third world loans are inevitable.[17] But bankers are still stuck. They have no desire to pull profitable loans out of the third world, but only to insure prompt loan servicing.

Clearly, bankers would like borrowing government to follow "sensible" economic policies thereby insuring prompt repayment of their debts. They are, however, unable, by and large, to impose such policies on borrowers. Industrialized governments are also hesitant to unilaterally dictate economic policies to the LDCs. Therefore, public and private lenders are increasingly turning to the International Monetary Fund as a key actor controlling the LDC debt situation. As foreign debt mounted and LDC debt service ratio rose to between 25 and 45 percent, the IMF was increasingly promoted to the role of authority. As a major, ostensibly nonpolitical, actor the IMF lent and watched over huge sums of money. In Mexico, commercial banks were soothed when the Mexican government agreed to the IMF demand that it limit its 1977 borrowing from private foreign banks to $3 billion.[18] In June 1977 Gabriel Hauge, the Chairman of Manufacturers Hanover, suggested that banks and the IMF should cofinance international balance of payments loans. Although IMF officials immediately questioned the plan's feasibility, bank-IMF cooperation, tacit and otherwise, is increasing in regard to the formulation of prudent procedures for financing non-oil developing country needs.[19]

Since commercial bankers need third world loans to maintain their current profitability, they are eager for non-oil LDC economies to prosper.[20] Moreover, major LDC defaults could shake and perhaps topple large banks throughout the world. It is therefore sensible to examine past debt renegotiation mechanisms and their implications for future developments. Current "risky" situations should also be considered to better comprehend the potential political role of multinational banking institutions in world politics.

Debt Rescheduling and International Banks

Lending is a two-way street. Banks exert tremendous influence over nations through their ability to extend or deny credit. Banks' lending policies affect national policies and development. However, once banks have extended substantial sums to borrowers, they are, for all practical purposes, committed to the borrower through thick and thin. When huge sums are involved, banks are unlikely to cut their losses and run even though they have no wish to throw bad money after good. Traditionally, when nations have been unable to meet their payments, they have rescheduled their public debts and refinanced their private ones. Public and private lenders are firm because they control the borrower's credit-worthiness but understanding because default would be calamitous. In a game of brinkmanship, however, the threat of complete debt repudiation gives the borrower a clear advantage. The classic example, Russia's threat to default on French loans unless France joined Russia at the outbreak of World War I, illustrates this.[21]

THE CREDITOR CLUB MECHANISM

At the end of the 1960s almost no major Eurocurrency lending to non-oil LDCs had been undertaken. Offshore loans of more than 180 days were rarities. By 1975 almost half of all lending to non-oil LDCs came from private sources. By the end of 1976 about 40 percent of total loans outstanding to non-oil LDCs were private in origin. Yet, little of the principal from even the earliest medium-term Eurocurrency credits has been repaid. This shift in debt composition portends major changes in future rescheduling negotiations. Since 1956 there have been approximately 40 official multilateral debt renegotiations involving 11 developing countries.[22] LDC debtors included Argentina, Brazil, Chile, Ghana, India, Indonesia, Peru, Turkey, and Zaire.[23] Official national and international institutions working under the auspices of an official creditor club almost always occupied center stage in debt renegotiations. Private lenders did not participate in these proceedings although they have sometimes refinanced their own obligations in parallel meetings.

Normally countries threatened by perilously high debt servicing requirements seek relief through the credit club mechanism after establishing a link with the IMF. Paris has been the most frequent host for such negotiations, which are usually chaired by the French Ministry of Finance. Facts are analyzed and umbrella agreement between creditor countries and debtor nations are negotiated. The resolution of differences is usually based on the principle of equal treatment of all creditors and generally sets the tone of subsequent bilateral and private agreements.

Debt rearrangement may consist of (a) a moratorium allowing for temporary suspension of debt service payments; (b) a debt refinancing under which creditors provide debtors with new loans to make possible the continuation or resumption of debt service payments; (c) a debt rescheduling providing for the rephasing of payments of principal and interest on outstanding loans; and (d) debt cancellation.[24] Such arrangements have depended on the creditor clubs' case-by-case approach and focused on conditionality and the mutual interests of creditors and debtors in reaching settlements.[25]

The IMF has played a critical role in many creditor club negotiations by providing assessments of debtor nations' economic situation. The IMF may also provide technical assistance to debtor nations and survey the implementation of the debtor's financial program for creditors. Twice the IMF has also helped debtor nations prepare for private debt renegotiations and then attended the meetings.

While most creditor countries have been pleased with the functioning of creditor clubs, the proliferation of lending to LDCs and the possibility of more frequent renegotiations have provoked a search for new methods. At the 1977 Conference on International Economic Cooperation, Europe and the United States proposed more formal guidelines for future creditors clubs. These proposals were rejected by the developing countries, which would, by and large, have preferred some sort of generalized debt relief. No new agreement emerged.

The growing volume of private lending to non-oil LDCs has also made it necessary to consider private creditor clubs to deal with overextended debt. Although private bankers have not until now participated in official creditor clubs, official lenders have, on occasion, made their agreements with debtors contingent on the willingness of the latter to reach agreement with their private creditors. Frequently, these secondary meetings closely parallel the results of the official creditor clubs, but usually rely on refinancing more than rescheduling. Thus, in Chile in 1972, substantial amounts of bank credits were negotiated by private banks outside the Paris club framework but on terms closely related to official guidelines.[26]

As important as these structures are for the continued economic prosperity of debtors nations and private lenders, it is critical to link the non-oil LDC debt difficulties of the mid-1970s to the wider picture. What are the implications of such problems for the stability of the banking system and for overall relations between industrialized and developing nations? By looking critically at the linkages in creditor-debtor relationships in several cases, it is possible to begin drawing wider conclusions. We shall examine Zaire, the only major nation to directly default and require creditor clubs in the past four years; Indonesia, an OPEC nation nonetheless brought to the brink of default; Peru and Turkey, the most recent flare-ups; and Brazil and Mexico, the two largest LDC debtor nations.

LOANS AND NEGOTIATIONS: ZAIRE

As more banks entered the international fray and undercut established market leaders, large banks wished to find relatively safe, profitable arenas where less experienced interlopers would be fearful to tread. Large banks, faced with handling massive liquidity after 1973, were attracted to Zaire as a potential borrower for their accumulating funds. For those banks, Zaire was a test case. Its rich copper bounty and seemingly unending mineral wealth promised to make Zaire "the Brazil of Africa." On the other hand, its people were poor, its infrastructure primitive, and its birthrate high. Still, the prospect of stable government and high copper, cobalt, and zinc exports persuaded some large commercial banks to consider financing Zaire's growth.

In 1973 fifteen Japanese banks participated in thirty-three separate Eurocurrency loans to Zaire to help assure Japanese access to Zaire's mineral wealth. No other nation's private banks were nearly as active. American and European banks were reluctant to be shut out of this market so they too participated in loans to Zaire, particularly Belgian banks with their traditional involvement in the country. Indeed, any foreign bank with some sort of permanent office in Zaire found it extremely difficult to avoid participation in Zaire's money-raising efforts.[27] U.S. and European banks with representation in Zaire continued to raise money for the country in 1974 and 1975. Significantly, Japanese banks, which were pressed by difficulties in the aftermath of Herstatt's collapse in mid-1974 and were free of entangling investments, did not participate in publicized loans to Zaire after 1973. By the time Zaire faced severe repayment problems in 1975, the Japanese were not making new commitments, but other foreign banks were by then more deeply involved.

Zaire's economy was disrupted by the Angolan civil war, which crippled the transport of copper. The war also impoverished the government of Zaire, which was sending material aid to one faction. Falling copper prices in 1974 and 1975 and Zaire's inept handling of newly nationalized industries siphoned away foreign exchange and left the economy in shambles by late 1975. Banks refused to enter into new agreements and cancelled a previously negotiated but unsigned loan in early 1976 when foreign investors in a new mining project abandoned it.[28] Private banks were left holding approximately $500 million in loans to Zaire, which the government was unable to repay.

In the spring of 1976, after extensive technical aid and advice from the IMF, Zaire announced an economic stabilization plan, requested an official creditors club for the purpose of general debt rescheduling, and expressed willingness to meet with its private creditors. Citibank, Zaire's largest private creditor, organized the private negotiations. Citibank's Dr. Irving Friedman who had previously worked with the IMF and World Bank became the private banks' chief negotiator. In November 1976 commercial creditors agreed to allow Zaire to postpone payment of 85 percent of its 1975 and 1976 source loans for three years and then stretch repayment over another seven years. The remaining 15 percent would be stretched over a three year peiod. Zaire agreed to negotiate with the IMF for eligibility to draw $110 million, which would allow it to begin repaying private creditors. In return, Citibank agreed to make its "best effort" to assemble a $250 million short-term loan, to be used to speed Zaire's industrialization and not to repay the $250 million due to private banks through 1978.

Once the agreement was reached to refinance rather than reschedule, Zaire's government changed tactics. The government insisted that the $250 million be a medium-term, 5-7 year loan rather than the originally negotiated 6 month trade credit. Zaire paid its past interest, but placed the owed principal in a blocked account at the Bank for International Settlements and refused to release it until the $250 million was committed. The banks' "best effort" pledge was deemed insufficient. Zaire used its debt to hold the private banks hostage until the $250 million were delivered. Given the political uncertainties raised by the outbreak of hostilities in Zaire's copper-rich Shaba province, Citibank had not raised the $250 million by early 1978.[29] About a year after the original agreement, Irving Friedman declared before a Senate subcommittee that Zaire was "broke, as broke as any country in the world."[30]

Surprisingly, Zaire's problems have had little effect on the rate and nature of lending elsewhere. Bankers perceived Zaire as a possible new profit source with distinct prospects and problems separating it from other non-oil LDC borrowers. Significantly, despite provocation, commercial banks have not declared Zaire to be in formal default on its debts. Apparently, problems in Chile, Argentina, Peru, and Turkey have been far more important to commercial banks' decision-making concerning LDC loans. Citibankers in particular have attacked the notion that loans to developing nations are in trouble and likely to create massive problems.[31]

LOANS AND NEGOTIATIONS: INDONESIA

In 1977 OPEC member Indonesia's state-owned oil company, Pertamina had tremendous financing difficulties. On November 4, 1976, the day before the Zaire package was announced, Morgan Guaranty indicated that Indonesia might technically be in default on two loan agreements totaling $850 million.[32] While no payments to the American-led syndicates had been omitted, the world's commercial bankers shivered collectively.

Morgan Guaranty, along with Citibank a traditional lead bank for Indonesia, estimated that at the close of 1976 Indonesia had medium- and long-term private debts of approximately $3.44 billion, about 65 percent owed to U.S. banks.[33] U.S. banks have been the dominant and continuing source of funding for Indonesia since 1973. While banks from other nations participated and even comanaged Eurosyndicates, particularly in 1975, they were secondary actors. Japanese banks, more insular in their operations, were American bankers' only real competition.

Pertamina accounted for 72 percent of Indonesia's export earnings in 1975 and for 40 percent of total government revenues. It was a power unto itself, largely unhindered and unchecked by the central government. Pertamina engaged in a wide range of activities including hotels, steel, tankers, and rice estates. It even, for a time, acted as an autonomous development agency financing its own investments from foreign loans and its own earnings. However, Pertamina had insufficient funds to mount its development program without outside funding. Expenses for developing its petroleum reserves are gigantic. Not surprisingly, Indonesia tapped private sources for Pertamina's needs.

In March 1975 a single private lender decided not to refinance its loans to Pertamina past their maturity date. Cash flow problems resulted in a technical default. When the figures were totaled, Pertamina's foreign debt, as of May 1976, was tabulated at $10.5 billion.[34] Pertamina's mismanagement created serious problems for Indonesia's economy and credit-worthiness. Relations between lenders and Pertamina further deteriorated because the company refused to disclose details of its cash flow and repayment capabilities.

At the height of its mismanagement, Pertamina consistently borrowed short-term funds to finance medium- and long-term needs. Bankers apparently assumed that Indonesia's potential wealth protected them and that the government would intervene if necessary to assure eventual repayment. Too little time was spent assessing Pertamina's management and cash flow since its loans were backed, in essence, by Indonesia's future, not by Pertamina. Bank hopes were justified.

The Indonesian government, rather than ruining its credit rating, assumed Pertamina's obligations. It enforced strict new regulations over Pertamina. New loans had to be negotiated and signed by the Bank of Indonesia on behalf of the Ministry of Finance. Pertamina's import and export operations were brought under direct central bank control, export earnings being deposited to the central bank's account. Non-oil projects were canceled or channeled into other governmental departments. Pertamina was also required to make regular, detailed financial reports to the Bank of Indonesia concerning all aspects of its operations. Furthermore, to soothe creditors and unravel Pertamina's activities, Indonesia hired Arthur Young Associated to make a complete financial accounting and retained the investments banks Kuhn, Loeb; Lazard Freres; and S. G. Warburg as financial advisors to the Bank of Indonesia. Finally, the central bank turned to the renegotiation of tanker loans.

Aside from Pertamina's development debts, tanker loans were the most serious, potentially embarrassing situation dividing Indonesia from its international backers. The most publicized problem concerned a suit filed in July 1976 by Bruce Rappoport, Chairman of Inter Maritime Management of Geneva, for payment of $1.25 billion owed to him for providing Indonesia with oil tankers. Since standard loan clauses said, in effect, that if Pertamina or Indonesia failed to repay any loan, all its debts were considered in technical default, Morgan Guaranty and Citibank raised the prospect that Indonesia might be in technical default on its borrowings.[35]

Throughout 1977 Rappoport and the Indonesian government negotiated while foreign creditors watched closely. Indonesia staunchly pushed its position until Rappoport's resistance wavered.[36] More importantly, commercial bankers chose to ride out the storm without demanding formal rescheduling. While the Zaire model was fresh in bankers' minds, private creditors preferred to work out the problems without a formal confrontation. Indonesia's immediate prospects were brighter than Zaire's and the amount of funds at stake were far greater. Liquidity-choked bankers wanted to keep open the possibility of continued Indonesian borrowing without threatening it with massive IMF intervention in its domestic economic policy-making. Indonesia rescheduled credits in 1966, 1967, 1968, and 1970, but never for more than a few hundred million dollars and always on highly concessionary terms. These public refinancings were not as dangerous to Indonesia's economy and development plans as the potential rescheduling of Pertamina's huge debt. Both bankers and government officials were pleased to avoid formal antagonism and relieved when the shipping difficulties began receding. Apparently, Indonesia's OPEC status and large indebtedness helped persuade bankers not to opt for formal debt renegotiations. The politicization and increased media coverage which such a negotiation would have spurred were undesirable for all. In sum, private creditors and the government eagerly avoided confrontation to insure continued or increased future interaction.

LOANS AND NEGOTIATIONS:
OTHER PROBLEM COUNTRIES

Although only Zaire has called a creditors' club since 1974, it has not faced trouble alone. Argentina approached financial collapse in 1976, called for rescheduling, but persuaded banks to extend more funds by ousting Mrs. Peron and imposing an austere new economic program. Peru attempted to avoid IMF constraints by raising private funds in 1976, but when commercial banks soured on their unfamiliar regulatory role, Peru submitted to IMF economic supervision to assure continued financial support. The head of the IMF visiting team, effectively acted as the Peruvian minister of finance.[37] In late 1977 Turkey, burdened by extremely short maturities on its outstanding borrowings, tottered on the brink of financial collapse.

Commercial banks also became concerned about lending to socialist nations. U.S. banks have lent quite heavily to Eastern Europe and the Soviet Union, but avoided China, North Korea, and Albania. In the 1970s western bankers regarded Eastern Europe and the Soviet Union as ideal borrowers. They paid their debts on time, with a minimum of fuss. The image of the trustworthy Communist, however, was dashed when North Korea went into technical default on loans to Swedish, French, Russian, and Japanese banks in late 1975.[38] This event troubled even those bankers with no exposure in North Korea. Western financial institutions, many approaching their Eastern European and Soviet lending limits, started worrying that Communist borrowers might become unwilling or unable to service their debts.[39]

As shown in the examples of Zaire and Indonesia, commercial banks have displayed remarkable restraint and patience in dealing with recent problem debts. Nations have been generously allowed to stretch out their debt payments and rework their debt structure. While Zaire and Peru have had trouble raising new capital, other nations have continued borrowing while working out difficulties. While troubled borrowing nations have submitted to some outside economic supervision, they have maintained strong bargaining positions. Commercial creditors, after all, have not been able to force repayment, have not wanted repayment, and have been choked with liquidity anyway. They have been content with the situation as long as they had confidence in eventual debt servicing.

Except for oil-rich Indonesia, nations with debt servicing difficulties, have not been the largest borrowers in the system. Several questions remain unanswered. Are bank loans to Brazil, Mexico, or other major borrowers in danger? How strong are these nations' bargaining positions? How would trouble in Brazil or Mexico affect the international financial system? What are the likely political roles of private banks if Brazil, Mexico or other key nations founder?

LOANS AND POTENTIAL PROBLEMS:
BRAZIL AND MEXICO

A recent American Express study estimates that one out of four dollars borrowed abroad by LDCs in 1977 will go for debt servicing. By 1980, one out of every two dollars will be used to repay old debts.[40] Brazil and Mexico are by far the largest LDC borrowers, accounting for 44 percent of all outstanding loans to banks by non-oil developing countries. Brazil's total external debt is estimated to be between $25 and $30 billion, of which $13 billion are owed to U.S. banks. Its 1977 debt service burden was approximately $5.3 billion, or 40 percent of its total export earnings. Even with the recent quadrupling of coffee prices and increasing economic diversity, Brazil needed to raise more than $5 billion to finance its 1977 payments deficit. Mexico's external debt is only marginally smaller, around $26 billion, half owed to U.S. banks, and debt servicing eats up about 30 percent of its total export earnings. In addition, the 40 percent devaluation of the peso in 1976 meant that Mexico's servicing requirements became much heavier because its major financial obligation to foreigners are denominated in dollars.[41]

American banks claim that risk splitting would minimize their losses in even a major national default. This assumption is questionable. Brazilian profits alone accounted for 13 percent of Citibank's total 1976 earnings (compared to 28 percent in the U.S.). Chase Manhattan made 78 percent of its more meager 1976 earnings abroad and listed Brazil as its fourth largest exposure after Japan, the United States, and the United Kingdom.[42] Mexican profits for these and other major U.S. banks are only slightly smaller. In addition, some banks have placed more than 10 percent of their capital, the U.S. legal lending limit, in Mexico and Brazil by extending credit to several ostensibly independent government agencies or government enterprises. Should either country repudiate its debts or be unable to meet its payments, the entire U.S. banking structure would be threatened. Therefore, banks study developments in Brazil and Mexico closely even as they continue to extend them credit.

Not surprisingly, American banks have been the key lenders to Brazil and even more to Mexico.[43] Whether banks can or want to curtail their lending to non-oil LDCs is a major question. An August 1977 Senate committee report concluded, "The fact is, the big banks are now so deeply enmeshed in the whole deficit financing process that they cannot afford to say 'no,' either to their major depositors or to their major borrowers."[44] Though many banks have reached or almost reached their lending limits to non-oil LDCs, they must continue to slowly expand their lending to these nations or face the strong possibility of severe repayment problems. There is no short-term escape from this dilemma. The problem is heightened by the existence of "cross-default clauses," which throw a borrower who is in official default against any single creditor, into automatic default on all its loans. Any bank then can call its outstanding loans for immediate repayment. If, as is likely, the the borrower is unable to pay, the whole system could collapse. This was one reason that banks were extremely cautious not to declare Zaire, Indonesia, or Peru to be *officially* in default.

Neither Brazil nor Mexico have requested or desired rescheduling of their loan obligations. Indeed, their international borrowing has continued to climb. When many developing nations advocated some form of general debt forgiveness at the Conference on International Economic Cooperation in Paris in 1976 and 1977, these two nations quietly but forcefully opposed this initiative. Brazil and Mexico believed that a forgiveness motion, if pressed too far, would isolate them from their private creditors at a time when they were eager to continue borrowing. Richer LDC borrowers perceived debt rescheduling as an exercise which would mainly benefit India, Pakistan, and several other nations with large public but almost no private loans outstanding.[45] Richer borrowers feared that even a solely public debt rescheduling would discourage further private lending.

From private bankers' perspective, Mexico and Brazil have and will continue to exert great attraction. Mexico has two great advantages. Its newly discovered petroleum reserves promise to return it to its former prominence as an energy exporter. If the petroleum fields test out and can be tapped, Mexico will have little difficulty repaying its vast borrowings. American lenders also are attracted by Mexico's contiguous border with the United States. Most creditors feel that the U.S. government is so involved with Mexico's economy that it would aid the Mexican government and U.S. lenders if disaster struck. As a result, Mexico is almost always the first developing nation with which U.S. banks become involved. It is the gateway to Latin America and the testing ground for novice lenders.

Even while encouraged by Mexico's economic potential and geographic position, international creditors worry about Mexico's recent economic performance, its lopsided reliance on future oil wealth, and its underlying, potentially explosive, social problems. Banks are uncertain of its financial officials and perceive the government planning mechanism as overly rigid. Social and economic disarray could scuttle the economy, distract the government, and make it difficult to continue servicing foreign debts.

Commercial banks are not totally reassured about Mexico's prospects. Their high liquidity levels and the profitability of the loans, press them towards further lending. While margins have fallen in 1976 and 1977, banks have resisted the pressure to emulate 1976's lengthening of terms. Thus in mid-1977 when Nacional Financiera, Mexico's development agency, wished to raise at least $200 million, the agency adopted a "renewal" technique. It wanted ten year money but realized that it would be difficult to raise and so offered potential lenders the option to withdraw or roll-over their loans every two years. In effect, the Mexicans attempted to negotiate a two-year loan which creditors could renew four times.[46]

Brazil, the other huge LDC borrower of private funds, faces different problems and opportunities than Mexico. It lacks Mexico's proven oil reserves, but is nonetheless incredibly rich in resources and increasingly diverse in output. While it has borrowed more money than Mexico, the maturities of these debts are spaced carefully to assure that they do not come due for repayment simultaneously.[47] In addition, Brazil estimates and publishes its global debt and not just its external public or state-guaranteed debt. Across all categories of debt, Brazil's situation looks brighter. Foreign commercial bankers are also pleased by Brazil's conscientious willingness to disclose its exact debt position and work with creditors to rationalize the lending and repayment of funds and by the openness and accessibility of Brazilian officials.[48] These factors ease the red tape involved in creating a lending syndicate and improve Brazil's attractiveness to lenders. Brazil also is working scrupulously with the IMF to control its domestic economy and has experimented with six month, renewable bankers' acceptances. So far, the major issue of renewable acceptances for Petrobras (the Brazilian Oil Company) has been rolled-over successfully.[49] Indeed, most bankers like the "feel" of the Brazilians and slightly prefer to lend to Brazil than to Mexico despite the former's lack of oil reserves.

To summarize, although private lending to Brazil and Mexico are unlikely to continue growing as rapidly in the future, commercial bankers remain willing to finance these nations because their prospects remain strong. Banks are also so committed to these countries' eventual success that they can only marginally discourage further loans. Creditors, however, are cautious to spread risks as widely as possible, to work against lengthening loan terms, and to take as much of their profits as possible up front. Thus, despite incomplete data, it is nonetheless clear that the ratio of managers to participants in publicized Eurocurrency loans to both Mexico and Brazil has increased steadily since 1973, more than doubling in three years.[50] Fewer banks will participate in syndicates without receiving a share of the lucrative management fee. As a result, the average number of managers required to raise a fixed sum of money has increased in recent years. However, commercial creditors seemingly have separated their experiences in Zaire, Indonesia, and Eastern Europe from their Latin American lending. Geographic divisions within commercial banks and bankers' perception that Zaire was a failed experiment and Indonesia a special oil-laden case partially account for this separation. In addition, Western bankers are more often at home with the mentality and business operations in Latin America, where their experience is longer and their confidence remains, perhaps unjustly, high. Nonetheless, the vast loans raised abroad by Mexico, Brazil and other richer developing nations have created a system of mutual hostages. Without continued bank support, many nations' economies could disintegrate. Without borrowers' cooperation, industrialized nations' economic stability and numerous large banks' survival could be threatened. This reciprocal hostage situation has important implications for international political relations between developed and developing nations in the next decade.

Lending, Debt, and the New
International Economic Order

While the history of actual default in the post-World War II era is encouraging, the longer view is less heartening. Charles Kindleberger feels that a longer view of LDC debt indicates that

> productive loans in developing countries are not very productive and do not stay long out of default. The reasons are several. In the first place, the lending occurs in bursts, often called "manias," precipitated if not caused by some shock to the system, whipped up by euphoric excitement, overdone, with the borrower typically getting less than it is committed for, and being forced to suspend debt service in the next recession.[51]

Banks prefer lending for cash flow-generating projects which will allow borrowers to meet their obligations. They prefer not to finance consumption and infrastructure, are uneasy about financing payments deficits, and would rather not refinance previous loans. However, since banks are essentially lending to countries and not to discrete LDC borrowers, fungibility makes strict accounting impossible. Given banks' need to lend, the amounts already extended, and the potential inability of nations to repay their debts, it seems probable that debt and debt rescheduling may become the preeminent issue in relations between the industrialized and developing worlds in the next decade. What role will bankers play?

At the CIEC meetings many non-oil LDCs demanded that some plan for general debt forgiveness be adopted. As proposed, the program would have covered official debts and also, if possible, private debts. The industrialized nations with some covert LDC aid successfully fought this initiative. Mexico, Brazil, and other LDCs with extensive private debt realized that such a move could not be completely successful without totally isolating LDCs from further private lending, and the whole idea was buried. The private bankers, who watched the CIEC meetings nervously, obviously opposed the LDC initiative.

Instead, richer LDCs are seeking ways to insure high prices for their commodity exports. Poorer LDCs are also pushing for this action.[52] Unlike debt forgiveness, high commodity prices would, in theory, benefit private overseas creditors.[53] The commercial banks have remained silent until now. They believe that higher commodity prices might be in their interest, but hesitate to become enmeshed in political negotiations. Banks hope that the proposed New International Economic Order is an economic, not a political thrust by the LDCs.[54] If economic, LDC success would lead to more certain debt servicing and eventual repayment. If the NIEO initiative is mainly political, LDC success might lock foreign financiers more deeply into a no-win situation.

In any event, commercial banks are extremely pleased by the IMF's recent resurgence. The IMF, at its nadir, was stripped of all initiating power by Nixon and Simon to protect U.S. dominance within the international monetary scene. Simon's departure and the deteriorating international debt outlook prompted an American policy shift. Since the U.S. officials had no wish to dictate domestic economic policy to LDCs, it accepted the IMF leadership on the debt issue. Managing Director Johannes Witteveen proposed stricter IMF supervision over nations borrowing heavily from the IMF but also a more generous special fund for dispersement as necessary among developing nations. This fund would backstop troubled borrowing nations. In effect, the IMF became a strict but kindly lender of last resort. Commercial bankers were delighted because the Witteveen facility inserted an additional layer of protection between themselves and third world default. Bankers were particularly pleased because the IMF provided long-run support. In case of short- or medium-run problem, there was some possibility that bankers might get out and leave the IMF holding the bag. Bankers were also pleased with IMF participation in managing borrowers' economies. They realized that their own bargaining position, once substantial funds were committed, was poor and therefore supported any move to stabilize third world economies and assure their continued economic survival.

While richer LDCs have gained substantial bargaining clout within Western financial circles which may strengthen their efforts to form a NIEO, Arab OPEC nations have made no comparable strides. Although Middle Eastern oil nations have earned billions of petrodollars since 1973, their influence within the banking system has been marginal. As conservative depositors in an overliquid market, they have been able to demand little. By mid-1974, some major banks refused to accept short-term OPEC deposits.[55] Simultaneously, Arab investment policies became more conservative after the Herstatt collapse. Since many Arab oil nations refused to deposit funds for long terms or with smaller, less secure institutions, favored bankers, in essence, told them how and where to invest their fortunes.

Arab OPEC power was also not manifest in their spending plans. While petrodollar investments were conservatively administered by a limited number of officials supported by foreign financial advisors, petrodollar purchases were wildly extravagant and wasteful. Bribery, greed, and waste made it impossible for Arab purchases to use their acquisitions to further specific policy goals. Recently, Arab governments have changed tactics. They are borrowing Eurofunds to lock Western technology and commitment into their development projects.[56] They place funds in the market and borrow them back to create an obligation to Western banks. While Arab OPEC nations may eventually tie bankers' fates to their future, they are unlikely to rival LDCs in importance for the politics of the international economic system in the next decade.

Many observers fear that Arab OPEC nations could undermine the monetary system by rapidly moving funds from currency to currency. Perhaps this is true, but the damage to Arab nations would be too great to contemplate. Even discounting possible invasion or food embargoes, Arab nations would nonetheless be slitting their own economic throats. They could not shift money fast enough to avoid massive devaluation of their capital and would probably find their funds frozen if they removed funds too incautiously. Although Arab assets helped persuade the United States to bury rhetorical threats of invasion and commercial banks to acquiesce in the Arab embargo of Israel, their influence was distinctly tempered.[57] They hesitate to invest money too openly or to buy control of major companies in industrialized nations since this might provoke increased public, union, and governmental hostility.[58] Neither did they overreact when California and other states forbade corporations to abide by the boycott of Israel. As long as world liquidity remains great, Arab nations cannot take the offensive against commercial banks or developed' nations except at tremendous costs to their nations and economies. If and when excess liquidity is absorbed, banks may continue to find their best interests lie in siding with non-oil developing nation borrowers.

Summary and Concluding Thoughts

In summary, bankers from industrialized nations, even as they protest the credit-worthiness of non-oil LDC borrowers, have fallen prey to these borrowers. The banks are hostages. At first glance, it is startling that they are willing hostages. On the one hand, they seek to maximize their repayment possibilities. To this end LDC prosperity supported by high commodity prices and IMF domestic economic supervision help bankers. On the other hand, it is frequently overlooked that bankers would not wish to cancel their LDC loans. These loans are profitable at a time when other opportunities are vanishing. They are likely to remain profitable in the foreseeable future. Thus, while experimental lending to Zaire ran into substantial problems, this did not discourage bank lending to other developing nations. Bankers also did not declare Indonesia or Zaire in default for fear of launching domino defaults throughout the developing world. Instead, they moved to prop up LDC economies and reinforce the IMF's policing abilities and lending capabilities during crises.

LDC borrowers, however, are also hostages. Private creditors can turn off the funding tap and retard and disrupt the development dreams of borrowing

LDCs. Neither lenders nor creditors wish to destabilize the system since both currently benefit from the arrangement. Banks *need* to lend their funds to counteract the overliquidity and "overcompetitiveness" of the international financial system. Borrowing non-oil LDCs *need* the borrowed funds to continue their ambitious development projects. Both have made concessions to preserve the system. Private banks have searched for ways to bolster the LDC economies and probably would support NIEO demands for higher commodity prices even if this harmed their home nations' economic prosperity. Banks also refrained from the useless move of declaring national borrowers in formal default. At the same time, LDC borrowers allowed the IMF to exert limited control over their economies and moderately rearrange their development priorities to insure continued international credit-worthiness. This reciprocal hostage arrangement suggests that both borrowers and lenders will tiptoe along the precipice as long as possible.

Overall, however, non-oil LDCs have a stronger bargaining position. Default might topple the entire international monetary framework, institutions and all. While lenders could create domestic economic chaos in LDCs, they would probably relent in time, for in the short term, without LDC borrowers, the banking system might be choked by excessive liquidity. In the medium term, banks and governments can perhaps control the growth of the global money supply and limit the "overcompetition" in international banking.[59] In the short run, however, bankers need semisafe borrowers for their funds. Such borrowers are rare today among MNEs and industrial nation governments. The socialist world is looking increasingly unsafe. Non-oil LDCs may be the only available borrowers. If banks feel relatively confident of eventual repayment and prompt loan servicing, funds available to non-oil LDCs might increase rather than decline in coming years. Non-oil LDCs by exercising discretion in their dealings and listening serenely to outside advice, could persuade private borrowers to increase their loans. A little public relations by non-oil LDCs could convert a segment of the private financial community from uneasy hostages to active allies.

Debt will probably be the critical issue dividing the industrialized and non-industrialized world in the coming years. Commercial banks will be more than economic spectators. Their indirect power within the international monetary system may prove both subtle and important. Table 7.2 places this indirect influence into the context of previous chapter.

Table 7.2: Influence Employed by Banks in the International Monetary System

	Direct Influence	Circumventing Influence	Indirect Influence
Response to:	Existing or proposed policies or legislation.	Policies and legislation aimed at market participants.	Policies and legislation aimed at controlling the economic system.
Channels:	Lobbying Personnel transfer Public appeals Bribery	Capital flows Currency exchanges International structure	Capital flows Currency exchanges International structure
Strategy:	Persuasion	Evasion	Coercion
Impact on:	Policy-making	Policy effectiveness	Economic outcomes
Intent:	Conscious	Conscious at primary level. May have unintentional side effects.	Conscious or unintentional at both primary and secondary levels.
Influence at work during:			
Exchange Regulations	Persuaded officials to adjust policies to treat all banks fairly. Unable to persuade U.S. to remove constraints.	Learned to evade regulation, making them ineffective. Unintended expansion of banking, Euromarkets was important result.	Little or no indirect influence.
Exchange Crises	Gave advice which was largely ignored.	"Tools" created by evading exchange restraints used to wield indirect power.	Major impact on the development of crises, their timing, and resolution, particularly when low government will.
Monetary Reform	Gave advice which was largely ignored.	Little or no circumventing influence.	Along with MNCs, shaped the dimension of possible monetary reform with implicit threat to transfer funds.
LDC Loans	Asked governments and IMF to help protect loans by extending official credits and economic supervision.	Little or no circumventing influence.	In future, banks may try to influence developed nations to support LDC demands as a way to insure continued loan servicing by wealthier LDC borrowers.

NOTES

1. State Department estimates provided by Robert Ryan, Acting Deputy Assistant Secretary of State, April 14, 1977.

2. Morgan Guaranty, *World Financial Markets* (December 4, 1976): 4.

3. There have been a virtual deluge of articles in the financial press on bank lending to developing nations and its prospective risks. Even groups of political scientists have taken note. *Foreign Affairs* printed three separate articles on the topic in its July 1977 issue. Two panels on bank lending to developing countries at the joint meeting of the African and Latin American Studies Associations in Houston on November 3, 1977, drew large turnouts, and two more panels on the same topic for the International Studies Association meetings in late February, 1978, in Washington.

4. Cited in Emma Rothschild, "Banks: the coming crisis," New York *Review of Books* (May 27, 1976): 16.

5. Sanford Rose, "Why they call it 'fat city'," *Fortune* (March 1975): p. 108.

6. For a discussion of the mechanisms and risk-splitting possibilities of syndicate lending and consortium bank lending see, Jonathan Aronson, "Politics and the international consortium banks," *Stanford Journal of International Studies* 11 (Spring 1976): 59-66.

7. Cuba actually sued unsuccessfully in U.S. courts to recover the profits Citibank made on the expropriation. *First National City Bank* v. *Banco Nacional de Cuba,* 92 *Supreme Court Reporter* 1808 (1972).

8. This has not always been the case. A decade ago the idea of permanently rolling over loans to a customer would have been doubted by bankers and attacked by government regulators much more quickly.

9. Teresa Hayter, *Aid as Imperialism,* (Harmondsworth, England: Penguin, 1971).

10. Adlai Stevenson, for instance, ran a series of hearings on Eximbank policies in Chile and elsewhere which have brought into serious question the continued existence of the institution.

11. The classic set of recommendations, the report of Lester Pearson's Commission on International Development, *Partners in Development* (New York: Praeger, 1969) was composed by a panel of experts largely from industrialized nations.

12. Robert Ryan, April 14, 1977.

13. Interviews with representatives of Bank of America, United California Bank, and Wells Fargo Bank, Los Angeles, October 1977.

14. *Wall Street Journal,* January 12, 1977.

15. Interviews with representatives of Bank of America, United California Bank, and Wells Fargo Bank, Los Angeles, October 1977.

16. A particularly interesting early study of this sort which concentrated on domestic lending is: Hyman Minsky, "Financial resources in a fragile financial environment," paper prepared for the 17th annual Forecasting Conference of the American Statistical Association, New York, April 18, 1975.

17. In 1976 U.S. banks did, for a time, take an active role in overseeing the Peruvian economy as part of the conditions for a major syndication. All parties were dissatisfied. The exercise is unlikely to be repeated.

18. Interview with United California Bank official, October 1977.

19. *Wall Street Journal,* June 9, 1977 and June 10, 1977.

20. The serious question remains of whether it is so important that certain LDC borrowers prosper that banks would be willing to neglect the interests of their home countries to assure such prosperity.

21. Herbert Feis, *Europe: The World's Banker, 1970-1914* (New York: W.W. Norton, 1965): 210-224.

22. Statement of Under Secretary for Economic Affairs, Richard Cooper, before the Subcommittee on International Finance of the Senate Committee on Banking, Housing and Urban Affairs, August 29, 1977: 4.

23. International Bank for Reconstruction and Development, "Multilateral debt renegotiations: 1956-1968," prepared by Patrick de Fontenay, April 11, 1969: 4.

24. Ibid.: 1.

25. Richard Cooper, statement: 5.

26. Ibid.: 6.

27. Interview with a representative of Bank of America, London, September 1974.

28. David O. Beim, "Rescuing the LDCs," *Foreign Affairs* 54 (July 1977): 727.

29. *Wall Street Journal,* January 7, 1977 and May 24, 1977.

30. Cited in *Barrons* (October 17, 1977): 12.

31. See, G. A. Costanzo, Vice-Chairman Citibank, "Is the third world a sound debtor?" New York *Times* editorial April 18, 1977; and Harold van B. Cleveland and W.H. Bruce Brittain, "Are the LDCs in over their heads?" *Foreign Affairs* 55 (July 1977): 732-750. It is worth noting that the Citibank argument is largely economic rather than political in nature.

32. *Wall Street Journal,* November 5, 1976.

33. Morgan Guaranty, *World Financial Markets* (June 1977): 7.

34. New York *Times,* June 29, 1976. This figure is all types of debts.

35. *Wall Street Journal,* November 5, 1976.

36. *Wall Street Journal,* August 9, 1977.

37. Interview with a representative of United California Bank, Los Angeles, October 1977.

38. These difficulties were first announced in the *Far Eastern Economic Review,* October 1975. North Korea presents a special problem to lenders; it is not a member of the IMF and does not provide lending banks extensive economic data. In addition, it is not a member of COMECON and therefore cannot be pressured through that group.

39. New York *Times,* June 6, 1976; *Wall Street Journal,* February 22, 1977; and Richard Portes, "East Europe's debt to the West: interdependence is a two-way street," *Foreign Affairs* 55 (July 1977): 751-782.

40. U.S. Congress, Senate, Committee on Foreign Relations, "International debt, the banks, and U.S. foreign policy." Report for the Subcommittee on Foreign Economic Policy. Prepared by Karin Lissakers. 95th Cong., 1st sess., 1977: 51.

41. Ibid.: 54.

42. Ibid.: 56.

43. American Express Euromoney Syndication Guide of reported bank participations in Eurocurrency syndications.

44. "International debt, the banks, and U.S. foreign policy": 61.

45. Conversations with Robert Ryan, Department of State.

46. *Wall Street Journal,* June 13, 1977.

47. "Brazil: the lenders and the borrowers," *Euromoney* (June 1976): 48.

48. "Should international banks continue to lend to Brazil?" *Euromoney* (May 1976): 16.

49. Conversation with a representative of Wells Fargo, April 1977.

50. Amex Euromoney Syndication Guide, computed by author.

51. Charles Kindleberger, "Debt situation of the developing countries in historical perspective," paper for a symposium at the Export-Import Bank on Developing Countries' Debt, April 21, 1977, mimeo: 8.

52. LDC demands for NIEO are laid out in the Manila Declaration, UNCTAD 1976.

53. However, L. N. Rangarajan's figures, in his *Commodity Conflict: The Political Economy of International Commodity Negotiations,* (Ithaca: Cornell University Press, 1978) indicate that many LDCs might actually be hurt by general, high commodity prices.

54. Stephen Krasner has been developing the thesis that the NIEO is an almost purely political rather than economic initiative by the LDCs.

55. Interviews with representatives of several American banks in London, October 1974.

56. Interview with a representative of United California Bank, October 1977.

57. Geoffrey Barraclough, "Wealth and power: the politics of food and oil," New York *Review of Books,* August 7, 1975.

58. See, Jonathan Aronson, "The response to Arab and Japanese investment in the United States: a comparison paper," presented at the International Studies Association Meetings, St. Louis, March 1977.

59. See, "The closed currency 'club'," *Business Week* (October 24, 1977): 114-115.

Chapter 8

CONCLUSIONS

Bank pressure on officials *in many issue areas* did increase in the past decade. Bank power over outcomes in the monetary sphere similarly increased. Differences in bank power over outcomes have been dealt with throughout this book and seem related to the growth of the Euromarkets. It is less clear why the level of pressure emanating from banks differed so dramatically on different issues over time. Structural considerations help explain differences in pressure from issue to issue, but do not explain apparent shifts in the magnitude of bank pressure over time on some issues. If these shifts could . be predicted, officials in governments would have considerably more flexibility in deciding whether to allow themselves to be persuaded by private pressure or resist it.

Bank Competition and Pressure

At the outset, it was suggested that changes in the relationship of major private actors or the entry of new actors into the markets alters the magnitude of private pressure exerted on government policy-makers. If so, a close examination of the internal dynamics of private bank competition as well as of the relations between public and private sectors is needed. In particular, the main elements affecting the level of bank-induced pressure on government officials must be analyzed. Pressure may be direct, may build when bank activities force government officials to spend time working on issues, or may force regulators to change policies by making them inefficient or counterproductive.

In theory, increasingly stringent government regulations provoke private opposition in the form of increased direct and circumventing private pressure on officials to alter, relax, or eliminate regulations. In addition, when international developments alter bank profit or planning environments, the level of bank pressure probably will shift. Developments hindering bank operations will result in greater bank pressure while those favoring banks should lead to a relaxation of pressure. However, when political considerations interfere or economic resolve is high, rising direct bank pressure may induce even greater government determination to resist and thus be counterproductive. More subtly, expanding profit opportunities may lead to ardent competition within the banking system and a wave on unintended bank pressure on officials.

Finally, the link between the perceived likelihood of systemic collapse and the level of private pressure, mutes private influence during perceived *system* crises. Since system maintenance is more important to private executives than short-term profit maximization, they reorient their objectives and reduce their pressuring when stability is threatened. Where governments hesitate to support system stability, however, banks may exert considerable direct pressure on them to do so.

Throughout, it is important to remember that the banking system is an integrated whole. It is erroneous to view initiatives and problems in one part of banks' business as isolated from others. Competition in one area presses banks into other fields. Difficulties in a particular type of activity stimulate the search for greener pastures. Thus the potentials and crises surrounding bank activities in foreign exchange and Eurocurrency operations are integrally connected to banks involvement in tanker funding, real estate investment trusts, diversification of business lines, and lending to socialist and developing nations.

INTERNAL PRIVATE SECTOR COMPETITION

Simply stated, it appears that a rapid increase in the intensity of bank competition generates increased direct and indirect pressure on government officials dealing with issues related to the markets in which the competitive shift took place. In practice, an "increase in the intensity of competition" takes place when new, potentially profitable markets open following changes in government regulations or oligopoly control. For example, until January 1, 1976 New York City banks were barred from opening upstate branches. When the new law took effect, the intensity of competition increased. Similarly, the tenfold expansion of U.S. banks active abroad increased the competition in international capital markets.

Rapid changes in a market's competitive intensity may initiate destabilizing processes within the market and focus officials' attention on market issues. The bargaining position between the established oligopolists and the would-be interlopers is central to this process. If the oligopoly triumphs, bank-government relations are unlikely to change greatly. If the oligopoly bends or breaks under the newcomers' initiatives, increased private pressure on governments is likely to follow. Within the international banking system, at least until Herstatt, smaller newcomers were often able to induce large banks to change their policies to combat competition. Since mid-1974, the competition for limited, prime business in a highly liquid environment continued to create minicrises requiring substantial government attention.

The American antitrust tradition is grounded in a fundamental distrust of monopoly power. Based on the experience of the last half of the nineteenth century, in which oligopolies grew while eliminating their rivals, this tradition assumes that large established firms will squash their newer, smaller competitors in the absence of controls. Oligopolists in any industry are likely to be the first to break into profitable new areas. Smaller firms wait in the wings, estimating whether they could successfully enter these new areas. Antitrust laws prohibit an industry oligopoly from preventing smaller companies' entry into an area, though frequently the leaders attempt to do so anyway.[1] In most industries the oligopoly cannot be widely challenged since huge entry costs and existing regulations preclude effective, widescale competition.

However, in industries, such as banking, where small oligopolies never emerged, there are few economies of scale deterring would-be interlopers. Indeed, regulators and regulations prevent the development of an effective oligopoly.[2] A little equity, a little expertise, and a good credit rating was all that was needed to enter London in the 1960s. U.S. exchange regulations and high reported international bank profits persuaded many regional bankers to take the plunge. The bevy of new banks eager to grant credit at marginally better rates to win a London business base forced established banks to follow their leads. Antitrust fears and visibility prevented larger banks from refusing to lend to the newcomers on the interbank markets. Indeed, the newcomers were not so small, usually over $1 billion in assets, and were not completely dependent on international operations for profits. Since regulators would move to insure their continued existence, established banks could not bar them from the market.

In international banking, the competitive maelstrom usually develops as follows. The oligopoly establishes itself in a new market. Fear of losing ground to competitors insures that almost all major industry leaders will enter any new business development.[3] Business and profits are divided among the oligopolists. If profits are substantial, a second tier of firms takes note and begins planning their entry into the market. Often, as in banking in Europe, the imposition or removal of government regulations stimulates the second wave to enter the fray. At any rate, new arrivals, after spending heavily on capital outlays, often discover that the best customers are already locked into contracts with established market leaders. Why should customers choose second rank banks over larger, proven institutions? Only a better price will lure them away. Therefore, newcomers often cut their margins to attract business. They also seek to widen their customer base and to exploit opportunities underutilized by oligopolists. Thus, small banks used foreign exchange markets for profits before large banks. If profit opportunities are less bright than they first appeared, few newcomers will turn around and head for home. American executives are notoriously optimistic and entrepreneurial. Particularly during the go-go years of the 1960s they expected to conquer every dragon they faced.[4] In addition, prestige and egos precluded retreat even if economically justified.[5] Therefore, new banks often cut prices and margins. Business quality deteriorates. This forced newcomers and oligopolists to search for new profit centers. Sometimes movement to overlapping margins, and accepted lower-quality customers. Oligopolists could have refused to follow, but normally chose not to buck the tide. Once the oligopoly surrendered, customers demanded the better price. Reluctantly, large banks let margins and business quality deteriorate. This forced newcomers and oligopolists to search for new profit centers. Sometimes movement to overlapping markets was spontaneous, at other times it was planned.

Margins and business quality can sink only so far. Without profits, stagnation and bankruptcy are inevitable. But, in an isolated market competition can run wild, making everyone unprofitable. Each bank makes profits elsewhere to offset the losses, and nobody will be the first to admit defeat. This pattern resembles the widely publicized overcompetition by foreign automobile manufacturers in Brazil.[6]

Another option is often open. Competitors may try to turn the game to make profits from corporate or governmental customers in spillover areas. Thus, as Euromarket spreads for corporate borrowers fell, foreign exchange margins increased. Similarly, one-way foreign exchange bets pressured governments and profited MNCs and banks after 1967. Some pressure directed against government officials by private actors might never have occurred if lending spreads had remained adequate.

Obviously, private pressure cannot grow endlessly. An abatement process must exist. Similarly, cutthroat competition must end, particularly when none of the firms can easily be driven from the field. Unfortunately, there is seldom an easy way out, even though all players would benefit if margin cutting ceased. However, since executives believe that their banks would be even worse off if they lost the business altogether, no bank trusts the others sufficiently to be the first to break off.[7]

Fortunately, competition is not an either/or situation. The transition period between sensible competition and complete collapse is a time of crisis in which alterations are possible. When competition threatens to destroy either the competitors or the system in which they compete, private firms suddenly perceive the strengthening of existing structures as their paramount need. They withdraw from the fray and expect governments to straighten things out. In addition, large oligopoly members regain their bargaining advantage since smaller firms can no longer command respect in the aftermath of failure. This breathing spell from pressure allows governments to act and permits the private firms to order their own priorities. Smaller participants are excluded from dealings or withdraw for their own safety. Customers return to quality suppliers even at slightly higher prices. Existing relationships are rationalized and a group of private actors, which may be larger than the original oligopoly, is certified as solid. From there, the process may begin again in different arenas or even in the same markets.

How well does this scenario describe the developments in the international banking and monetary systems since 1958? Does it adequately describe bank behavior in the United States? Can this scenario help predict future areas in which bank pressure on officials is likely to rise? These questions must be explored.

FOREIGN EXCHANGE, EUROMARKET, AND LDC LENDING COMPETITION

A changing competitive situation characterized the foreign exchange and Euromarkets in the late 1960s and early 1970s. As profit possibilities became obvious and Euromarket margins were narrowed, the foreign exchange market was converted from a service to a profit center for major banks. By 1967 or 1968 the interbank borrowing rate for all banks in London converged to a single level, which allowed small banks to compete actively for funds. In addition, the size of credits expanded, terms increased, spreads narrowed, and quality deteriorated. Prime customers demanded the best rate offered. Nonprime borrowers began to raise money more easily. MNCs and governments in need of funds found willing lenders in the buyer's market of the late 1960s and early 1970s.

Narrowing margins induced greater volume lending since no reserve requirements were demanded by authorities. Bank leverage ratios increased markedly. Banks were also attracted by new profit possibilities in the foreign exchange realm after 1967. Smaller newcomers attempted to garner foreign exchange earnings before older, larger banks because they needed profits while establishing their other business. Active bank profit-seeking placed additional indirect pressure on government authorities trying to defend parities. Possibly, had newer banks not been driven abroad by exchange regulations of the 1960s, the U.S. could have defended the dollar longer. Without regional banks operating abroad, a large balance of payments deficit could more easily have been tolerated since fewer banks and corporations would have been the focus of speculation.

Why did government authorities and large banks tolerate small banks' disruptive behavior? It seems that while profits were abundant, large banks acquiesced in small banks' manipulations. In addition, large banks were fearful of antitrust actions being brought against them because the former had no convenient excuse to act to exclude interlopers. Simultaneously, government officials were otherwise distracted. Compared to balance of payments and exchange rate problems, officials perceived small banks' activities as unimportant. Large banks, which were examined more closely, were found to be behaving honorably, in nonspeculative fashion. Since many newcomer margin cutters were based in Europe, U.S. authorities also had difficulty seeing the whole picture.

As Euromarket spreads narrowed, unsound economic policies in the U.S. and competition among banks for profits and business rapidly transformed the foreign exchange markets from a hedging market into a sharply fluctuating, profit-oriented dice game where banks and MNCs indirectly influenced government policies and the outcome of international monetary development. This competitive shift did not immediately affect bank pressure against exchange regulations, but led to increased indirect influence related to monetary crises and reform. The search for earnings predisposed dealers to find profitable exchange crises and thereby forced government officials to spend more time worrying about the markets and their behavior. Similarly, the demand for a potentially profitable flexible exchange rate system may have been partially responsible for the March 1, 1973 run on the mark, which buried the possibility of a return to fixed rates.

Only the threatened collapse of the banking system in the aftermath of Herstatt persuaded large banks to agree with the already reluctant MNCs that too much flexibility was dangerous. Herstatt also allowed them to reassert their control over smaller market members with MNC and government support. Top officials demanded that banks be dealt with according to their soundness. This push was echoed by MNCs, which were no longer ready to deal with any bank. In this regrouping, the notoriously conservative Arab OPEC nations helped large banks reassert their control by depositing their funds only with the largest, safest institutions. Significantly, top executives of unscathed smaller banks also commanded their subordinates to cease speculative activities which could undermine their solvency. As a result of this, Euromargins began to widen and terms began to shorten. Small banks became less active internationally for a time. Most significantly, the volume of foreign exchange speculation, particularly speculation for banks' own books decreased markedly. This was reflected in lower foreign exchange profits for major and minor banks in 1975 than in 1974. The competition declined somewhat by the January 1976 Jamaica monetary accord, but by 1976 both the foreign exchange and Euromarkets had regained most of their former robustness. However, it appears that less outright speculation for banks' own profits was taking place in these areas. Nevertheless, in the Euromarkets a new and dangerous problem was developing.

THE PROCESS REPEATED: AREAS TO WATCH OVERSEAS

Does this competitive scenario recur in other settings? Does the breakdown of oligopolistic control of a market frequently result in increased indirect pressure on governments to act? Is this pattern evident elsewhere in international or domestic banking or in the operation of other industries?

The cleansing of the Euromarkets and foreign exchange markets after Herstatt did not obviate the need for profits. Indeed, the glut of petrodollars forced banks to find new ways to invest funds. Loan demand in Europe and the United States sagged somewhat during the recession of 1974-1975. Profit-making by smaller banks became more difficult and necessitated the search for new profit areas. Even the partial recovery of Euromarket margins did not help the smaller banks too much because the best customers were dealing mostly with the larger banks.

In the absence of strong domestic loan demand, small and large banks therefore turned to new groups of customers previously downplayed by international lenders. Heavy lending for oil tanker construction, to socialist nations, and to the richer developing nations were undertaken. It is questionable whether these fields would have developed as rapidly or as competitively without the stimulus of heavy competition and overliquidity. The drive for profits may bend bankers' judgment. Tanker loans were stimulated by the 1967 closure of the Suez Canal and the growing energy demands in industrialized nations. Many of these loans soured when industrial nations stepped up their domestic production and instituted conservation drives after the 1973 oil embargo. Banks misread the demand for tankers and many lost heavily in shipping construction loans.[8]

Bankers now realize that their tanker lending and energy development loans depend on the economic viability of the borrowers and on political stability in the Middle East. This may have induced bank and oil company pressure on the U.S. government to soften its antagonistic rhetoric towards Arab oil-producing nations. More indirectly, tanker loan losses focused Treasury and Federal Reserve attention on the banks and helped convince regulators to seek more stringent bank controls. However, the magnitude of lending and losses cramped neither bankers nor government regulators severely. It did make energy and shipping issues more salient to some middle-level officials, stir up interest in stricter Euromarket regulations, and encourage talk of a firm safety net for banks caught by political events.

A second growing area is bank lending to socialist nations. In a peculiar perversion of views, capitalist bankers considered Communist, government-guaranteed loans extremely safe. Poland, Yugoslavia, East Germany, and the Soviet Union have all received substantial financing from Western banks. Led by Chase Manhattan, a number of U.S. banks have opened offices in China and the Soviet Union. Small American banks are now beginning to move slowly into this area. However, in the wake of North Korea's default to European banks, bankers are seriously concerned.[9] Large scale communist defaults would inevitably create chaos for the monetary system and tension among nations.

A third dramatic new departure in commercial bank lending involves credits for richer non-oil developing nations. Major banks are earning a substantial portion of their profits in these nations. Loan demand, even at high spreads, continues strong. Significantly, a major acceleration in these loans followed Herstatt and the cutback in foreign exchange speculation. It is clear, however, that even with good intentions, many of these nations will be forced to reschedule the loans. The credits are for shorter durations than comparable World Bank financing and the proportion of nations' exchange earnings being devoted to debt repayment is rising precariously.[10] Still, banks continue to search for new borrowers. Walter Hoadley, a senior Bank of America economist was among the first to warn of the danger that the next major financial crisis "will occur in 1976 among Third and Fourth World Nations with large accumulated maturing debts that they cannot pay without massive assistance."[11] Indonesia, Peru, Turkey, and Zaire's debt problems flared and subsided in 1976-1977 and might easily recur.

Still, a learning process is evident. Banks try to protect themselves by spreading their political and economic risks. Syndicates composed of banks of many nations and consortium banks owned by banks of many nations split and spread the risk in large loans. Massive country defaults would automatically involve governments from many nations. This strategy is closely related to one employed by Kennecott in Chile. By involving Chilean nationals and companies from many nations in their operations, they made it sensible for Chile to compensate the company rather than fight the world. Anaconda, which insisted on going it alone, was not so lucky.[12] Still, loans will be lost. Larger banks will survive with only slight injury, but smaller institutions could be hurt badly. The experience of the Western American Bank stands out as a stark warning. Despite its sound international parentage, WAB took risks to establish itself by guaranteeing the placement of syndicates before finding syndicate participants. WAB also issued long-term, fixed-interest Eurobonds just before interest rates rose. In September 1974, WAB's parents were forced to rescue their wayward child. Trying to break into the oligopoly too quickly almost bankrupted WAB. In response, the Bank of England demanded letters of comfort from parents of other London consortia.

WAB forced down rates and threatened system profitability and stability. Small banks, having learned their lesson, can also destabilize situations through their caution. In dealing with each new country, smaller banks are the last in and the first out. Since they are smaller-scale participants in most Eurosyndicates, they are likely to pull out all their funds if frightened. Larger banks with wider involvement in economies cannot disassociate themselves from countries and economies so quickly. Thus, in Turkey in 1977, several large banks "inherited" positions from smaller banks which chose not to roll-over their short-term loans. Large banks became more committed to Turkey than they wished because failure to roll-over the entire debt would have forced Turkey to admit that it could not repay its debt.[13]

Part of the problem faced by smaller banks fighting for their share of the profits is beyond their control. Central banks may allow small banks to fail, but will protect the banking giants. The large banks, particularly in France, therefore can safely allow their leverage to rise. Small banks, forced to match larger institutions' loan to equity ratio, may be caught by a sudden liquidity squeeze. Yet, they begin with the disadvantage of having to break into a market already controlled by larger institutions. Unless they are fortunate, their efforts to establish themselves can lead to their own demise and to serious problems for larger oligopoly members as well.

Unfortunately, the genie is out of the bottle. Economics alone is unlikely to persuade many U.S. banks to withdraw from London. When a crisis hits, central banks and private firms turn to the large, established banks as a nucleus of stability. In the shorter run, however, it appears possible that small banks competing for a finite amount of "good" business will induce crisis situations in diverse areas of international banking. Already by early 1978 loan margins had dropped to pre-Herstatt levels. The small follow the oligopoly; profit margins decline; quality declines; a crisis alleviates the pressure and reestablishes the position of the oligopoly in the stricken area. Refusing to go home, smaller banks search for new profit centers and often trigger another round of competition, crisis, and restructuring. No end is in sight.

BANK COMPETITION IN THE UNITED STATES

Shifting competitive environments have also appeared in the United States. On a general level, the quality and riskiness of U.S. domestic bank operations deteriorated after the mid-1960s. It appears that bank lending has become riskier and that the underlying strength of the banking industry has deteriorated sharply in the past ten years. In this period total bank liabilities have grown far faster than total demand deposits and financial net worth, but far slower than banks bought funds. At the same time a greater proportion of loans have been made to borrowers unable to repay them from cash flows on operations into which they are placed. And loans to debtors without the capacity to repay even the interest on their borrowings from generated cash flow are on the rise.[14] These trends reflect increased nationwide bank competition in recent years. The introduction of the one-bank holding company allowed large banks to establish nonbanking subsidiaries throughout the United States to compete with many types of financial institutions. The electronic transfer of funds issue threatens to increase national bank competition further. Sleepier, smaller, regional banks have been forced to scramble to avoid losing business to larger outsiders. Some of this scrambling is excellent for customer service but it has led to problems. The Franklin National Bank tried to expand its successful Long Island operations into New York City, found little good business, and lowered its lending standards. Losses spiraled outwards in many areas leading to large losses and a forced sale to the European-American banking group.

Large banks, of course, make errors too. Many established real estate investment trust subsidiaries in the early 1970s and were severely burned when land values in Southern retirement communities nosedived. Hugh losses were suffered, frequently because bankers put in charge of the Real Estate Investment Trusts were novices concerning real estate speculation and development. Smaller banks which followed the large ones into REITs suffered huge reversals as well. Characteristically, the large banks digested their losses more easily than their smaller rivals.

A change in the competitive positions between firms is not, however, the root of all evil. While smaller banks followed the larger ones into Penn Central and W. T. Grant, they did not create the problem. Banks lost more money than necessary, however, when they tried to revive these moribund organizations with capital transfusions, but that was a conscious strategy. Similarly, internal bank competition had little to do with the financing problems of New York City and other state and local governments in 1975. When banks finally turned off the spigot, they had already accepted far more municipal paper than they thought prudent. Government pressure put them into an insoluble bind. On the one hand, Federal Reserve officials pressured bankers to accept more municipal paper while cautioning the bankers not to accept high risk customers.[15]

It must be stressed that changes in the private competitive situation do not invariably lead to identical types of pressure on government officials.

International competition between U.S. firms may create pressure with intergovernmental and system implications. Domestic competition, on the other hand, is likely to force officials to devote more time to a topic and subject them to increased direct pressure from opposing competitive groups. In this sense, the domestic case is a subset of the wider pressures spilling over in international competitive confrontations.

Policy Implications and Research Needs

This work has yielded some indication of how big banks, little banks, and government authorities interact. However, far more work needs to be done to establish the basic relationships between banks and governments before policy claims can be accepted with anything approaching conviction. More work is critical in helping determine the appropriate relationship between public and private actors in the economic system.

If changes in competitive situations can lead to disturbing problems for market participants and regulatory authorities, who is to blame and what steps can be taken to deal with this? Within the international banking realm, it appears that although large and small banks must both accept some blame, most of the confusion was created by government authorities. But large banks, and particularly Citibank, through their activities, created what might be called the "Citibank syndrome." Their success abroad was so spectacular and so well publicized that smaller banks were convinced they could copy Citibank's aggressive style without their depth of experience and without as many competent executives. Their success enticed smaller, regional banks to emulate Citibank at home and abroad. Adopting Citibank's go-go style frequently resulted in short-term profits, but when recession struck in 1974, imitators were burned. Although Citibank slipped through unscathed, its two chief regional imitators, North Carolina National Bank and Citizens and Southern in Atlanta suffered substantial reverses.

Obviously, Citibank did not force others to follow its lead. Smaller, regional banks must accept more of the blame for their tendency to risk too much on scant information and insufficient experience. When their profit pictures started to dim and their customers began demanding international services, they jumped on the international bandwagon without sufficient care and planning. Once abroad, their can-do optimism precluded retrenchment. Only crises, in part stimulated by their own activities, could induce them to return to their former, conservative styles or to pull out of the international marketplace.

At least at the initial stages, however, the governments were usually the critical actors changing the competitive climate in the markets. Officials inadvertently encouraged private sector behavior which they could not subsequently control as in the promulgation of U.S. exchange regulations between 1963 and 1968. Once the international banking and Euromarket system was established, banks confounded governments' domestic and international monetary policies.

It is impossible to turn back the clock. Removing regulations does not reverse the effects of these regulations. Thus, the Eurocurrency business is now established and unlikely to return to New York. Longer-term Eurobond financing has similarly found a niche outside the United States. The idea of forcing over 100 banks to withdraw from their international activities is preposterous. If new U.S. regulations forced the withdrawal of American bank branches and subsidiaries from abroad, the resulting chaos would far overshadow difficulties involved with the regulation of existing Euromarkets.

Arthur Okun in a recent series of lectures struggled with the seemingly unavoidable tradeoff between equality and efficiency.[16] Unwilling to forfeit either, Okun came down for a compromise solution embracing neither socialism nor free markets. Unfortunately, none of the probable policy alternatives are terribly attractive. Ideally, a solution should be found that allows for competition, entry into new markets, and does not protect oligopoly members simply because they happen to be the largest, the first on the scene, or most reactive to government wishes to protect the monetary system.[17] Simultaneously, authorities must become more attentive to the activities of smaller companies without sufficient experience and expertise to operate successfully in all markets. These companies and their risk taking appear to be a major market destabilizing force. Greater state control of banks promises no bonanza of stability. The nationalized French banks, the state-owned regional banks of Germany, and the Japanese banks, which are closely tied to the Japanese government, have been at least as reckless as private commercial banks in the past decade in international banking affairs. In addition, there is a real possibility that a closely controlled, nationalized banking system would not be efficient and would not seek growth possibilities to benefit the world economy. Control, if it seriously hinders economic growth, is expensive.

At the root of the U.S. policy-making problem is the difficulty of regulating over 14,000 commercial banks through a complex system of overlapping authorities which leaves gaping loopholes. Some believe that had national bank branching flowered in the 1930s, as A. P. Giannini planned, the number of U.S. banks today would be far smaller.[18] However, while there is likely to be a slow attrition and gradual drop in the number of U.S. banks, it is unlikely to decline sufficiently to preclude the difficulties discussed here. The desirability of a United States with 100 giant banks is debatable, but it seems probably that the costs involved in making the transformation from the existing to a more compact system would be too large for the transformation to be seriously contemplated.

If a return to free markets or even to a pre-Euromarket environment would be costly and unlikely, some policy changes still seem reasonable. Many difficulties which plagued banks in recent years crept up unnoticed by both bankers involved and the responsible regulators. Regardless of the shape of regulatory organizations, a major step towards early detection of problems would be a move towards more thorough exposure of relevant bank dealings. This has already begun in the foreign exchange markets and has proven helpful in avoiding exchange volatility based on collusion and manipulation rather than on the economic prospects of currencies. It is important, however, not to confuse better information with more information. Government officials must carefully consider what information they need and what they do not. The type of information disclosed should be sharpened for usefulness, not increased. It may prove sensible to combine regulatory agencies with overlapping authority to make lines or responsibility clearer.

It should be noted, that those fearful of the political manipulation of bank regulation and monetary policy believe that greater authority should rest with the politically independent Federal Reserve System. However, legislators in recent years have demanded that Federal Reserve policies should be placed under closer Congressional scrutiny and control. A struggle between Congress and the Federal Reserve concerning central bank independence is underway.

More importantly, an atmosphere of mutual trust and cooperation must be restored and better lines of communication between public and private actors built. If banks intend to continue their international expansion, they must consider the political implications of their activities before acting. If government authorities hope to build an efficient, stable monetary system, they must consider the implications of their policies for private actors, the likely response of private actors to their actions, and the impact of these responses on the viability of their plans. A useful first step would be to broaden the communication channels between government agencies, private enterprises, and public interest groups. Publicizing the information and views of diverse groups might lead to greater consideration of the proper role of private enterprises in the economy and of the desirable role for private organizations and public interest groups in the foreign economic policy-making process.

NOTES

1. See, Mark Joelson, "International antitrust: a look at recent developments," *William and Mary Law Review* (Spring 1971): 565-579; and Raymond Vernon, "Anti-

trust and international business," *Harvard Business Review* (September-October 1968): 78-87.

2. However, the concentration of assets in the largest fifty banks has increased markedly in recent decades.

3. Yair Aharoni, *The Foreign Investment Decision Process* (Cambridge: Harvard University Press, 1969): 65-68.

4. John Brooks, *The Go-Go Years* (New York: Weybright and Talley, 1973) is an excellent description of go-go gone wild.

5. A London cliché held that small banks wanted to be the second to leave London. Not until 1975, however, were there departures. Then three small U.S. regionals (Central National Bank of Cleveland, Houston Citizens, and Northwest National Bank of Minneapolis) closed their London representative offices. No mass exodus has followed, however.

6. J. Wilner Sundelson, "U.S. automotive investments abroad," in Charles Kindleberger (ed.) *The International Corporation:* 245-246.

7. See, Mancur Olson, *The Logic of Collective Action* (Cambridge, Mass.: Harvard University Press, 1974) for a thorough general discussion of this dilemma.

8. See, Nicholas Faith, "How the world tankers slump may affect banks' balance sheets," *Euromoney* (June 1976): 14-16.

9. See, New York *Times,* June 6, 1976.

10. Emma Rothschild, "Banks: the coming crisis," New York *Review of Books* (May 27, 1976): 16-22. Also see, New York *Times,* June 14, 1976.

11. New York *Times,* December 17, 1975.

12. Theodore Moran, *Multinational Corporations and the Politics of Dependence: Copper in Chile* (Princeton, N.J.: Princeton University Press, 1975).

13. Interview with a representative of Wells Fargo Bank, October 1977.

14. Hyman Minsky, "Financial resources in a fragile financial environment," paper presented to the 17th annual forecasting conference of the New York Chapter of the American Statistical Association, New York, April 18, 1975: 5.

15. Frank Morris, President, Federal Reserve Bank of Boston at a seminar at the Harvard Center for International Affairs, January 16, 1976.

16. Arthur Okun, *Equality and Efficiency: The Big Tradeoff* (Washington, D.C.: Brookings Institution, 1975).

17. Charles Schultze's lectures at the same forum two years later published as *The Public Use of Private Interest* (Washington, D.C.: Brookings Institution, 1977) begin to address possible strategies.

18. One key fact in international banking today is that most countries have four or five dominant commercial banks while the U.S. supports many, many more.

BIBLIOGRAPHY

Books

ABELL, P., ed. *Organizations as Bargaining Influence Systems*. New York: Halsted, 1975.

AHARONI, Y. *The Foreign Investment Decision Process*. Cambridge, Mass.: Harvard University Press, 1966.

ALIBER, R. *The International Market for Foreign Exchange*. New York: Praeger, 1969.

———. *The International Money Game*. New York: Basic Books, 1973.

ALLISON, G. *Essense of Decision: Explaining the Cuban Missile Crisis*. Boston: Little, Brown, 1971.

ARMSTRONG, H. F. *Peace and Counter Peace: From Wilson to Hitler*. New York: Harper and Row, 1971.

AUBREY, H. G. *The Dollar in World Affairs*. New York: Praeger, 1964.

BAGEHOT, W. *Lombard Street: A Description of the Money Market*. New York: Scribner and Armstrong, 1873.

BARNET, R. and R. Müller, *Global Reach: The Power of the Multinational Corporations*. New York: Simon and Schuster, 1974.

BAUER, R. A., I. de S. POOL, and L. A. DEXTER. *American Business and Public Policy: The Politics of Foreign Trade*. Chicago: Aldine-Atherton, 1972.

BELL, G. *The Euro-Dollar Market and the International Financial System*. New York: Macmillan, 1973.

BERGSTEN, C. F. *Dilemmas of the Dollar*. New York: Council on Foreign Relations, 1976.

———. *The Future of the International Economic Order: An Agenda for Research*. Lexington: D. C. Heath, 1973.

———. *Reforming the Dollar: An International Monetary Policy for the United States*. New York: Council on Foreign Relations, 1972.

BETER, P. *The Conspiracy Against the Dollar*. New York: George Braziller, 1973.

BHAGWATI, J. N. ed. *Economies and World Order*. Toronto: Macmillan, 1972.

BLOCK, F. *The Origins of International Economic Disorder*. Berkeley: University of California Press, 1977.

BRITTAN, S. *Steering the Economy: The Role of the Treasury*. London: Secker and Warburg, 1969.

BROOKS, J. *Business Adventures*. New York: Weybright and Talley, 1969.

———. *The Go-Go Years*. New York: Weybright and Talley, 1973.

BROWN, W. A. *The International Gold Standard Reinterpreted, 1914-1934*. 2 vols. New York: National Bureau of Economic Research, 1940.

CAIRNCROSS, Sir A. *Control of the Long Term Capital Markets.* Washington, D.C.: Brookings Institution, 1973.

CALLEO, D. and B. ROWLAND. *America and the World Political Economy.* Bloomington: Indiana University Press, 1973.

CAREY, O., ed. *The Military-Industrial Complex and U.S. Foreign Policy.* Pullman: Washington State University Press, 1969.

CHANDLER, L. *Benjamin Strong: Central Banker.* Washington, D.C.: Brookings Institution, 1958.

CLARKE, S. *Central Bank Cooperation: 1924-1931.* New York: Federal Reserve Bank of New York, 1967.

COHEN, S. D. *International Monetary Reform, 1964-1969.* New York: Praeger, 1970.

COLEMAN, J. C. *The Mathematics of Collective Action.* Chicago: Aldine, 1973.

CONYBEARE, J. "United States foreign economic policy and the international capital markets: the case of capital controls, 1963-1974." Ph.D. dissertation, Harvard, 1976.

COOMBS, C. *The Arena of International Finance.* New York: John Wiley, 1976.

COOPER, R. *The Economics of Interdependence: Economic Policy in the Atlantic Community.* New York: McGraw-Hill, 1968.

DAHL, R. *Modern Political Analysis.* Englewood Cliffs, N.J.: Prentice-Hall, 1963.

de ROOVER, R. *The Rise and Decline of the Medici Bank, 1397-1494.* Cambridge, Mass.: Harvard University Press, 1963.

EINZIG, P. *The Euro-Dollar System: Practice and Theory of International Interest Rates.* New York: St. Martin's, 1970.

–––. *The Fight for Financial Supremacy.* London: Macmillan, 1932.

–––. *Foreign Dollar Loans in Europe.* New York: St. Martin's, 1965.

–––. *Foreign Exchange Crises: An Essay in Economic Pathology.* New York: St. Martin's, 1970.

–––. *The History of Foreign Exchange.* New York: St. Martin's, 1962.

FAYERWEATHER, J. *The Mercantile Bank Affair.* New York: New York University Press, 1974.

FEIS, H. *Europe the World's Banker, 1870-1914.* New York: W. W. Norton, 1965.

FRIEDMAN, M. *Essays in Positive Economics.* Chicago: University of Chicago Press, 1953.

––– and A. SCHWARTZ. *A Monetary History of the United States, 1867-1960.* Princeton, N.J.: Princeton University Press, 1963.

FROHLICH, N., J. A. OPPENHEIMER, and O. YOUNG. *Political Leadership and Collective Goods.* Princeton, N.J.: Princeton University Press, 1974.

GARDNER, R. *Sterling-Dollar Diplomacy.* New York: McGraw-Hill, 1969.

GILPIN, R. *U.S. Power and the Multinational Corporation.* New York: Basic Books, 1975.

HALM, G., C. F. BERGSTEN, and F. MACHLUP, eds. *Approaches to Greater Flexibility of Exchange Rates: The Bürgenstock Papers.* Princeton, N.J.: Princeton University Press, 1970.

HALPERIN, M. *Bureaucratic Politics and Foreign Policy.* Washington, D.C.: Brookings Institution, 1974.

HAMMOND, B. *Banks and Politics in America.* Princeton, N.J.: Princeton University Press, 1960.

–––. *Sovereignty and an Empty Purse: Banks and Politics in the Civil War.* Princeton, N.J.: Princeton University Press, 1970.

HAYTER, T. *Aid as Imperialism.* Harmondsworth, England: Penguin, 1971.

HIRSCH, F. *Money International.* Harmondsworth, England: Penguin, 1967.

HIRSCH, F. *The Pound Sterling: A Polemic.* London: Victor Gollancz, 1965.

–––. *Social Limits to Growth.* Cambridge, Mass.: Harvard University Press, 1977.

HOLMES, A. *The New York Foreign Exchange Market.* New York: Federal Reserve Bank of New York, 1959.

HOYT, E. P., Jr. *The House of Morgan.* New York: Dodd, Mead, 1966.

JAMES, M. and B. JAMES. *The Biography of a Bank: The Story of Bank of America N.T. & S.A.* New York: Harper and Brothers, 1954.

JOHNSON, B. *The Politics of Money.* New York: McGraw-Hill, 1970.

JOSEPHSON, M. *The Robber Barons.* New York: Harcourt, Brace, and World, 1934.

KELLER, M. *The Life Insurance Enterprise, 1885-1910.* Cambridge, Mass.: Harvard University Press, 1963.

KEOHANE, R. and J. NYE, Jr., eds. *Power and Interdependence.* Boston: Little, Brown, 1977.

–––. eds. *Transnational Relations and World Politics.* Cambridge, Mass.: Harvard University Press, 1972.

KELLY, J. *Bankers and Borders.* Cambridge, Mass.: Ballinger, 1976.

KINDLEBERGER, C. P. *The World Depression 1929-1939.* Berkeley: University of California Press, 1973.

–––. ed. *The International Corporation: A Symposium.* Cambridge, Mass.: MIT Press, 1970.

–––. *Power and Money.* New York: Basic Books, 1970.

KROOS, H., ed. *Documentary History of Banking and Currency in the United States.* 4 vols. New York: McGraw-Hill, 1969.

LANDES, D. S. *Bankers and Pashas: International Finance and Economic Imperialism in Egypt.* New York: Harper and Row, 1969.

League of Nations. (Nurkse, R.). *The International Currency Experience.* Geneva: League of Nations, 1944.

LEES, F. A. *International Banking and Finance.* New York: John Wiley, 1974.

LENIN, V. I. *Imperialism: The Highest Stage of Capitalism.* Peking: Foreign Language Press, 1965.

LEVITT, K. *The Silent Surrender: The Multinational Corporation in Canada.* New York: St. Martin's, 1970.

LITTLE, J. S. *Euro-Dollars: The Money Market Gypsies.* New York: Harper and Row, 1975.

McRAE, H. and F. CAIRNCROSS. *Capital City: London as a Financial Center.* London: Eyre Methuen, 1973.

MAGDOFF, H. *The Age of Imperialism: The Economics of U.S. Imperialism.* New York: Monthly Review Press, 1969.

MAISEL, S. *Managing the Dollar.* New York: W. W. Norton, 1973.

MANDEL, E. *Decline of the Dollar: A Marxist View of the Monetary Crisis.* New York: Monad Press, 1972.

MATTINGLY, G. *Renaissance Diplomacy.* Boston: Houghton Mifflin, 1971.

MAYER, M. *The Bankers.* New York: Weybright and Talley, 1974.

MEYER, R. H. *Bankers' Diplomacy: Monetary Stabilization in the Twenties.* New York: Columbia University Press, 1970.

MOGGRIDGE, D. E. *The Return to Gold: 1925.* Cambridge, England: Cambridge University Press, 1969.

MORAN, T. *Multinational Corporations and the Politics of Dependence: Copper in Chile.* Princeton, N.J.: Princeton University Press, 1974.

MOSTERT, N. *Supership.* New York: Warner, 1975.

MYERS, M. *A Financial History of the United States.* New York: Columbia University Press, 1970.

ODELL, J. "Sources of foreign policy change: the United States in the international monetary system," Ph.D. dissertation, University of Wisconsin, 1976.

OKUN, A. *Equality and Efficiency: The Big Tradeoff.* Washington, D.C.: Brookings Institution, 1975.

OLSON, M. *The Logic of Collective Action.* Cambridge, Mass.: Harvard University Press, 1974.

OYE, K. "Bargaining, belief-systems, and bullion: the evolution of international monetary politics," Ph.D. dissertation, Harvard University, 1978.

Partners in Development (The Pearson Report). Report of the Commission on International Development. New York: Praeger, 1969.

PHELPS, C. *The Foreign Expansion of American Banks: American Branch Banking Abroad.* New York: Ronald Press, 1927.

POLANYI, K. *The Great Transformation.* Boston: Beacon, 1957.

RANGARAJAN, L. N. *Commodity Conflict: The Political Economy of International Commodity Conflict.* Ithaca: Cornell University Press, 1978.

ROBBINS, S. and R. STOBAUGH. *Money in the Multinational Enterprise: A Study of Financial Policy.* New York: Basic Books, 1973.

ROBINSON, S., Jr. *Multinational Banking.* Leiden, Netherlands: A. W. Sijthoff, 1972.

ROLFE, S. and J. BURTLE. *The Great Wheel: The World Monetary System: A Reinterpretation.* New York: Quadrangle, 1973.

SAFIRE, W. *Before the Fall.* New York: Doubleday, 1975.

SCHACHT, H. *My First 76 Years.* New York: Wingate, 1955.

SCHATTSCHNEIDER, E. E. *Politics, Pressure and the Tariff.* New York: Prentice-Hall, 1935.

SCHLOSS, H. H. *The Bank for International Settlements: An Experiment in Central Bank Cooperation.* Amsterdam: North Holland, 1958.

SERVAN-SCHREIBER, J.-J. *The American Challenge.* Translated by Ronald Steel. New York: Avon Books, 1969.

SMITH, A. *Supermoney.* New York: Popular Library, 1972.

The Smithsonian Agreement and Its Aftermath: Several Views. New York: Council on Foreign Relations, 1975.

SOLOMON, R. *The International Monetary System, 1945-1976.* New York: Harper and Row, 1977.

STENTON, D. M. *English Society in the Early Middle Ages.* Harmondsworth, England: Penguin, 1965.

STERN, S. *The United States in International Banking.* New York: Columbia University Press, 1951.

STRANGE, S. *International Monetary Relations,* Vol. 2 in Andrew Schonfield (ed.) *International Economic Relations in the Western World 1959-1971.* London: Oxford University Press, 1976.

–––. *Sterling and British Policy.* New York: Oxford University Press, 1971.

TRIFFIN, R. *Gold and the Dollar Crisis.* New Haven, Conn.: Yale University Press, 1961.

VERNON, R. *Storm over Multinationals.* Cambridge, Mass.: Harvard University Press, 1977.

–––. *Sovereignty at Bay.* New York: Basic Books, 1971.

WILKINS, M. *The Emergence of Multinational Enterprise: American Business Abroad from the Colonial Era to 1914.* Cambridge, Mass.: Harvard University Press, 1970.

WILLIAMS, B. H. *Economic Foreign Policy of the United States.* New York: McGraw-Hill, 1929.
WILSON, H. *A Personal Record: The Labour Government 1964-1970.* Boston: Little, Brown, 1971.
WONNACOTT, P. *The Canadian Dollar, 1948-1962.* Toronto: University of Toronto Press, 1965.
YEAGER, L. *International Monetary Relations.* New York: Harper and Row, 1966.

Articles and Papers

"After all the dire predictions of calamity, confidence and liquidity have returned to the scene." *Forbes,* June 1975, pp. 29-30, 74-78.
ARONSON, J. D. "The response to Arab and Japanese investment in the United States: a comparison." Paper presented at the meetings of the International Studies Association, St. Louis, March 1977.
–––. "Politics and the international consortium banks." *Stanford Journal of International Studies* (Spring 1976): 42-69.
–––. "The multinational corporation, the nation-state, and the international system: a bibliography." *A Current Bibliography on African Affairs* 7 (Fall 1974): 378-436.
ASCHINGER, F. E. "The Eurodollar market in times of crisis." *Euromoney* (November 1969): 12-14.
ASHBY, D. "The $300 billion super-dollar market." *The Banker* 124 (May 1974): 449-454.
AUBREY, H. G. "Behind the veil of international money." *Princeton Essays in International Finance* 71 (January 1969): 1-32.
BALL, G. "Multinational corporation and nation-states." *Atlantic Community Quarterly* 5 (Summer 1967): 247-253.
BARRACLOUGH, G. "Wealth and power: the politics of food and oil." New York *Review of Books,* August 7, 1975, pp. 23-30.
BARRASS, A. "Afloat in a sea of controls." *The Banker* 123 (June 1973): 613-620.
BEIM, D. O. "Rescuing the LDCs." *Foreign Affairs* 55 (July 1977): 717-731.
BEMAN, L. "How it all came apart in the Eurodollar market." *Fortune* 91 (February 1975): 85-87, 168-174.
BLACKHURST, R. "Spot markets under floating rates." *The Banker* 126 (January 1976): 29-31.
BLOOMFIELD, A. "Short term capital movements under the pre-1914 gold standard." *Princeton Studies in International Finance* 11 (July 1963): 1-104.
BRADSHAW, R. "Foreign exchange operations of U.S. banks." Paper presented at the 11th annual conference on bank structure and competition, Chicago, Federal Reserve Bank of Chicago, May 12, 1975.
"Brazil: the lenders and the borrowers." *Euromoney* (June 1976): 48-54.
BRIMMER, A. "American international banking: trends and prospects." Paper presented at meetings of the Bankers Association for Foreign Trade, Boca Raton, Florida, April 2, 1973.
–––. "Prospects for commercial banks in international money and capital markets: an American perspective." Paper presented at the conference on World Banking, London, January 17, 1974.
–––. "Capital flows, bank lending abroad, and the U.S. balance of payments." Remarks before the American Bankers Association School for International Banking, Boulder, Colorado, July 17, 1974.

BRIMMER, A. "Commercial bank lending abroad and the U.S. balance of payments." Remarks at a symposium on the international monetary system in transition, Chicago, Federal Reserve Bank of Chicago, March 16, 1972.

–––. "Multi-national banks and the management of monetary policy in the United States." Paper presented at a joint session of the American Economic Association and the American Finance Association, Toronto, December 28, 1972.

–––. "Capital outflows and the United States balance of payments: review and outlook." Paper presented at the Federal Reserve Bank of Dallas, February 11, 1970.

–––. "The Euro-dollar market and the United States balance of payments." Paper presented at the London School of Economics, London, November 17, 1969.

–––. "Monetary policy and the allocation of commercial bank credit." Lecture at the Vermont-New Hampshire School of Banking, Dartmouth, Hanover, New Hampshire, September 11, 1966.

BRUNSDEN, P. "The Edge Act in U.S. banking." *The Banker* 123 (February 1973): 143-152.

BURTLE, J. "Toward the international monetary system the multinational corpora-*Business* 9 (Spring 1974): 61-67.

––– and A. TECK. "Judgment on floating rates." *The Banker* 124 (September 1974): 1053-1056.

BURTLE, J. "Toward the international monetary system at the multinational corporations should want and why." Paper presented at the Center for International Studies, MIT, Cambridge, October 25-27, 1973.

CHALMERS, E. "Keeping out hot money." *The Banker* 121 (February 1971): 132-137.

CLEVELAND, H. van B. and W.H.B. BRITTAIN. "Are the LDCs in over their heads?" *Foreign Affairs* 55 (July 1977): 732-750.

COHEN, B. J. "Major issues of world monetary reform." Paper prepared for the Commission on Critical Choices for America, August 1974, mimeo.

COOMBS, C. "Some thoughts on international money." *The Banker* 125 (December 1975): 1481-1487.

–––. "Interview." *The Banker* 117 (November 1966): 740-749.

COOPER, J. "How foreign exchange operations can go wrong." *Euromoney* (May 1974): 4-7.

COOPER, R. "Prolegomena to the choice of an international monetary system." *International Organization* 29 (Winter 1975): 169-209.

–––. "Economic interdependence and foreign policy in the seventies." *World Politics* 24 (January 1972): 159-181.

COSTANZO, G. A. "The Eurodollar: villain or victim?" *Euromoney* (June 1971): 24-28.

"Crises in the foreign exchange markets." Conference sponsored by the Investment and Property Studies Ltd. and the *International Currency Report,* London, July 10, 1974, transcript.

"The currency crisis: Germany and the Euro-currency pool." *The Banker* 121 (June 1971): 10.

DAHL, F. "International operations of U.S. banks: growth and public policy implications." *Law and Contemporary Problems* 32 (Winter 1967): 100-130.

DELBRIDGE, R. "Foreign exchange dealings in banks." *Arthur Anderson Chronicle,* April 1975, pp. 39-54.

DESPRES, E., C. KINDLEBERGER, and W. SALANT. "The dollar and world liquidity." *Economist* (February 5, 1966): 526-529.

de VRIES, R. "A banker's view of overseas activities of banking organizations and the role of regulations." Paper presented at a conference on "A view of banking and bank regulations." Minneapolis, Federal Reserve Bank of Minneapolis, March 27, 1973.

de VRIES, R. "Charting a new course in U.S. international banking regulation." *Bankers Magazine* 155 (Automn 1972): 75-81.

DUFEY, G. "The Eurobond market: its significance for international financial managements." *Journal of International Business Studies* 1 (Spring 1970): 65-81.

ENG, M. "U.S. international banking: challenge and opportunity." *Bankers Magazine* 154 (Spring 1971): 79-88.

ETHIER, W. and A. BLOOMFIELD. "Managing the managed float." *Princeton Essays in International Finance* 112 (1975): 1-27.

FAITH, N. "How the world tankers slump may affect banks' balance sheets." *Euromoney* (June 1976): 14-16.

FITZSIMONS, R. "Who are the 'currency speculators?'" *The Banker* 121 (November 1971): 1277-1281.

FOWLER, H. "National interests and multinational business." *California Management Review* 8 (Fall 1965): 3-12.

FRIEDMAN, M. "The case for flexible exchange rates," in *Essays in Positive Economics,* pp. 157-203. Chicago: University of Chicago Press, 1953.

GILBERT, M. "The size of the Eurodollar market." *Euromoney* (August 1971): 12-15.

GILPIN, R. "The politics of transnational economic relations." *International Organization* 25 (Summer 1971): 398-419.

HALL, W. "Swift: the revolution round the corner." *The Banker* 123 (June 1973): 633-639.

HART, J. "Three approaches to the measurement of power in international relations." *International Organization* 30 (Spring 1976): 289-305.

HAUGE, G. "Changes in U.S. regulations: impact on the markets." *Euromoney* (Spring 1973): 25-26.

HELDRING, F. "A curb on the Eurocurrency market." *Euromoney* (March 1973): 42-43.

HIRSCH, F. "The Bagehot problem" London, 1974, mimeo.

––– and D. HIGHAM. "Floating rates: expectations and experience." *Three Banks Review* 102 (June 1974): 3-34.

"How did we ever get here? a banker's diary, 1964-1973." *The Banker* 123 (September 1973): 1005-1012.

HYMER, S. "The internationalization of capital." *Journal of Economic Issues* 6 (March 1972): 91-111.

–––. "The multinational corporation and uneven development," in *Economic and World Order,* pp. 113-139. Edited by J. N. Bhagwati. Toronto. Macmillan, 1972.

"Imprudence and over-prudence in foreign exchange." *International Currency Review* 6 (July-August 1974): 5-13.

JOELSON, M. "International antitrust: a look at recent developments." *William and Mary Law Review* 12 (Spring 1971): 565-579.

KATZ, S. "The emerging exchange-rate system (early 1974)," Discussion Paper No. 46, Division of International Finance, Board of Governors of the Federal Reserve System, May 23, 1974.

KATZENSTEIN, P. "International relations and domestic structures: foreign economic policies of advance industrial states." *International Organization* 30 (Winter 1976): 1-45.

KAUFMAN, H. "Banks may be all the better for a few restrictions." *Euromoney* (June 1976): 70-75.

KEOHANE, R. O. and J. NYE, Jr. "Introduction: complex politics of Canadian-American interdependence." *International Organization* 28 (Autumn 1974): 595-607.

———. "Transgovernmental relations and international organization." *World Politics* 27 (October 1974): 39-62.

———. "World politics and the international economic system." In *The Future of the International Economic Order: An Agenda for Research,* pp. 115-179. Edited by C. Fred Bergsten. Lexington, Mass.: D. C. Heath, 1973.

KEOHANE, R. O. and V. D. OOMS. "The multinational firm and international regulation." *International Organization* 29 (Winter 1975): 169-209.

KINDLEBERGER, C. P. "Debt situation of the developing countries in historical perspective." Paper for a symposium at the Export-Import Bank on Developing Countries Debt, April 21, 1977.

———. "The benefits of international money." *Journal of International Economics* 2 (September 1972): 425-552.

———. "The case for fixed exchange rates, 1969." In *The International Adjustment Process,* pp. 93-108. Proceedings of a Conference Sponsored by the Federal Reserve Bank of Boston in October 1969. Boston: Federal Reserve Bank of Boston, 1970.

KLOPSTOCK, F. H. "The wiring of the Eurodollar market." *Euromoney* (August 1970): 16-20.

KOSZUL, J. P. "American banks in Europe." In *The International Corporation: A Symposium,* pp. 273-289. Edited by Charles P. Kindleberger. Cambridge, Mass.: MIT Press, 1970.

KRAMER, G. "Borrowing on the international capital markets." *Columbia Journal of World Business* 9 (Spring 1974): 73-77.

LANYI, A. "Political aspects of exchange rate systems." In *Communication in International Politics,* pp. 423-446. Edited by Richard Merritt. Urbana: University of Illinois Press, 1967.

LINDERT, P. "Key currencies and gold 1900-1913." *Princeton Studies in International Finance* 24 (August 1969): 1-85.

LOW, W. "Euro-study: a review of the Euro-money and Euro-capital market: 1973-1974." London: International Insider, January 1974.

MACHLUP, F. "Five errors about the Eurodollar system." *Euromoney* (July 1972): 8-14.

———. "The magicians and their rabbits." *Morgan Guaranty Survey,* May 1971, pp. 3-13.

———. "Eurodollar creation: a mystery story." *Banca Nazionale del Lavoro Quarterly Review* 94 (September 1970): 219-260.

MAIN, J. "The first real American bankers." *Fortune* 75 (December 1967): 143-147, 196, 198.

MAKIN, J. "Capital flows and exchange rate flexibility in the post-Bretton Woods era." *Princeton Essays in International Finance* 103 (February 1974): 1-25.

"Medium-term Eurocurrency bank credits." Conference sponsored by the Investment and Property Studies Ltd., London, October 25, 1974, transcript.

MINSKY, H. "Financial resources in a fragile financial environment." Paper presented at the 17th annual forecasting conference of the New York chapter of the American Statistical Association, New York, April 18, 1975.

MORAN, T. "Transnational strategies of protection and defense by multinational corporations: spreading the risk and raising the cost for nationalization in natural resources." *International Organization* 27 (Spring 1973): 273-287.

MORSE, C. J. "The evolving monetary system." *Finance and Development* 11 (September 1974): 13-16.

MORSE, E. "Transnational economic forces." *International Organization* 25 (Summer 1971): 373-397.

NICHOLS, J. "Roosevelt's monetary diplomacy in 1933." *American Historical Review* 56 (January 1951): 295-317.

NYE, J., Jr. "Multinational corporations in world politics." *Foreign Affairs* 53 (October 1974): 153-173.

O'BRIEN, Sir L. "The Eurodollar market: controls are not the answer." *Euromoney* (June 1971): 8-12.

ODELL, J. "U.S. officials and the emergence of flexible exchange rates: an analysis of foreign policy change." Paper presented at the meetings of the International Studies Association, Toronto, February 1976.

PORTES, R. "East Europe's debt to the West: interdependence is a two-way street." *Foreign Affairs* 55 (July 1977): 751-782.

PRINGLE, R. "Why American banks go abroad." *Bankers Magazine* 150 (Autumn 1967): 48-58.

RODRIGUEZ, R. "What were the U.S. multinational companies doing during the international monetary crisis?" Harvard, December 8, 1975, mimeo.

ROOSA, R. "Approaching international reform." In *The Smithsonian Agreement and Its Aftermath*, pp. 13-40. New York: Council on Foreign Relations, 1972.

ROSE, S. "Why they call it 'fat city.'" *Fortune* 89 (March 1975) 106-110, 164-167.

———. "Capital is something that doesn't love a wall." *Fortune* 83 (February 1971): 100-103, 110-112.

ROTHSCHILD, E. "Banks: the coming crisis." New York *Review of Books* May 27, 1976, pp. 16-22.

RUSSELL, R. "The need for regulation of multinational banking." Paper presented to the International Affairs Fellowship program, May 14, 1976.

———. "Public policies toward private international financial flows." Paper presented at the meetings of the International Studies Association, St. Louis, March 22, 1974.

———. "Crisis management in the international monetary system, 1960-1973." Paper presented at the meetings of the International Studies Association, New York, March 16, 1973.

———. "Toward explaining the politics of international monetary reform." Revision of a paper presented to the meetings of the American Political Science Association, New Orleans, September 7, 1973.

———. "Transgovernmental interaction in the international monetary system." *International Organization* 27 (Autumn 1973): 431-464.

SALANT, W. "The post devaluation weakness of the dollar." *Brookings Papers on Economic Activity* (1973: 2): 481-497.

Salomon Brothers. "United States multinational banking: current and prospective strategies," prepared by Thomas Hanley. New York: Salomon Brothers, June 1976.

"Should international banks continue to lend to Brazil?" *Euromoney* (May 1976): 16-19.

SPENCER, W. I. "Who controls MNCs?" *Harvard Business Review* 53 (November-December 1975): 97-108.

STOPPER, E. "The conflict of monetary and social policies." *Euromoney* (February 1971): 14-16.

STRANGE, S. "The market as actor and environment." Paper presented at the meetings of the International Studies Association, New Orleans, September 7, 1973.

———. "The politics of international currencies." *World Politics* 23 (January 1971): 215-231.

SUNDELSON, J. W. "U.S. automotive investments abroad." In *The International Corporation: A Symposium,* pp. 243-271. Edited by Charles P. Kindleberger. Cambridge, Mass.: MIT Press, 1970.

"SWIFT to add new speed and security to international banking." *Forbes,* June 1975, p. 87.

TAYLOR, H. "The banking lobby: a papier mache monster." *Bankers Magazine* 153 (Spring 1970): 74-78.

TEW, B. "Are some banks more equal than others?" *The Banker* 124 (October 1974): 1195-1198.

"Those bank failures and losses." *The Banker* 124 (August 1974): 905-909.

TRIFFIN, R. "The Smithsonian standards and its aftermath." In *The Smithsonian Agreement and its Aftermath,* pp. 54-63. New York: Council on Foreign Relations, 1972.

———. "The evolution of the international monetary system: historical reappraisal and future perspectives." *Princeton Studies in International Finance* 12 (1964): 1-83.

VAGTS, D. "The multinational enterprise: a new challenge for transnational law." *Harvard Law Review* 83 (February 1970): 739-792.

VAN AGTMAEL, A. W. "Evaluating the risks of lending to developing countries." *Euromoney* (April 1976): 16-30.

VAN VLIERDEN, C. M. "New era in international banking." *The Banker* 121 (February 1971): 146-149.

———. "International commercial banks: a link between two systems." *Euromoney* (July 1971): 12-14.

VERNON, R. "A skeptic looks at the balance of payments." *Foreign Policy* 5 (Winter 1971-1972): 52-65.

———. "Antitrust and international business." *Harvard Business Review* 46 (September-October 1968): 78-87.

WAGNER, R. H. "Dissolving the state: three recent perspectives on international relations." *International Organization* 28 (Summer 1974): 435-466.

WATSON, A. "Back to gold—and silver." *Economic History Review* 20:1 (1967): 1-34.

WHITMAN, M.V.N. "The current and future role of the dollar: how much symmetry?" *Brookings Paper on Economic Activity* (1974:3): 539-591.

WRIGHT, G. and M. A. MOLOT. "Capital movements and government control." *International Organization* 28 (Autumn 1974): 671-688.

YASSUKOVICH, S. "The growing political threat to international lending." *Euromoney* (April 1976): 10-15.

———. "Dilemmas of Euromarket regulation." *The Banker* 123 (April 1973): 368-371.

Governmental and International Organizational Documents

Bank for International Settlements, *Annual Report.*

Bank of England, *Quarterly Bulletin.*

Board of Governors of the Federal Reserve System, *Annual Reports.*

Board of Governors of the Federal Reserve System, *Federal Reserve Bulletin.*

Board of Governors of the Federal Reserve System, *Minutes of the Federal Open Market Committee Meetings,* 1967.

COOMBS, C. "Treasury and federal reserve foreign exchange operations." Federal Reserve Bank of New York, *Monthly Review,* semiannually.

HORSEFIELD, K. et. al. *The International Monetary Fund 1945-1965.* 3 vols. Washington, D.C.: IMF, 1969.

International Bank for Reconstruction and Development. "Multilateral debt renegotiations, 1956-1968." Washington, D.C.: IBRD, April 1969.

International Monetary Fund, *Annual Reports.*

International Monetary Fund, *International Financial Statistics.*

International Monetary Fund, *Reports on Exchange Restrictions.*

U.S. Congress. House. Committee on Banking, Currency, and Housing. *Financial Institutions and the Nation's Economy: Compendium of Papers Prepared for the FINE Study.* 2 vols. 94th Cong., 2nd sess., 1976.

U.S. Congress. House. Committee on Banking, Currency and Housing. *International Banking: A Supplement to a Compendium of Papers Prepared for the FINE Study.* 94th Cong., 2nd sess., 1976.

U.S. Congress. House. Committee on Banking, Currency and Housing and Joint Economic Committee. *Exchange Rate Policy and International Monetary Reform: Report of the Subcommittee on International Trade, Investment and Monetary Policy of the Committee on Banking, Currency and Housing and by the Subcommittee on International Economics of the Joint Economic Committee.* 94th Cong., 1st sess., 1975.

U.S. Congress. House. Committee on Banking, Currency and Housing and Joint Economic Committee. *International Monetary Reform: Hearings before the Subcommittee on International Finance of the Committee on Banking, Currency and Housing and the Joint Economic Committee.* 93rd Cong., 1st sess., 1973.

U.S. Congress. House. Committee on Banking and Currency. *Balance of Payments, 1965: Hearings before a subcommittee of the House Committee on Banking and Currency.* 89th Cong., 1st sess., 1965.

U.S. Congress. House. Committee on Foreign Affairs. *Direct Investment Controls: Hearings before the Subcommittee on Foreign Economic Policy of the Committee on Foreign Affairs.* 91st Cong., 1st sess., 1969.

U.S. Congress. Joint Economic Committee. *Making Floating Part of a Reformed Monetary System: Report of the Subcommittee on International Economics.* 93d. Cong., 2nd sess., 1974.

U.S. Congress. Joint Economic Committee. *Gold and the Central Bank Swap Network: Hearings before the Subcommittee on International Exchange and Payments.* 92d Cong., 2nd sess., 1972.

U.S. Congress. Joint Economic Committee. *Gold, SDR's, and Central Bank Swaps: Report of the Subcommittee on International Exchange and Payments.* 92d Cong., 2nd sess., 1972.

U.S. Congress. Joint Economic Committee. *How Well Are Fluctuating Exchange Rates Working? Hearings before the Subcommittee of International Exchange and Payments.* 92d Cong., 2nd sess., 1972.

U.S. Congress. Joint Economic Committee. *The Balance of Payments Mess: Hearings before the Subcommittee on International Exchange and Payments.* 92d Cong., 1st sess., 1971.

U.S. Congress. Joint Economic Committee. *The Euro-Dollar Market and Its Public Policy Implications: Economic Policies and Practices Paper No. 12.* Prepared by Ira O. Scott Jr. 91st Cong., 2nd sess., 1970.

U.S. Congress. Joint Economic Committee. *The Multinational Corporation and International Investment: Hearings before the Subcommittee on Foreign Economic Policy.* 91st Cong., 2nd sess., 1970.

U.S. Congress. Joint Economic Committee. *A Review of Balance of Payments Policies: Hearings before the Subcommittee on International Exchange and Payments.* 91st Cong., 1st sess., 1969.

U.S. Congress. Joint Economic Committee. *The U.S. Balance of Payments. Hearings.* 88th Cong., 1st sess., 1963.

U.S. Congress. Senate. Committee on Finance. *Economic Implications of Massive International Capital Flows: Hearings before the Subcommittee on International Finance and Resources.* 93d Cong., 2nd sess., 1974.

U.S. Congress. Senate. Committee on Banking, Housing and Urban Affairs. *Hearings on Whether to Amend the Par Value Modification Act.* 93d Cong., 1st sess., 1973.

U.S. Congress. Senate. Committee on Finance. *Implications of Multinational Firms for World Trade and Investment and for U.S. Trade and Labor.* 93d Cong., 1st sess., 1973.

U.S. Congress. Senate. Committee on Finance. *The International Financial Crisis: Hearings before the Subcommittee on International Finance and Resources.* 93d Cong., 1st sess., 1973.

U.S. Congress. Senate. Committee on Finance. *The International Monetary Crisis: Materials prepared for the Subcommittee on International Finance and Resources.* 93d Cong., 1st sess., 1973.

U.S. Congress. Senate. Committee on Foreign Relations. *International Debt, the Banks, and U.S. Foreign Policy: Report for the Subcommittee on Foreign Economic Policy.* Prepared by Karin Lissakers. 95th Cong., 1st sess., 1977.

U.S. Congress. Senate. Committee on Foreign Relations. *Direct Investment Abroad and the Multinationals: Effects on the U.S. Economy: Report for the Subcommittee on Multinational Corporations.* Prepared by Peggy Musgrave. 94th Cong., 1st sess., 1975.

U.S. Congress. Senate. Committee on Foreign Relations. *Multinational Corporations in the Dollar Devaluation Crisis: Report on a Questionnaire: Staff Report of the Subcommittee on Multinational Corporations.* Prepared by Vivian Lewis. 94th Cong., 1st sess., 1975.

U.S. Department of Commerce. *Statistical Reporter,* "Report of the Advisory Committee on the Presentation of Balance of Payments Statistics," June 1976, 221-238.

U.S. Department of Commerce. *Foreign Direct Investment Program: Selected Statistics.* 1972.

U.S. Department of Commerce. *1971 Business Statistics.*

U.S. Department of Commerce. *U.S. Direct Investments Abroad, 1966. Part 1: Balance of Payments Data.*

U.S. Department of Commerce. *Survey of Current Business.*

U.S. Department of the Treasury. *Recommendations for Change in the U.S. Financial System.* Revised 24 September 1973.

U.S. President. *The 1973 International Economic Report of the President.*

U.S. President. *United States International Economic Policy in an Interdependent World: Compendium of Papers.* 2 vols. July 1971.

U.S. President. *Economic Reports of the President.*

U.S. President. *Public Papers of the President.*

Newspapers and Periodicals

American Banker. (American Express-Euromoney Syndication Guide.)
Bank of America Archives.
Barrons.
Business Week.
Business Europe.
Financial Times.
New York *Times.*
San Francisco *Chronicle.*
Times (London).
Wall Street Journal.

INDEX

ABOUT THE AUTHOR

JONATHAN DAVID ARONSON received an M.A. in Applied Economics and a Ph.D. in Political Science from Stanford University. He spent the 1975-1976 academic year as a graduate research associate at the Center for International Affairs at Harvard University. Subsequently, he became an Assistant Professor and Director of the Mid-Career Masters Program at the School of International Relations of the University of Southern California, where he teaches courses in the area of international political economy. Professor Aronson is currently editing a volume on international lending and developing nations and is a member of a transnational research team that is beginning an examination of the impact of the international insurance industry on the world political economy.

SELECTED BOOKS WRITTEN UNDER THE AUSPICES
OF THE CENTER FOR INTERNATIONAL AFFAIRS,
HARVARD UNIVERSITY

The Soviet Bloc, by Zbigniew K. Brzezinski (sponsored jointly with the Russian Research Center), 1960. Harvard University Press. Revised edition, 1967.

The Necessity for Choice, by Henry A. Kissinger, 1961. Harper & Bros.

Strategy and Arms Control, by Thomas C. Schelling and Morton H. Halperin, 1961. Twentieth Century Fund.

United States Manufacturing Investment in Brazil, by Lincoln Gordon and Engelbert L. Grommers, 1962. Harvard Business School.

Foreign Aid and Foreign Policy, by Edward S. Mason (sponsored jointly with the Council on Foreign Relations), 1964. Harper & Row.

How Nations Negotiate, by Fred Charles Iklé, 1964. Harper & Row.

Public Policy and Private Enterprise in Mexico, edited by Raymond Vernon, 1964. Harvard University Press.

The Troubled Partnership, by Henry A. Kissinger (sponsored jointly with the Council on Foreign Relations), 1965. McGraw-Hill Book Co.

Problems of National Strategy, ed. Henry Kissinger, 1965. Frederick A. Praeger, Inc.

Arms and Influence, by Thomas C. Schelling, 1966. Yale University Press.

Planning without Facts: Lessons in Resource Allocation from Nigeria's Development, by Wolfgang F. Stolper, 1966. Harvard University Press.

Export Instability and Economic Development, by Alasdair I. MacBean, 1966. Harvard University Press.

Europe's Postwar Growth, by Charles P. Kindleberger, 1967. Harvard University Press.

Agrarian Socialism, by Seymour M. Lipset, rev. ed., 1968. Doubleday Anchor.

Aid, Influence, and Foreign Policy, by Joan M. Nelson, 1968. The Macmillan Company.

International Regionalism, by Joseph S. Nye, 1968. Little, Brown & Co.

Political Order in Changing Societies, by Samuel P. Huntington, 1968. Yale University Press.

The Brazilian Capital Goods Industry, 1929-1964 (sponsored jointly with the Center for Studies in Education and Development), by Nathaniel H. Leff, 1968. Harvard University Press.

Economic Policy-Making and Development in Brazil, 1947-1964, by Nathaniel H. Leff, 1968. John Wiley & Sons.

German Foreign Policy in Transition, by Karl Kaiser, 1968. Oxford University Press.

The Logic of Images in International Relations, by Robert Jervis, 1970. Princeton University Press.

Europe's Would-Be Polity, by Leon Lindberg and Stuart A. Scheingold, 1970. Prentice-Hall.

Taxation and Development: Lessons from Colombian Experience, by Richard M. Bird, 1970. Harvard University Press.

The Kennedy Round in American Trade Policy: The Twilight of the GATT? by John W. Evans, 1971. Harvard University Press.

Korean Development: The Interplay of Politics and Economics, by David C. Cole and Princeton N. Lyman, 1971. Harvard University Press.

Peace in Parts: Integration and Conflict in Regional Organization, by Joseph S. Nye, Jr., 1971. Little, Brown & Co.

Sovereignty at Bay: The Multinational Spread of U.S. Enterprise, by Raymond Vernon, 1971. Basic Books.

Transnational Relations and World Politics, edited by Robert O. Keohane and Joseph S. Nye, Jr., 1972. Harvard University Press.

The Politics of Land Reform in Chile, 1950-1970: Public Policy, Political Institutions, and Social Change, by Robert R. Kaufman, 1972. Harvard University Press.

Organizing the Transnational: The Experience with Transnational Enterprise in Advanced Technology, by M. S. Hochmuth, 1974. Sijthoff (Leiden).

Economic Nationalism and the Politics of International Dependence: The Case of Copper in Chile, 1945-1973, by Theodore Moran, 1974. Princeton University Press.

The Andean Group: A Case Study in Economic Integration among Developing Countries, by David Morawetz, 1974. MIT Press.

Big Business and the State: Changing Relations in Western Europe, edited by Raymond Vernon, 1974. Harvard University Press.

Economic Policymaking in a Conflict Society: The Argentine Case, by Richard D. Mallon and Juan V. Sourrouille, 1975. Harvard University Press.

No Easy Choice: Political Participation in Developing Countries, by Samuel P. Huntington and Joan M. Nelson, 1976. Harvard University Press.

The Politics of International Monetary Reform—The Exchange Crisis, by Michael J. Brenner, 1976. Ballinger Pub. Co.

The International Politics of Natural Resources, by Zuhayr Mikdashi, 1976. Cornell University Press.

The Oil Crisis, edited by Raymond Vernon, 1976. W. W. Norton & Co.

Perception and Misperception in International Politics, by Robert Jervis, 1976. Princeton University Press.

Power and Interdependence, by Robert O. Keohane and Joseph S. Nye, Jr., 1977. Little, Brown.

Soldiers in Politics: Military Coups and Governments, by Eric Nordlinger, 1977. Prentice-Hall.

The Military and Politics in Modern Times: On Professionals, Praetorians, and Revolutionary Soldiers, by Amos Perlmutter, 1977. Yale University Press.

Bankers and Borders: The Case of the American Banks in Britain, by Janet Kelly, 1977. Ballinger Pub. Co.

Shattered Peace: The Origins of the Cold War and the National Security State, by Daniel Yergin, 1977. Houghton Mifflin.

Storm Over the Multinationals: The Real Issues, by Raymond Vernon, 1977. Harvard University Press.

Political Generations and Political Development, ed. Richard J. Samuels, 1977. Lexington Books.

Raw Materials Investments and American Foreign Policy, by Stephen D. Krasner, 1978. Princeton University Press.

Commodity Conflict: The Political Economy of International Commodity Negotiations, by L. N. Rangarajan, 1978. Cornell University Press and Croom Helm (London).